ACKNOWLEDGMENTS

The author gratefully acknowledges the work of Joan Brigham, associate professor of art at Emerson College, and her students who in 1982 pounded the city's pavements to compile *What's Up?*—a booklet listing public art in the cities of Boston, Cambridge, and Chelsea—as well as the work of Netta Lynn Davis and Stephanie Berman in expanding that list under the auspices of Mary Shannon, executive director of the Boston Art Commission.

Other resources to whom this book owes a debt include UrbanArts, Arts on the Line, Cambridge Arts Council, the Artists Foundation, Lowell Historic Preservation Commission, the Massachusetts Art Commission, the Quincy Historical Society, the Brockton, Danforth, DeCordova, and Rose Art Museums, the Boston Museum of Fine Arts, the Boston Public Library, the Bostonian Society, the Essex Institute, the Museum of the National Center for Afro-American Artists, the Addison Gallery, the Massachusetts Historical Society, the Museum of Our National Heritage, Mount Auburn and Forest Hills Cemeteries; art specialists at Babson College, Boston College, Boston University, Harvard University, Massachusetts Institute of Technology, Framingham State College, Northeastern University, Pine Manor College, Tufts University, Wellesley College, Wheaton College; the Crabtree Trust, the staff of *Folio*, Massport, the Metropolitan District Commission, Milton Academy, Roxbury Latin School, Newton Arts in the Park, the Pilgrim Society, numerous arts lottery council chairpersons, many executives, executive secretaries, and public relations people, the artists themselves, and, most important, to countless reference librarians in public libraries for their willing assistance. Finally, not least, thanks to Prof. Bonnie Grad of Clark University for her helpful perusal of the manuscript, and to the New England Sculptors Association for its aid and sponsorship.

Publication of this book is made possible in part by a grant from the Boston Globe Foundation and in part by support from the Massachusetts Arts Lottery as administered by:

Andover Arts Council
Arlington Arts Council
Brookline Council for the Arts & Humanities
Burlington Arts Council
Chelsea Arts Council
Concord Arts Council
East Bridgewater Arts Council
Framingham Arts Lottery Council
Gloucester Arts Council
Lawrence Arts Lottery Council
Lexington Council for the Arts
Lynn Arts Lottery Council
Arts in Malden

Marshfield Local Arts Council
Needham Arts Lottery Council
Newton Arts Lottery Council
North Andover Arts Council
Peabody Arts Council
Quincy Arts Council
Revere Council on the Arts
Scituate Arts Council
Walpole Arts Lottery Commission
Waltham Arts Lottery Council
Wellesley Local Arts Council
Weston Arts Council
Woburn Arts Council

A GUIDE TO
PUBLIC ART
in Greater Boston
From Newburyport to Plymouth

Marty Carlock

THE HARVARD COMMON PRESS

HARVARD AND BOSTON

MASSACHUSETTS

Author's Comment

The initial intention of this guide was to produce a complete list of *all* the public works in the greater metropolitan area that centers on Boston, an area that stretches from Newburyport to Milford to Plymouth and includes such communities as Lowell, often considered demographically separate from Greater Boston. Two years' research revealed that "complete" was too large an order in a vital art scene that sees new works sited almost weekly. The author will welcome additions and corrections; readers are encouraged to write Marty Carlock, c/o Harvard Common Press, 535 Albany St., Boston, MA 02118. Please include a telephone number.

All photos are by the author except those otherwise credited.

Information contained in this guide may have been edited for style and space considerations. We apologize for any discrepancies resulting from these adjustments and regret any inconvenience caused by inaccurate information. Every effort has been made to insure accuracy in the guide, but we cannot assume responsibility for any errors.

Sponsored by New England Sculptors Association, 55 Smith St., Dover, Mass. 02050.

The Harvard Common Press
535 Albany Street
Boston, Massachusetts 02118

COPYRIGHT © 1988 BY THE HARVARD COMMON PRESS

Library of Congress Cataloging-in-Publication Data

Carlock, Marty.
  A guide to public art in greater Boston.

  1. Public art—Massachusetts—Boston Metropolitan
Area—Guide-books.   I. Title.
N6535.B7C37   1988   917.44'610443   88-4727
ISBN 0-916782-94-8 (pbk.)

INTRODUCTION

Curious countercurrents affect Boston's attitudes about the visual arts. On one hand, this metropolitan area is home to the Center for Advanced Visual Studies, an institution marching at the vanguard of techno/art, dedicating itself to the synthesis of art and scientific technology. On the other hand, the Boston Museum of Fine Arts, venerable arbiter of the city's visual art, spent most of this century ignoring contemporary work. The Institute of Contemporary Art has dedicated its resources to showing, not collecting, contemporary work, and owns no permanent collection.

Boston boasts the oldest arts commission in the country, yet if the connoisseur is looking for famous names Boston's public art takes a back seat to that of Philadelphia. Here monuments have been the mode. Walter Muir Whitehill commented in his book *Boston Statues* that the erectors of our public works, generally the Legislature or the Boston Art Commission, have never "shown great devotion to any abstract principles of selection."

The Commonwealth's Arts Lottery, now five years old, has injected new blood into the arts, and new thinking. Currently there are two schools of thought about public art; one tending toward site-integrated art, and one favoring "plop art." (Theorists work through a gradation from "site-dominant" to "site-adjusted" to "site-specific" to "site-determined" art, but for our purposes we can consider the two extremes.) "Plop," or site-dominant, art is a term given to works that were created independently of the site, usually by one of the stars of the international art world, and plopped down in some open space with varying degrees of acceptance and success. This method is rather out of fashion just now with those who commission public art. M.I.T. has a collection of very good plop art, some of which is accepted to the degree that it is routinely climbed on and sat upon; some of which is openly disliked and occasionally disfigured by the student body. To its credit, M.I.T. saw to it that its new List Arts Center integrated site-responsive art and architecture (perhaps too thoroughly—few would recognize the color tiles on the building as art by internationally known colorist Kenneth Noland).

Site-determined art is designed for a specific site, often with input from the neighborhood which will live with it. Local involvement sometimes even takes the form of hands-on creation, as in the children's tiles in the Davis Square subway station, the Rosenberg ceramics in Newton, Lynn, and at Villa Victoria housing project, and in the community mural recently completed in Chinatown. At times the neighborhood's opinions limit the artist's vision too strictly, diminishing the formal qualities of the art: North Cambridge's brickworker made of brick or, for example, Lechmere Canal Park's totem of faces. At times the art is so thoroughly integrated as to be invisible, like that of the List Center, or like Sennot Park's *Sun Arc*, indistinguishable from totlot climbing equipment.

When it works, site-specific art is wonderful: Harries' cast-bronze debris at Haymarket, Haas' architectural murals, Rosenberg's Puerto Rican *Betances Mural*, Dorrien's mock-architectural fragment in Cambridge's

Winthrop Park, Biegun's cookie-cutter ceramic at a pre-schoolers' play-ground in Weston, Shaner's poetry underfoot on the Davis Square subway platform. Its best quality is its wit, a quiet wry appropriateness that leaves the viewer surprised and a bit dazed to find something so perfectly suited to its place.

It occurs to most viewers to ask, "Who are these people, anyway?" Who are the artists who are privileged to place their concepts and visions into our daily lives, and who are the powers that have chosen them? More than most guides, this book lays out the artist's credentials for public inspection. When it is known, the person or institution which commissioned the work is listed. Who the people within those institutions are, the people who are choosing, commissioning, and shaping our aesthetic environment today, would have to be the subject of another book, and a fat one.

This book rejects the concept that "fine" art should have exclusive command of the viewer's attention. The trend toward participatory and community art can only be encouraged; from such beginnings artists and art audiences come. For the benefit of students of aesthetic history, the guide stars some works as "must see". (A star before a name indicates an artist of historical importance; a star before a title indicates the author's opinion that the work is worth seeing.) Lack of a star does not imply that the work or artist is inferior, however. Other than that, the author has endeavored in most cases (not quite all) to leave personal opinion aside and to content herself with explaining artists' intentions and concepts, describing the processes of making art, and researching the reasons for a particular work's presence on a particular site and the history of the persons or events commemorated.

Museum of Science

North End

Gov't. Center   Quincy Market   Water-front

Beacon Hill
State House

King's Chapel

Charles River Esplanade

Boston Common

Commonwealth Ave.

Downtown

Back Bay

Public Garden

China-town

CONTENTS

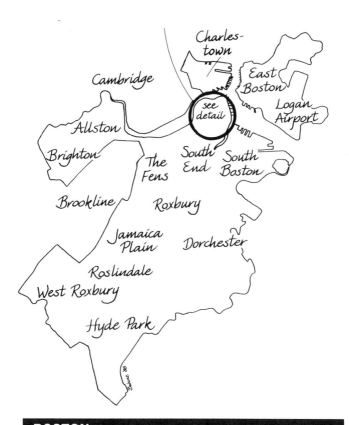

BOSTON

CAMBRIDGE

OTHER CITIES AND TOWNS

Boston

DORRIEN, PORTAL AND STELE, CLIVE RUSS PHOTO

EAST BOSTON

At Logan Airport:

★ PORTAL AND STELE, 1985. Stone, four pieces, h. 6½'–14'.
Harborwalk, airport ferry landing (Maverick St.).
Carlos Dorrien (*see* Waltham [Bentley College]: *Portal*).

GEN. EDWARD LAWRENCE LOGAN, 1956. Bronze, larger than life.
Mall at entrance to airport.
Joseph A. Coletti (1893–1973).

Coletti's family emigrated to Quincy from Italy when the future
sculptor was two years old. His father worked in the granite industry,
and the son had a job as a tool sharpener for a time. He attended
Massachusetts College of Art and Harvard; he assisted John Singer
Sargent with the sculptural elements of his murals at Boston Public
Library and in the rotunda of the Museum of Fine Arts. Coletti served
for six years as chairman of the Massachusetts Art Commission.

Lawyer, judge, and soldier, the airport's namesake is portrayed in
uniform. In civilian life he was a Boston city councilman, legislator,
and municipal court judge; in his military role he saw duty in the
Spanish–American War on the Mexican border, as a colonel of the
101st Infantry during World War I, and as lieutenant general in the
National Guard. Coletti's granite bas-relief carvings, art deco style, on
the base are more interesting than the statue itself.

(DETAIL FROM BASE)

4 BOSTON

★ WINDWHEELS, 1982. Stainless steel with diffraction grating, h. 16'–20' (varies as sculpture moves).
To be re-sited; temporarily at Hyatt Regency Hotel, Cambridge, during terminal reconstruction.
William Wainwright (1924–   ).

Indiana-born, Wainwright attended Purdue, Cornell, and the Chicago Institute of Design, then did graduate work at M.I.T. He is a registered engineer and architect; among his mentors was modern-design guru Buckminister Fuller. Now a resident of Brookline, Wainwright has taught graphics and architecture at Harvard School of Design and has been a visiting artist at Massachusetts College of Art.

One of a dozen publicly sited Wainwright works in Greater Boston, *Windwheels* employs diffraction grating that results in prismatic color changes as kinetic parts move in the wind. Funded by friends of the artist and City Life, Boston.

PASSING REFLECTIONS, 1986. Mirror arrays, h. 9' × 45'.
North and south ends of Terminal C, upper level.
James Scawright.

Scawright's intention with his reflective materials is to employ the passing scene as part of the work, the patterns of motion and color changing as people move by. Commissioned by Massport.

AUDIOKINETIC SCULPTURES, 1986. Multimedia, h. 7' × 9' × 9'.
Upper level, Terminal C.
George Rhoades (*see* Museum of Science: *Archimedian Excogitation*).

CLOUD THE TRAVELER, 1985. Polyester sailcloth, approx. 100 units each 34″ square, spaced 14″ apart.
Ceiling, upper level, Terminal C.
Susumu Shingu (*see* Waterfront [New England Aquarium]: *Echo of the Waves*).

The fabric units are suspended and balanced so that they move with the air stream from the air conditioning system.

LADIES PREPARING NEWLY WOVEN SILK, 1981. Photo replicas from Chinese scroll painting, h. each 6' × 3½'.
Terminal C, pier B corridor.
Emperor Hui Tsung (1082–1135).

Although this scroll is attributed to the emperor himself, it is thought to be a copy of an earlier work. Magnified thirty-one times, the photo replicas are taken from a Chinese handscroll in the Asiatic collection of the Boston Museum of Fine Arts, which houses an oversized Polaroid camera for fine-arts reproduction. Funded by Polaroid Corp. and the Boston Museum of Fine Arts.

BOSTON AIRBORNE: HISTORY TAKES A FLIGHT, 1981. Mural, h. 11' × 35'.
Corridor connecting Terminals D and E.
Elizabeth Carter (*see* Cambridge [Central Sq.]: *Floating Down Mass. Avenue*).

Carter's illusionistic mural contains imagery from Boston's aviation history. Figures include Charles Lindberg, who landed here, Amelia Earhart (born in Medford, a Boston suburb), and Elsie Mackay. Funded by Massport and Townscape, Inc.

BANNERS
Terminal E (International Terminal).

These banners were fabricated by sailmaker Ted Hood (formerly of Marblehead), known for his sails for world-class international competitions such as the America's Cup race.

TWIRLING, 1975. Bronze.
Mariana Pineda (1924–   ).
Heritage House, Sumner St. Elderly Housing, Maverick Sq.

One of the Bunting Institute's early fellows in the 1960s, Pineda has since taught sculpture at Boston University, Boston College, and Newton College of the Sacred Heart. She studied sculpture at Cranbrook Academy, Bennington College, University of California at Berkeley, Columbia University, and in Paris. Pineda may be termed an expressionist/realist whose figures contain strong emotional impact. Among her public commissions is an eight-foot bronze of Lili'uokalani, last queen of Hawaii, commissioned by that state for its capitol building. Funded by Boston Redevelopment Authority, 1% for Art.

COMMEMORATIVE RELIEF OF NODDLE ISLAND, 1975. Bronze, h. 8′ × 4′.
Heritage House, Sumner St. Elderly Housing, Maverick Sq.
Ted Barbarossa (*see* Arlington: *Uncle Sam*).

What is East Boston today was once Noddle Island; this bas-relief recapitulates the area's history from its beginnings, including the era of clipper ships, the early airport (Lindberg is shown landing here), and problems of the present day. Funded by 1% for Art.

CALLAHAN AND SUMNER TUNNEL MEMORIALS, 1956. Bronze relief on granite.
Entrance facades (west end, Callahan Tunnel; east end, Sumner Tunnel).
Joseph Coletti (*see* above: *Gen. Edward Lawrence Logan*).

It is certain that Coletti did the bas reliefs on the Callahan Tunnel facade (he signed the portrait), and it is as good a guess as any that he may also have done those on the earlier Sumner Tunnel; no records have been found. Opened in 1961, the Callahan Tunnel paralleled the much older Sumner Tunnel, dating from 1934 and named for Gen. William Sumner of Roxbury (1780–1861), adjutant general of Massachusetts 1818–35. The Callahan Tunnel is named in memory of the son of William F. Callahan, chairman of the Massachusetts Turnpike Authority, which took over the tunnels in 1959.

CHARLESTOWN

WILLIAM PRESCOTT, 1881. Bronze, larger than life.
Bunker (Breed's) Hill, Monument Ave. and High St.
★ William Wetmore Story (*see* Dorchester: *Edward Everett*).

The first major engagement between British and colonial American forces occurred on Breed's (miscalled Bunker) Hill in June of 1775. The entrenchments were dug overnight under the command of Col. William Prescott (1726–1795). As the fighting and the weather grew hot, the colonel shucked his uniform for a broadbrimmed hat and light coat, and is thus immortalized here. Commissioned by the Bunker Hill Monument Association.

JOSEPH WARREN, 1857. Marble, larger than life.
Bunker Hill, inside the Park Service building.
★ Henry Dexter (1806–1876).

It is instructive to compare this rather old-fashioned marble statue, in the style of the early 1800s, to Story's livelier *Prescott* outside. Known early in his career as "the blacksmith sculptor," Dexter was apprenticed to that trade and practiced it, but was drawn to art. After some mediocre attempts at painting, he discovered clay and a natural bent for portrait modeling. He shortly became Boston's most popular portrait sculptor, taking the likenesses not only of Bostonians but of visitors such as Charles Dickens. In 1859 he undertook an ambitious journey to visit every state and the Capitol, to portray the governor of each state and the President, James Buchanan. In 1861 he exhibited the fruit of the undertaking, thirty-two busts, in Boston, but his timing was terrible: The Civil War eclipsed his achievement; the collection was donated to the National Museum and forgotten.

The most famous American casualty at the battle of Bunker Hill, Dr. Warren is remembered by a better statue at Roxbury Latin School. Commissioned by the Bunker Hill Monument Association for the 75th anniversary of the battle.

WIND SCULPTURE, 1978. Stainless steel, h. 25' × 3' × 3'.
Charlestown High School.
Michio Ihara (*see* Lowell: *Pawtucket Prism*).

BIRNHAM WOOD, 1970. Welded steel, h. 11½'.
Fire station, 525 Main St., Sullivan Sq.
Robert Amory (*see* Downtown: *Helion*).
Funded by 1% for Art.

SUNDIAL, 1987. Bronze, three life-size figures and thirteen bas-relief elements on granite sundial, h. 1½' × diam. 10'.
Hayes Square, Bunker Hill and Moulton Sts.
Lu Stubbs (*see* Brookline: *Three Women*).

Craftspeople of Colonial days are pictured on the face of the sundial. Funded by the Browne Fund.

UNTITLED, installation planned spring, 1988.
Thompson Square, Main St. and Dexter Row.
Jeffrey Schiff (1952–   ).

Jeffrey Schiff has drawn a good deal of critical attention for his collaborative performance and installation art, but he also makes permanent objects combining concrete, lead, stone, steel, and wood. Assistant professor of sculpture at Wesleyan, he is a graduate of Brown and holds a master's degree from UMass/Amherst. In 1985 he was awarded a Boston/Kyoto Sister City grant enabling him to study temples and tea houses in Japan. Among his fellowships have been three from the National Endowment for the Arts, three from the Artists' Foundation, and the Rome Prize from the American Academy in Rome. Schiff has also taught at Boston College, Massachusetts College of Art, Clark University, and Rhode Island School of Design. His work is owned by La Jolla Museum of Contemporary Art, UMass/Amherst, and the University of Connecticut.

This environment, combining granite, bronze, brick, and trees, will feature a double font which spills water into basins on both sides. Funded by the Browne Fund.

MUSEUM OF SCIENCE

ARCHIMEDIAN EXCOGITATION, 1987. Steel, percussion instruments, billiard and bowling balls, h. 26'.
Atrium stairwell.
George Rhoads (1927–   ).

A multi-faceted artist, George Rhoads has been a printmaker, cera-micist, muralist, advertising artist, medical illustrator, and toy designer. As an art student in Paris he developed the first innovation in centu-ries in the ancient Japanese art of origami (paper-folding); he folded an elephant, ears and all, from a single sheet of paper. Rhoads is a member of a generation of sculptors who began as engineers before turning to art. He attended engineering school at the University of Wisconsin while in the U.S. Army in 1943, but finished with a B.A. at University of Chicago and moved on to the Art Institute of Chicago and then to studies in Paris. Rhoads now lives in Ithaca, N.Y.

Rhoads' audiokinetic (sound/motion) works use machinery to lift balls to the top of a system through which they travel by gravity. Sev-eral random distribution mechanisms along the track introduce variety into their action. This work is actually three separate systems stacked atop one another. The top two use candlepin bowling balls whose journeys through the maze activate pendulums and turn wheels and windmills, as well as creating sounds. The bottom system uses billiard balls. Rhoads' audiokinetic sculptures are installed in shopping cen-ters in half-a-dozen cities in this country and Canada, at the Port Au-thority Bus Terminal in New York, and at Logan Airport's Terminal C.

CONSTELLATION, 1975. Cor-ten steel, h. 8'.
  To be relocated at Science Museum, 1988; formerly at MBTA Auditorium station exit.
  Dennis Kowal (see Wellesley [Babson College]: *Ominous Icon #6* and *Yaddo Study*).

HUMAN CONNECTIONS, 1987. Polarized light mural, h. 27' × 25'.
  Lobby, Omni Theater.
  Austine Wood–Comarow (1942–   ).

Daughter of a United Nations official, Austine Wood attended ele-mentary school in Germany, high school and art school in Switzer-land, and Swarthmore College before graduating from Indiana University in 1964. After beginning her work with polarization, she studied color with Eduardo Vilches in Chile and took a graduate de-gree (M.F.A.) at Syracuse University. She now maintains a studio in California and works under the name "Austine." Her Polage murals, some interactive with the viewer and some not, are located across the country, including three in the Kodak Pavilion at Epcot Center (Disney World) in Florida.

In 1967 Wood–Comarow invented the technique of Polage (a trade-marked term), or polarized collage, by sandwiching clear colorless cel-lulose (cellophane) between polarized filters. Color is created by the angle of one polarized layer to another, the filters acting as prisms to break white light into its component colors. Thus some areas seem white until a polarizing filter is rotated to the proper position; others, completely light-blocked, appear black. Rather than an entire rainbow, the interacting filters reveal a segment of the spectrum, a short range of color cycles as the angle of polarization changes. Both hand-held and mechanized filters are provided here so viewers can experiment with color changes. The 140 disks hanging in front of the work form what the artist calls "pixels" of visual information. For clear portions of the mural, they provide the second polarized filter that creates color. Wood–Comarow sees an analogy between Polage and music, because it incorporates the dimension of time. This mural depicts the history of our civilization in the context of communication. It is funded by Polaroid Corp., the Boston company that invented the polarizing filter.

CHARLES RIVER ESPLANADE

GEN. GEORGE SMITH PATTON, JR., 1955. Bronze, heroic size.
Near Hatch Shell, west of Longfellow Bridge.
★ James Earle Fraser (1876–1953).

Fraser lived for a time as a boy on the Dakota frontier, an experience that marked his art with a predilection for heroes and victims. A pupil of Augustus Saint-Gaudens, Fraser was designer of the Buffalo Nickel and of sculpture at the Supreme Court and National Archives buildings in Washington. He is best known for *End of the Trail*, the melodramatic portrayal of a defeated Plains warrior on an exhausted pony. At Fraser's death *End of the Trail* was considered the best-known sculpture in America. This work is a duplicate, the original being at the U.S. Military Academy at West Point. Another copy is in Hamilton. Commissioned by the Commonwealth.

Patton (1885–1945), colorful and eccentric commander of the American Third Army in Europe during World War II, was married to Beatrice Ayer, daughter of wealthy Boston textile manufacturer Frederick Ayer. (Their son George, also a U.S. Army general, was born in Boston and retired to exurban South Hamilton.) Recklessly brave (and accident-prone), Patton survived action against Pancho Villa's troops on the Mexican border, in France in World War I, in North Africa, Sicily, and Western Europe in World War II, only to die as the result of injuries suffered in a jeep accident in Germany after the war.

DAVID IGNATIUS WALSH, 1954. Bronze bust on granite monument.
Near Hatch Shell.
Joseph A. Coletti (*see* East Boston/Logan Airport: *Gen. Edward Lawrence Logan*).

Lawyer and Democratic politician, Walsh (1872–1947) was elected Lieutenant Governor in 1913, Governor in 1914, and U.S. Senator in 1919. The motto above his head, "Non sibi sed patriae," translates, "Not for self but for country." Commissioned by the Metropolitan District Commission.

GEN. CHARLES DEVENS, 1893–1896. Bronze, larger than life.
Near Hatch Shell.
★ Olin Levi Warner (1844–1896).

Connecticut-born Olin Warner made his way to Paris at the age of twenty-five, but within three years had to return to America because of political unrest in France. Lack of patronage and discouragement plagued him, although in time he was recognized for his sensitive portrait medallions. He was among the group that established the Society of American Artists in 1877. Commissioned to design bronze doors for the Library of Congress, Warner died in mid-task as a result of a bicycle accident in Central Park.

Devens (1820–1891), a Worcester lawyer who entered the Union Army as a major, won the brevet rank of major-general. Devens was later a judge in the state Supreme Judicial Court and U.S. Attorney General under President Hayes. Fort Devens in Ayer, still an active U.S. Army base, is named for him. Originally sited on Bowdoin St. behind the State House, this statue was displaced in 1950 by a parking lot. Commissioned by the Commonwealth.

MAURICE J. TOBIN, 1958. Bronze, life-size.
Near Hatch Shell.
Emilius R. Ciampa (b. 1896).

Ciampa came to Boston from Italy at the age of ten, studied at North Bennett Street Industrial School and briefly at Massachusetts Normal Art School. He served in France in World War I and later was in charge of art projects for Northern Art Stone Corp. of New York. Living and teaching in Medford after 1928, he executed a number of memorials and bas-relief portraits.

Tobin (1901–1953) was a protégé of the legendary Mayor of Boston, James Michael Curley. In the 1938 election, in what Curley forces termed unprecedented treachery, Tobin ran against and defeated his political mentor, winning the Mayor's office and serving until 1944, between Curley's last two terms. Tobin was Governor of Massachusetts from 1946 to 1947; in 1948 he became Secretary of Labor under President Truman. The former Mystic River Bridge now bears his name. Those who knew him say Tobin was imposing and "movie-star handsome"; if so, it is puzzling that this unimposing and unhandsome rendering was accepted. Commissioned by the Commonwealth.

ARTHUR FIEDLER, 1984. Aluminum, h. 6'4".
  Ralph Helmick (1952–   ).

  Cambridge sculptor Ralph Helmick earned a B.A. from the University of Michigan in 1974 and an M.F.A. from the Boston Museum School in 1980. This monumental head is built up of cut-out layers of aluminum in varying thicknesses, a distinctive technique originated by Helmick.
  Famed and beloved conductor of the Boston Pops orchestra for fifty years, 1929–1979, Arthur Fiedler founded the free Esplanade concerts still performed summer evenings at the nearby Hatch Shell. Funded by contributions from Store 24, the Browne Fund, the Permanent Charity Fund of Boston, David G. Mugar, J. F. White Contracting Co., the Alcoa Foundation, and Bank of Boston.

LOTTA FOUNTAIN, 1939. Granite, h. 6'.
  Dog sculpture above a tiled drinking basin for animals.
  J. W. Ames and E. S. Dodge, architects.

  Legend persists that this is a memorial to a specific dog: a trick dog, a dog that rescued someone from drowning in the Charles River Basin, or one of the sled dogs who heroically took diptheria vaccine to Nome in 1925. In 1940, however, a year after its dedication, the writer of a column in the *Boston Herald* told a young reader that "it is not a memorial to a real dog."
  The fountain is a bequest of actress and animal-lover Lotta Crabtree (1847–1924), who as a child was the Shirley Temple of the Golden West. Lotta had taken dancing lessons and done so well that the manager of a log theater in Rabbit Creek, Cal., persuaded the child's mother to let her appear onstage. Said to be petite and vivacious, with red-gold hair and brown eyes, "Little Lotta" was so engaging that the miners threw silver dollars and bags of gold dust at her feet, and her career was launched. She learned to play the banjo and began to act, earning enough money (which her mother shrewdly

invested) that she died a wealthy woman. She owned racehorses late in life and was said to be "a ready contributor" to any cause to aid animals. She died in Boston; her trust still supports animal rescue efforts.

★ TRIMBLOID X, 1970. Cor-ten steel.
Esplanade at Clarendon St.
David Kibbey (1940–   ).

Vermont-born, Kibbey studied art at Boston University, Cummington School for the Arts, and Rhode Island School of Design. He has taught art at a number of colleges, including the University of New Hampshire, Windham College, and Hampshire College, and has been director of exhibitions at M.I.T. *Trimbloid X* is one of a series of geometric forms Kibbey fabricated while in Boston. He now designs and builds one-of-a-kind furniture in Oakland, Cal. Funded by Summerthing and Project '70.

NORTH END

★ WATER STAGE, 1986. Mixed media fountain.
Atrium, Tip O'Neill Bldg., Causeway St. (next to North Station).
Mary Miss (1944–   ).

Environmental artist Mary Miss was an "Army brat," moving frequently throughout childhood because of her father's military career. His interest in history led to visits to old forts, mines, and Indian sites in the American West, to castle ruins, medieval towns, and war ruins in Germany, all strong impressions for Miss. Her interests widened to include Japanese culture, Pueblo Indian structures, and Italian fortified hill towns. She studied sculpture at the University of California and at Colorado College, then moved to New York and began building room-sized structures. Her first exhibition was at the Whitney Museum in 1970, and in 1973 she was included in the Whitney Biennial. Her work is always designed specifically for the site: in 1986 she built a construct in the Fogg Museum at Harvard (temporary), and another in the entry of the Danforth Museum in Framingham (permanent). Although many of her installations are temporary, permanent ones such as this are increasingly commissioned.

HANGING CRYSTAL MOBILE, 1986.
Atrium, Tip O'Neill Bldg.
Jane Kaufman (1938–   ).

Born in New York City, Kaufman attended New York University and Hunter College, then taught in the city's public high schools for a decade. She won a Guggenheim Fellowship in 1974 and another from the National Endowment for the Arts in 1979. Kaufman has taught at Lehman College in the Bronx, Bard College, Brooklyn Museum Art School, and Queens College, and has been a visiting artist at Michigan State, Syracuse University, the University of Colorado, the Art Institute of Chicago, Cooper Union, and others.

PAINTERS PAINTING, 1978. Mural, h. approx 12′ × 60′.
MBTA Elevated at Causeway and Canal Sts.
Miroslav Antic (1947–   ).

Born in Yugoslavia, Antic studied at the Academy of Fine Arts in Belgrade. He has been living and working here since the early 1970s; in 1980 he held a fellowship from the Artists Foundation. Funded by MBTA.

LEAVES 'N LINKS, 1978. Mural, h. 9′ × 70′.
MBTA Elevated at Causeway and Haverhill Sts.
Karen Moss (1944–   ).

Brookline artist Karen Moss studied painting at Rhode Island School of Design, then earned a master's degree from the Tufts/Boston Museum School program. She has held a grant from the Artists' Foundation and has taught at the Museum School, Massachusetts College of Art, Wheelock College, and Harvard summer school. Her paintings are owned by the Museum of Fine Arts, Addison Gallery of American Art, Rose and Decordova Museums, Vassar College, and many corporations. Funded by MBTA.

CALLAHAN TUNNEL MEMORIAL, 1956 (*see* East Boston/Logan Airport: *Callahan and Sumner Tunnel Memorials*).

★ ASAROTON (Unswept Floor), 1976. Bronze pavement inserts, assorted sizes, in area 55′ × 10′ × 9″ deep.
Pavement at Hanover and Haymarket Sts.
Mags Harries (*see* Chelsea: *Bellingham Square*).

Embedded in the asphalt at a busy outdoor market street crossing, these cast bronze objects intrigue and puzzle tourists walking the 'Freedom Trail to the Revere House. Harries' bronze detritus is cast

(DETAIL)

from real garbage and items found in the street: fish, flowers, newspapers, gloves, stepped-on strawberries and squashed corn cobs. *Asaroton* refers to a Greco-Roman floor mosaic technique dating to 200 B.C. Commissioned to commemorate the U.S. Bicentennial.

CHILDREN'S MOSAICS, 1975. Ceramic tile.
Inside pedestrian underpass from Haymarket to Cross St.

These ceramic tile mosaics were designed, fabricated, and installed by neighborhood children, as a project of Christopher Columbus Community Center.

★ GEORGE WASHINGTON, 1815. Marble.
Christ Church, Salem St.
Christian Gullager (d. 1827).

During his progress through New England in 1789, the general paused in Portsmouth, N. H., to sit for two hours for Gullager, a Danish artist who immigrated circa 1781. The resultant oil portrait is now owned by the Massachusetts Historical Society. In 1790 Gullager produced a plaster bust, from which this bust is derived; its distinction is that it appears to be the first Boston portrait work by a sculptor working in America. Gift of Shubael Bell, senior warden of Christ Church.

PAUL REVERE, 1940. Bronze, equestrian, larger than life.
At Paul Revere Mall behind Old North Church, between Salem and Hanover Sts.
★ Cyrus E. Dallin (1861–1944); (*see* Fenway [Boston Museum of Fine Arts]: *Appeal to the Great Spirit*).

Paul Revere (1735–1818) owes his romantic image to a poem written by Longfellow more than fifty years after he rode out of Boston in 1775 to rouse the militia for the battles of Lexington and Concord. He was in fact caught by a British patrol and never reached Concord, although his companion, Dr. Samuel Prescott, who joined him in Lexington and knew the local shortcuts, did. By profession Revere was a silversmith, engraver, maker of copper ship hull sheathing, and owner of a brass foundry (Revere bells still hang in the steeples of a number of New England churches).

This is the final large work of Dallin, a sculptor better known for his equestrian Indian statues, one of which stands in front of the Boston Museum of Fine Arts. Funded by the George Robert White Fund.

WATERFRONT

At New England Aquarium (Central Wharf, off Atlantic Ave. at Milk St.):

★ ECHO OF THE WAVES, 1983. Steel and fiber-reinforced plastic, h. 45′ at rest; 65′ with wings extended (*see* back cover photo).
Susumu Shingu (1937–   ).

Popularly called *The Whale*, this work is among the city's most impressive. Its majestic swimming motions imitate in an abstract but recognizable way the movements of nature's largest creatures, yet it moves for hours without repeating the same configuration. Although the wings are responsive to subtle movements of air, the artist has employed aerodynamic techniques to damp their motion in heavy weather.

An aesthetic idea new in this century is moving, or "kinetic" sculpture, introduced by a group including Calder, Duchamp, and Tinguely. Working in the kinetic mode, the Japanese-born Shingu adds a dimension from his Oriental heritage, a sensitivity to and a reverence for the rhythms of nature. The rhythms of each individual spirit, Shingu says, must grow and "change joyfully," and will do so best when intertwined with the rhythms of the natural world: streams flowing, grass swaying, the alternations of night and day. His works are "expressive conduits which connect us with the deeper life forces of nature," one associate comments.

Shingu studied at Tokyo University of the Arts and at the Academy of Rome. Beginning with an exhibition entitled "Wind" in 1967, he has investigated modern engineering and materials technologies to express space, time, and motion in his work. His major sculptures sited in Japan number more than twenty. This, his second work in the United States, was created in association with Cambridge Seven Associates, an architectural firm. Gift of Mr. and Mrs. David Bakalar.

DOLPHINS OF THE SEA, 1980. Bronze fountain.
Aquarium plaza.
Katherine Ward Lane Weems (*see* Fenway: *Rhinoceros*.).

★ UNTITLED, 1972. Stainless steel. Four units, each h. approx. 15′ × 15′ × 17′.
Harbor Towers Plaza, India Wharf.
David von Schlegell (1920–   ).

Born in St. Louis, von Schlegell studied engineering at the University of Michigan and worked as an aircraft engineer before becoming an Air Force pilot in World War II. He studied painting at the Art Students League in New York, then began experimenting with wood, manipulating it by steaming and other boatbuilding techniques. In 1964 he began to work in aluminum, attempting to pare from his art the "excess of emotion" he saw in abstract expressionism. In earlier, more referential works critics saw a tension between engineering and love of nature, between a romantic sensibility and a coolly mechanistic art. Von Schlegell has taught at Yale, Cornell, the School of Visual Arts, and the University of California at Santa Barbara; museums owning his work include the Whitney in New York, the Hirschhorn in Washington, and those at Yale, Cornell, and Carnegie Institute.

Here von Schlegell has stripped his aesthetic to an engineering problem and has achieved a scale that, as he wished, relates to buildings, bridges, and the larger objects in our world. Funded by 1% for Art.

At Boston Harbor Hotel:

BOY WITH DOG, ca. 1905. Oil on canvas, 50″ × 34″.
Entrance foyer.
Charles W. Hawthorne (1872–1930).

A painter of portraits and figures, Hawthorne was raised in Richmond, Me. After studies with William Merritt Chase at Shinnecock, he founded the Cape Cod School of Art in Provincetown and taught there until his death.

THE CELLIST, ca. 1900. Oil on canvas, 45″ × 31″.
Main lobby.
★ Lilla Cabot Perry (ca. 1848–1933).

Painter, writer, and poet, Perry is credited with introducing Bostonians to the work of French Impressionist painters. She was one of the few American painters whose work was accepted in the Paris salons of the 1890s.

PORTRAIT OF MISS LA BARONNE DE R., ca. 1900. Oil on canvas, 46″ × 29″.
Main lobby.
Lilla Cabot Perry (see The Cellist above).

THE BREAKING WAVE, 1922. Oil on canvas, 25″ × 30″.
Entrance to Rowes Wharf Restaurant.
Soren Emil Carlson.

STILL LIFE. Oil on canvas, 29″ × 36″.
In hotel restaurant.
Severin Rosen.

BEACON STREET IN WINTER. Oil on canvas, 29″ × 36″.
Reception area.
A. C. Goodwin (1864–1929).

Born in Portsmouth, N.H., Goodwin was largely self-taught. He is considered a member of the Boston School, a group of realist/impressionists dating from the turn of the century to the present day.

THE U.S.S. CHESAPEAKE AND H.M.S. SHANNON, ca. 1815. Oil on canvas,
  20″ × 32″.
In Harborview Lounge.
Thomas Buttersworth.

   Thomas Buttersworth and his son James were both British marine
painters, and there is some uncertainty as to which one of them produced this painting, a chronicle of a naval battle that took place off
Boston on June 1, 1813. It is usually attributed to the father because
of the early date and the distinctive technique.
   The battle is one of the more famous in American history, the first
major loss of a U.S. warship in the War of 1812. The *Chesapeake*,
suffering from a reputation as an unlucky ship, had just been put under the command of Capt. James Lawrence and was refitting at Boston. The *Shannon*, part of increased British blockading efforts,
appeared off the coast; in the quaint etiquette of the day, its captain,
Philip Vere Broke, sent Lawrence a written invitation for a one-on-one
engagement of the ships. Despite a green and somewhat mutinous
crew—prize money from their last voyage had not yet been
distributed—Lawrence set sail and courageously attacked. Throngs
cheered his ship out of the harbor, and people climbed the heights of
Salem to get a distant view of the brief and disastrous engagement. In
the first exchange of fire Lawrence was mortally wounded and his two
officers disabled; the disorganized crew was easy prey for the British
boarding party. The bloodiest battle in naval history to that time, it
cost the British 84 casualties and the Americans 146.

QUINCY MARKET

★ SAMUEL ADAMS, 1873. Bronze, heroic size.
In front of Faneuil Hall, Congress St.
Anne Whitney (1821–1915).

   A native of Watertown, Anne Whitney in her thirties turned from
writing poetry to modeling portrait busts of relatives and friends. Self-
taught, she progressed to idealized figures with so much success that
the Commonwealth awarded her the commission to carve Samuel
Adams for the Statuary Hall at the federal Capitol. This is a replica of
that work, purchased by the city in 1880.
   Adams (1722–1803), political writer and revolutionary firebrand, is
credited with being one of the principal shapers of the American Revolution. He was among the first to oppose Parliament's power to tax
the colonies, a stubborn opponent of compromise with the mother
country, and chief promoter of the Boston Tea Party. Second cousin
to U.S. President John Adams, Samuel Adams after the Revolution
served as Lieutenant Governor and from 1794 to 1797 as Governor.
Funded by the Jonathan Phillips Fund.

WALTER MUIR WHITEHILL MEDALLION, 1976. Bronze.
Base of Samuel Adams statue.
From a drawing by Rudolph Ruzicka.

The dual-purpose memorial, perhaps a sample of New England frugality, occurs more than once in Boston. Here the base of Sam Adams' statue is employed to honor a citizen temperamentally and chronologically far removed from Adams. Whitehill (1905–1978), scholar, author of popular regional histories, and long director of the Boston Athenæum, was Boston's consummate cultivated man.

GRASSHOPPER WEATHERVANE, 1742. Sheet copper, gilt.
    Atop Faneuil Hall.
    Shem Drowne.

In colonial Boston, Drowne and his son Thomas were master tinsmiths living and working in the North End.

★ RED AUERBACH, 1985.
    Bronze, life-size.
    Quincy Market mall, south side.
    Lloyd Lillie (*see* Government Center and Environs: *James Michael Curley*).

Longtime coach and manager of the Boston Celtics basketball dynasty, Arnold "Red" Auerbach is depicted in a characteristic moment: seated on the bench at courtside, about to light his victory cigar, an insouciant gesture indicating he considers the game as good as won.

THE SPIRIT OF BOSTON, 1982. Stainless steel, granite, h. approx. 12'.
    Bostonian Hotel, North and Blackstone Sts.
    David Lee Brown (1939–   ).

Brown has been an instructor in sculpture at Cranbrook and a professor of design at Pratt Institute. He studied at Cass Tech, North Carolina School of Design, and Cranbrook; his work is at DeCordova Museum, the Hirschhorn, and Milwaukee Art Center. He lives on Long Island.

This fountain represents schematically the historic Boston waterfront.

Inside Faneuil Hall:

Access to this historic hall is gained via the middle door at the east end—the opposite end from where Samuel Adams stands. Sixteen portraits hang here, including that of Peter Faneuil himself, wealthy French Huguenot merchant who built the hall in 1742. Sculpture portrait busts include John Adams, John Quincy Adams, and Daniel Webster. Other works are:

WEBSTER'S REPLY TO HAYNE, 1851. Oil on canvas. 16′ × 30′.
  Over speakers' platform.
  George Peter Alexander Healy (1813–1894).

In the U.S. Senate in 1830, Senator Daniel Webster of Massachusetts rose to debate Senator Robert Young Hayne of South Carolina
on the issue of Nullification. Hayne contended that the Constitution
was a compact among the states, and that states had the power to
nullify any law of the federal government. Webster replied with a defense of the Union which, historians say, did more to unify the country
than any single utterance of any other man. His ringing "Liberty and
Union, now and forever, one and inseparable," resounded throughout
the nation. (For more about Webster, *see* Marshfield: *Webster, the
Farmer of Marshfield*.) In this hall Webster also delivered a famous
eulogy of John Adams and Thomas Jefferson, who died within hours
of each other on July 4, 1826.

Dealing loosely with history, Healy has included in the audience life
portraits of more than one hundred men and women famous at the
time. This work was commissioned by King Louis Philippe of France
to be hung at Versailles, but he was overthrown before it was finished. Anonymous gift to the City of Boston.

EAGLE, 1798. Painted artificial stone.
  On rear balcony.
  Attributed to Daniel Raynerd.

This 250-pound bird was designed for an early bank building by
Charles Bulfinch, architect of the New State House, who enlarged
Faneuil Hall in 1806. When the bank was razed in 1824, the eagle
was placed here. It is credited to Raynerd, Bulfinch's chief ornamental
plasterer. The medium is pulverized marble, white sand, hair for
binder, and lime putty.

MERCY OTIS WARREN, ca. 1763. Polaroid replica of oil painting, h. 51″ × 41″.
  John Singleton Copley (1737–1815).

The outstanding portraitist of Colonial America, Copley was born in
Boston of Irish parents and self-educated. In 1774, despite success in
his native city, he went first to Rome, then established himself permanently in London and was admitted to the Royal Academy. Less facile
than his later work, Copley's American portraits are considered far
stronger and more honest.

Playwright, poet, feminist, and political historian, Mercy Warren
(1728–1814) was a controversial figure in her time. Sister of James
Otis (*see* Downtown [Hotel Meridien]: murals), she received a thorough education by sitting in on her brother's classes. She married
James Warren, a legislator; she and her husband were friends of
John and Abigail Adams and other architects of the American Revolution. Her first published work was a satiric anti-British play in 1772;
her best-known book was *History of the Rise, Progress and Termina-
tion of the American Revolution* published in 1805. An anti-Federalist
pamphlet she wrote was wrongly attributed to Elbridge Gerry for a
century. Warren feared that the new Federal Constitution would create

another aristocracy and rob the people of their hard-won liberty; the quotation, "The origin of all power is in the people," is from her pen.

Because no woman's portrait hung in Faneuil Hall, a commission from the mayor's office was appointed to provide one to mark the bicentennial of the U.S. Constitution in 1987. Warren was chosen because of her political writings. The Copley original, owned by the Boston Museum of Fine Arts, was too valuable to lend; this fine-arts copy was produced by a room-size Polaroid camera at the museum.

GOVERNMENT CENTER AND ENVIRONS

JAMES MICHAEL CURLEY, 1980. Bronze double portrait statues, life-size.
Curley Memorial Park, Congress and North Sts.
Lloyd Lillie (1932–   ).

Lloyd Lillie has taken realism to its logical conclusion, bringing statues of public heroes down off their pedestals and placing them in naturalistic, accessible poses. Born in Washington, D.C., he attended the Corcoran School of Art there, won honors at the Boston Museum School, and was awarded a traveling scholarship with which he studied at the Accademia di Belle Arti in Florence. He is now a professor of sculpture at Boston University, where he has taught for twenty-four years. His other life-size sculptures occupy sites in Washington, St. Louis, Hardy, Va., Falmouth, and Quincy Market in Boston. Here the two statues represent the two sides of Mayor Curley: standing, the powerful, egotistic public figure; sitting on the park bench, the folksy Irish friend to all.

Curley was four times mayor of Boston, never in consecutive terms. His education was cut short at age ten, when his father died and he went to work to help support his family. In 1904 he won election as alderman while serving a ninety-day sentence in jail for fraudulently taking a civil service exam for a friend; it was said he read everything in the prison library while there. He was successively alderman, councillor, legislator, twice Congressman, and Governor 1935–36. His identity as mayor was indelible; his fourth term began in 1946. Funded by the Browne Fund.

WINTERBREATH FOUNTAIN, installation planned 1988.
City Hall Plaza, Tremont and Cambridge Sts.
Joan Brigham (1935–   ) and Christopher Janney (1950–   ).

Both Brigham and Janney have been Fellows of the Center for Advanced Visual Studies at M.I.T., a center dedicated to the melding of art and technology. Following his graduation from Princeton, Janney attended Dalcroze School of Music in New York and earned a master's degree in visual studies from M.I.T. He has been artist-in-residence at Massachusetts College of Art. Steam sculptor Joan Brigham is an associate professor of fine arts at Emerson College. Born in Oklahoma, she grew up in California, attended Pomona College and Harvard University, and settled in Cambridge. Interested in the dramatic possibilities of steam, she mastered the pipe-fitter's trade and, as a research fellow of the Center for Advanced Visual Studies at M.I.T., began to experiment with steam and water mist as artistic mediums. Brigham has made smaller kinetic solar-powered steam sculptures, but most of her work is performance art, often combining lasers, film projections, audio, electronic music, and viewer interaction by means of photocells.

Brigham and Janney in the early 1980s produced a collaborative work called *Steamshuffle* for First Night, Boston's New Year's Eve arts celebration. The work produced steam and electronic music when viewers broke a photoelectric beam. Since then the artists have labored to convert the non-working fountain here to similar interactive purposes, a water fountain in summer and a steam fountain in winter. City funds have been allocated for repair of the fountain, and the Browne Fund is to underwrite the steam, music, and pressure-sensitive panels which viewers can step on to activate the fountain.

★ THERMOPYLAE, 1966.
Bronze, h. approx. 15′.
City Hall Plaza, Cambridge
and New Sudbury Sts., outside
John F. Kennedy Bldg.
Dimitri Hadzi (*see* Brookline:
Primavera).

This work, like his *Elmo/MIT*, reflects Hadzi's interest in classical armor, history, and myth, stemming from his Greek heritage and his years working in Greece and Rome. The artist says the work was inspired by John F. Kennedy's book *Profiles in Courage*.

NEW ENGLAND ELEGY, 1966. Painting, h. approx. 6′ × 10′.
Overhead, entry corridor of John F. Kennedy Bldg.
★ Robert Motherwell (1915–   ).

A native of Washington state, Motherwell studied philosophy at Stanford and Harvard, then art history and archaeology at Columbia before deciding, at age twenty-six, to become a painter. Settling in New York City, he became associated with a cadre of abstract painters and with them founded a Greenwich Village art school called The Subjects of the Artist. His calligraphic shapes made him one of the elite of abstract expressionism; scarcely a contemporary museum in the country lacks an example. Motherwell has taught at Hunter College. Funded by 1% for Art.

FULL CIRCLE, 1966. Welded copper and steel, h. 8′.
Courtyard, John F. Kennedy Bldg.
★ Herbert Ferber (1906–   ).

Despite a degree in dentistry from Columbia, Ferber began studying at the Beaux Arts Institute of Design and determined to become an artist. At first he carved directly in wood and stone; after the mid-forties he turned to welding techniques and soon enlarged them to architectural scale. Expanding the spatial possibilities of large works, in 1961 he developed entire rooms, which the viewer entered in order to explore the sculpture from within—an early version of environmental and installation art. He has been a leader of abstract expressionism in sculpture, attuned to the endless possibilities of nonobjective form. Funded by 1% for Art.

SPRING, 1986. Acrylic, 6½′ × 30′.
   City Hall lobby, balcony.
   ★ Maud Morgan (1903–   ).

The grande dame of Boston art, Morgan was born Maud Cabot in New York, attended Barnard College, studied art in Paris in the 1920s (where she became a friend of Hemingway), and with Hans Hofmann in Munich in the 1930s. She and her husband Patrick Morgan taught at Phillips and Abbot Academies in Andover, numbering among their students painter Frank Stella and Minimalist Carl André. Although she never achieved the same international reputation, she knew and exhibited with such well-known names of the 1950s as Mark Rothko, Barnett Newman, and Jackson Pollock. She still works actively in her Cambridge studio.

This work is one of four, depicting the four seasons. Gift to the city from friends of the artist.

NANCY, A PASSAGE OF TIME, 1978. Cor-ten steel, h. 5′10″.
   Tremont and State Sts.
   Rick Lee (1946–   ).

Lincoln resident Rick Lee earned a bachelor of science in art at the University of Wisconsin and a master's in design at Goddard College in Vermont. He taught for a time at Belmont Hill School. Gift of Bertram and Ronald Drucker.

THE JUDGES' BENCH, 1983. Limestone, h. 6′.
   Pemberton Sq., between Suffolk County Courthouse, (Somerset St.) and Center Plaza (on Cambridge St., facing Government Center).
   Will Reimann (*see* Cambridge [Porter Square]: *Embroidered Bollards*).

This elaborate Ionic column, found in a junkyard, was salvaged from a downtown building. It has been hollowed out at the rear so it can be used as a speaker's rostrum; the idea was to bring activity to this often-deserted public space. Sponsored by Township Institute of Cambridge; funded by the Browne Fund.

RUFUS CHOATE, 1898. Bronze.
In Suffolk County Court House, Pemberton Sq.
★ Daniel Chester French (*see* Concord: *Minuteman*).

Choate (1799–1859), trained in the law, has been called one of the most scholarly of American public men. Born in Ipswich, valedictorian at Dartmouth College, Choate served in both houses of the Massachusetts legislature and in Congress before succeeding his friend Daniel Webster in the U.S. Senate. Gift of George B. Hyde.

MASSACHUSETTS ARTIFACT, 1975. Bronze, h. 30′ × 40′.
McCormick Bldg., 1 Ashburton Pl.
Alfred M. Duca (*see Computersphere* below and Back Bay: *Boston Tapestry*).

Its design influenced by a committee intent upon representing the diversity of the Bay State, this Duca bronze casting is less successful aesthetically than the *Boston Tapestry*. It is nevertheless intriguing as a treasure hunt. Interwoven with the seals of cities and towns are initials of eighty-nine of Massachusetts' most illustrious sons and daughters (all deceased at the time the sculpture was made)—from Tisquantum, "Tis," to the Plymouth Colony's most famous lovers, P.M. and J.A., to A.N.W. (philosopher), eec (poet) and L.F. (merchant founder of the world's most famous bargain basement). Further complicating the design are historic, cultural, ethnic, and institutional references, symbols of regional crafts, trades, and industries, animals both wild and domestic, and a few heroes and legends.

Among new art technology developed by Duca was foam vaporization casting, in which the artist carves an original in polystyrene foam, makes a sand mold around it, and pours in molten metal. Unlike other casting processes, this one permits the original to be left inside, because the styrofoam is vaporized and destroyed by the molten bronze. Duca devised another shortcut to carve the original: he drew his design on a block of styrofoam, then held it under a heat lamp; the dark drawing absorbed heat and melted enough to create an etched-out design, which was then cast in bronze by the foam vaporization process. Funded by 1% for Art.

HUMAN ELEMENT, 1981. Marble, h. 4′ × 7′ × 4′.
RKO General Building, New Sudbury St.
Gerald M. Sherman.
Funded by 1% for Art.

WALL RELIEF, 1973. Steel.
RKO General Building.
Anthony C. Belluschi and Craig D. Roney.
ICA open competition, funded by 1% for Art.

UPWARD BOUND, 1970. Brass, 30′ × 18′ × 15′.
> Overhead, in portico outside Hurley Employment Security Bldg., Staniford and Cambridge Sts.
> C. Fayette Taylor (1894–   ).

After a career as a professor of mechanical engineering at M.I.T., Fayette Taylor retired in 1965 and embarked on a new career in his former avocation, art. Through summer courses in Provincetown and Woodstock, a sojourn in Paris, and study with established artists in Boston and at M.I.T., Taylor had supplied himself with a complete art education, including life drawing, etching, and painting. After retirement, he began to draw upon his engineering skills to create sculpture in brass, steel, and stainless steel. A native of New York and a graduate of Yale, he divides his time between Brookline and Rockport.

MURAL, 1970. Plaster, painted. h. approximately 14′.
> State Service Center, Hurley Employment Security Bldg.
> Constantino Nivola (*see* Downtown: *Mural*).

This work and the one immediately below exemplify Boston's tendency, early in its public art renaissance, to seek second-tier New York artists in preference to local talent.

RICHARD CARDINAL CUSHING, 1981. Bronze bust, life-size.
> Cushing Plaza, New Chardon and Cambridge Sts.
> James Rosati (1911–   ).

Most recently on the faculty of Philadelphia Academy of Art, Rosati has also taught at Yale, Dartmouth, and the Vermont School of Art; he has as well been a Guggenheim Fellow. In addition to portrait sculpture, he produces small and large-scale abstractions. Gift of the clergy of the Archdiocese of Boston.

FALCON FORM VI, 1970. Cor-ten steel, h. 5′.
> Jewish Family and Children's Services Center, 31 New Chardon St.
> Herb Harrington.
> Funded by 1% for Art.

COMPUTERSPHERE, 1965–67.
> Cor-ten steel, diam. 8′.
> Government Center Post Office, 25 New Chardon St.
> Alfred M. Duca (*see* Back Bay: *Boston Tapestry*).

The artist believes this may be the first work ever done from a computer-generated design. Funded by 1% for Art.

SUDDEN PRESENCE, 1971. Cor-ten steel, h. approx. 9′.
> At Government Center Garage, New Chardon and Merrimac Sts.
> ★ Beverly Pepper (1924–   ).

Born in Brooklyn, Beverly Pepper studied at Pratt Institute and the Art Students League in New York, and in Paris. After working as art director for advertising agencies, she established herself in Rome in 1949 as an independent artist. Critics say her objects have an intrinsic power that alters the environment in which they are situated. She has spoken of the introspective nature of her work, "the inner reaches of a geometric form. . . . My structures create a relationship that is not clear to the viewer but is instead very private." Her sculpture is owned by the Smithsonian, M.I.T., the Fogg Museum, Dartmouth College, and the Hirschhorn Museum. Funded by 1% for Art.

MR. BIGNOSE COMES TO BOSTON, 1969.
141 Merrimac St.
Todd McKie (1944–   ).

McKie was not long out of Rhode Island School of Design (B.F.A., 1966) when he did this mural as part of Summerthing, a city-sponsored art program intended to defuse inner-city tensions. Now exhibiting as a ceramicist and painter, he is still partial to the whim and caprice seen in these figures. He says he has always thought of them as "the falling figures," and doesn't remember where the title came from. Funded by Summerthing.

DOUBLE BOSTON VENUS, 1987. Bronze, h. 7½'.
90 Canal St.
★ Jim Dine (1935–   ).

One of the stars of the international art scene, Dine was born in Cincinnati, Ohio, and settled on his identity as an artist at an early age. After earning a bachelor's degree in fine arts, he did graduate

GREG HEINS PHOTO COURTESY THE GUND COLLECTION

work at Ohio University and later attended the Boston Museum School. He has held guest and visiting artist positions at Yale, Oberlin, and Cornell School of Architecture. In the 1960s Dine was associated with Pop Art and was perhaps best known for his series of paintings of his bathrobe. His work has also included printmaking and collage/assemblage paintings in which brushes, paint pots, and other accoutrements were left attached to the canvas. In the 1970s Dine's work took a personal turn and became more difficult to define; during this decade he has begun to produce bronze sculpture and to design variations on the Venus de Milo concept.

Architect Graham Gund, one of Boston's foremost collectors of contemporary art, commissioned these sculptures from Dine after Gund's firm converted the eighteenth-century Bulfinch Building here to office space. This is the only outdoor work by Dine in New England; another Dine *Venus* stands in a plaza in San Francisco.

MENORAH and ETERNAL LIGHT, 1972. Welded steel.
Charles River Park Synagogue, Martha Rd.
Richard Bertram.
Commissioned by the congregation.

★ AFRICAN QUEEN, 1979. Oil on cotton duck, diptych, each unit h. $9' \times 8'$.
Main lobby, Massachusetts General Hospital, 55 Fruit St.
John McNamara (1950–   ).

Born in Cambridge, McNamara took a B.F.A. from Massachusetts College of Art in 1971, an M.F.A. in 1977, and began to garner a reputation as one of Boston's outstanding younger painters. Now a resident of Brookline, he has received three grants from the Massachusetts Council on the Arts and Humanities, an Award in the Visual Arts, and a fellowship from the National Endowment for the Arts. Gift of the artist.

BEACON HILL/STATE HOUSE

ARISTEIDES THE JUST and CHRISTOPHER COLUMBUS, ca. 1850. Stone.
Louisburg Sq. (off Mount Vernon St.).

Garden ornaments rather than works of artistic merit, these two stand in one of the most-visited tourist locations on Beacon Hill. Aristeides (ca. 530–468 B.C.) was an Athenian statesman, several times elected strategus (something like a secretary of war) of the city. His sobriquet was probably derived from his fair assessment of taxes when a confederation of city-states, the Delian league, was formed. Legend persists that these statues were shipped from Italy as ballast in a ship owned by Joseph Iasigi, who lived at 3 Louisburg Square. Gift of Joseph Iasigi.

MUSEUM: Boston Athenæum, 10½ Beacon St. Incorporated in 1807, the Atheneum is a private museum/library, but offers tours to visitors. Of interest to connoisseurs of public art are the original plaster model of Ball's equestrian Washington, and a number of busts and sculptures by nineteenth-century sculptors who effected large outdoor pieces as well. A second-floor gallery open to the public exhibits contemporary art.

At the State House:

A catalogue, *Art in the Massachusetts State House*, published in 1986 by the Massachusetts Art Commission, may be purchased at the book store. Only the more prominent works are listed here:

THE BEACON HILL MONUMENT, 1898. Granite and bronze, h. 52'.
    Bowdoin St., parking lot behind the State House.

   This shaft is a re-creation of the 1790 original, the first monument in America to the War of Independence. In 1634 the General Court (legislative body) of the Massachusetts Bay Colony ordered a warning beacon erected atop the tallest of Boston's three hills (then sixty feet higher than it is now). In 1790 it was replaced by a Doric column topped with a gilt eagle and dedicated to the heroes of the American Revolution. The column was designed by Charles Bulfinch, America's first great architect, who next designed the "New" State House that still stands nearby as the front central portion of the vastly enlarged building. Bulfinch's monument was removed in 1811 when the top of the hill was cut down. The present version is a gift of the Bunker Hill Monument Association.

★ MARY DYER, 1959. Bronze, larger than life.
    South lawn, near east wing.
    Sylvia Shaw Judson (b. 1897).

   A Chicagoan, Judson attended the Art Institute of Chicago and then studied in Paris under Bordelle, Rodin's pupil. Her work is owned by the Museum of Modern Art, the Metropolitan Museum and the Philadelphia Museum of Art.
   Mary Dyer and her husband were among those settling in Rhode Island with Anne Hutchinson, although they later broke off and resettled in Newport. During a trip to England, Dyer became a Quaker and, in an early act of civil disobedience, felt compelled to challenge the

Boston colony's anti-Quaker laws enacted in the 1650s. Thrice jailed, once reprieved on the gallows, Dyer returned yet again and was finally hanged in 1660, one of four Quakers executed in the Boston colony during this period. Their deaths impelled King Charles II to overturn the laws, but whipping of Quakers continued until 1665. Funded by legacy of Zenas Ellis of Fair Haven, Vt.

JOSEPH HOOKER, 1903. Bronze, equestrian, larger than life.
    South lawn.
    ★ Daniel Chester French (*see* Concord: *Minuteman*) and Edward C. Potter (*see* Brookline: *Soldiers Monument*).

Major General Hooker (1814–1879) was commander of the Army of the Potomac defeated at Chancellorsville (thanks to Hooker's untimely caution) by Lee in 1863. Bostonians at first objected to the choice of Hadley native Hooker as an example of Union soldiery. But except for that disastrous lapse his military skills were enough to earn him the sobriquet "Fighting Joe"; he was twice wounded, and performed superbly as a subordinate commander for most of the war. French modeled the figure; Potter, the horse. Funded by an appropriation of the Commonwealth.

DANIEL WEBSTER, 1859. Bronze, larger than life.
    South lawn, Beacon St.
    ★ Hiram Powers (1805–1873).

Young Hiram migrated to Ohio with his family about 1818 to escape a famine in Vermont. Working odd jobs, Powers became a supervisor at a Cincinnati museum, where he learned to model clay. He traveled East, soliciting portrait bust commissions so successfully that President Jackson, Calhoun, and Webster all sat for him. Armed with further commissions, he and his family relocated permanently in Florence, Italy, then the center for American sculptors. His *Greek Slave* (begun in 1843), so popular that he produced it in nine versions, brought him international fame.

The first Webster statue shipped from Italy was lost at sea; a second casting reached Boston and was erected in 1859. Webster (*see* Marshfield: *Webster, the Farmer of Marshfield*) was a New Hampshire-born orator, Congressman and Senator, proponent of the Union, and Secretary of State under Harrison and Fillmore. Funded by Webster Memorial Committee.

HORACE MANN, 1865. Bronze, larger than life.
    South lawn.
    ★ Emma Stebbins (1815–1882).

Born in New York City, Stebbins first had a career as a painter; she was over forty when she went to Rome to study sculpture. Among her works is *Angel of the Waters*, a fountain in Central Park, N.Y.

Horace Mann (1796–1859), best known for his educational theories, was first a lawyer and Massachusetts legislator. As president of the state Senate in 1836–37, he pushed for creation of a State Board of Education, then became its first secretary. Although the board had little power, Mann skillfully turned the state's regressive school systems into a model for other states. Congressman from 1848 to 1852, Mann accepted the presidency of newly formed Antioch College in Ohio, a liberal school where he was able to extend his theories favoring non-sectarian, non-sexist education. Funded by a collection from Massachusetts school children and teachers.

ANNE HUTCHINSON, 1922. Bronze, larger than life.
South lawn, near west wing.
★ Cyrus E. Dallin (*see* Arlington: *Indian Hunter*).

Emigrating from England with her husband in 1634, Hutchinson became a leader among the women of the Massachusetts Bay colony and shortly challenged its theocracy by advocating "a covenant of grace," not "a covenant of works" (strict adherence to Biblical scripture). She had the support of Governor Vane (*see* Back Bay [Boston Public Library]: *Sir Henry Vane*) and some of the clergy, but when Vane was defeated in the election of the general court in 1637, she was tried, excommunicated, and exiled. She and her husband founded a colony of religious seekers in Rhode Island; after his death she formed another on Long Island, New York, where she was killed by Indians—an event Boston Puritans ascribed to divine retribution. Funded by Anne Hutchinson Memorial Association and State Federation of Women's Clubs.

HENRY CABOT LODGE, 1932. Bronze, heroic size.
South lawn, west end.
Raymond A. Porter (*see* Somerville: *Spanish War Memorial*).

The elder Lodge (1850–1924) was a Republican member of Congress for thirty-eight years, more than thirty of them in the Senate. He is remembered principally for his opposition to President Wilson and the League of Nations. Commissioned by the Commonwealth.

GEORGE WASHINGTON, 1826. Marble, heroic size.
In Doric Hall.
Sir Francis Chantrey (1781–1841).

Chantrey, a British neoclassical sculptor, was chosen to execute this work because no American sculptor was thought capable. First significant statue in Boston, it was commissioned to mark the 50th anniversary of American independence. Funded by a private committee.

JOHN ALBION ANDREW, 1871. Marble, larger than life.
Doric Hall.
★ Thomas Ball (*see* Boston Public Garden: *George Washington*).

Andrew (1818–1867) was governor of Massachusetts during the Civil War, a friend of Lincoln's, and effective supporter of the Union. A graduate of Bowdoin College and a lawyer, he based his strong antislavery stand on Unitarian religious convictions. Thanks to him, Massachusetts was the only northern state prepared for war; its troops were the first to go to the defense of the nation's capital. Andrew organized the first black regiments and fought successfully to have them paid on a par with white troops. Funded by public subscription.

WAR NURSES SCULPTURE, 1911. Bronze, heroic size.
  Nurses' Hall, State House.
  Bela Pratt (*see* Malden: *The Flag Defenders*).

WILLIAM FRANCIS BARTLETT, 1901. Bronze, larger than life.
  Hall of Flags.
  ★ Daniel Chester French (*see* Concord: *Minuteman*).

  Bartlett was twenty-one when the Civil War broke out; he volun-
  teered, and rose to general by the age of twenty-four. He was urged
  to run for governor, but died at the age of thirty-six, before he had the
  opportunity to seek office. This statue was intended for the State
  House grounds, but on acceptance in 1903 it was placed in Memorial
  Hall with Civil War battle flags. Flags of other wars have since been
  added.

ROGER WOLCOTT, 1906. Bronze, larger than life.
  Third floor, opposite main staircase.
  ★ Daniel Chester French (*see* Concord: *Minuteman*).

  Governor during the massive addition to the State House by
  Brigham in 1898, Wolcott championed the preservation of the Bulfinch
  section, which now houses Doric Hall, the old and new Senate cham-
  bers, and executive offices.

BOSTON COMMON

★ ROBERT GOULD SHAW AND THE 54TH MASSACHUSETTS REGI-
  MENT, 1897. Bronze bas-relief.
  Beacon St. at Park St.
  ★ Augustus Saint-Gaudens (1848–1907).

  A cobbler's son, born in Ireland but raised in New York, Saint-
  Gaudens began as a cameo-cutter, studied in Paris and Rome, and
  worked in New York and Cornish, N.H. Synthesizing vigorous naturalism and abstract ideals, he is best known for the enigmatic *Adams
  Memorial* in Washington, D.C.
  Scion of a prominent and idealistic Boston family, the twenty-six-
  year-old Shaw, already a veteran of Antietam and Cedar Mountain,
  was offered command of the first black regiment (the 54th Massachusetts) to fight for the Union. His 900 troops, first of 180,000 blacks to
  enlist, were trained near Boston. Assigned to the siege of Fort Wagner, South Carolina, Col. Shaw and his men paraded down Beacon
  Hill toward their transport ships just as their bronze counterparts do
  now. Outnumbered two-to-one in an assault on Fort Wagner in July,
  1863, the regiment was decimated; Shaw and his troops were uncere-
  moniously buried by the Confederates in a mass grave there. Some
  survived—Sgt. William Carney, thrice-wounded, snatched up the flag,
  rallied the regiment, and became the first black to receive the
  Congressional Medal of Honor.
  Saint-Gaudens took fourteen years to complete the work, taking
  pains to portray the soldiers hidden behind the horse in as much

detail as those readily seen. This work is thought to be the finest memorial in the city, and perhaps the finest war memorial anywhere. Funds raised by a citizens' commission.

BOSTON MASSACRE MONUMENT, 1888. Granite and bronze.
　　Tremont St.
　　Robert Kraus (1850–1902).

　　Records are oddly lacking regarding Kraus, who also sculpted the *Theodore Parker* now in Roxbury.
　　Names of the five Bostonians killed by British soldiers in the 1770 brawl are inscribed on the column behind a melodramatic Freedom, complete with flag, broken chain, eagle, and trod-upon British crown. One victim's hand, extending in high relief from the bronze plaque depicting the massacre, is kept polished by visitors who like to shake it. Many think they are shaking the hand of Crispus Attucks, famed as the first black to fall for this nation. But Attucks lies in the foreground, his protruding shoe toe also polished.

SOLDIERS' AND SAILORS' MONUMENT, 1877. Bronze and granite. h. 70'.
　　On Flagstaff Hill.
　　Martin Milmore (*see* Framingham: *Civil War Memorial*).

　　The four statues at the base represent Peace, the Sailor, the Muse of History, and the Soldier; the bas-relief plaques (now grotesquely vandalized) between them depict the departure and return of the forces, the Navy, and the work of the Boston Sanitary Commission. (In one plaque, Longfellow with his great beard can be seen accompanying the governor.) The figures at the base of the column represent the sections of the country, North, South, East, and West. The Genius of America stands at the top. The inscription was written by Harvard president Charles W. Eliot. Funded by the Commonwealth.

(DETAIL)

THE BREWER FOUNTAIN, 1855. Bronze.
　　Near Tremont and Temple Sts.
　　Paul Lienard, French sculptor (d. 1900).

　　Brought home by Beacon Hill resident Gardner Brewer from the Paris Exposition of 1867, this is one of several castings from the 1855 original. Modeled in the Renaissance style, which seeks to portray the classic beauty of the human body, the mythological figures at the base are Greek god of the sea Poseidon, his wife Amphitrite, sea-nymph Galatea, and her lover Acis. Gift to the city from Gardner Brewer.

THE PARTISANS, 1979. Cast metal, larger than life.
Near Charles and Beacon Sts.
Andrzei Pitynski (1947–   ).

Pitynski, born in 1947 in Ulanow, Poland, studied at the Academy of Fine Arts and the Museum of Fine Arts in Cracow, becoming conservator of sculpture at Jagiellonski University Museum in that city. He emigrated to New York in 1974, studying at the New York Art Students League and at Sculpture House. He shortly joined the Johnson Atelier/Technical Institute in Princeton, N.J., where he is supervisor of the modeling, resins, and moldmaking departments.

One of the most popular of Boston's outdoor works, *The Partisans* is technically here on temporary loan. A tribute to guerilla freedom fighters everywhere, beaten but still persisting, it is realistic enough to intrigue viewers and enigmatic enough to provoke questions. Installation sponsored by J. Seward Johnson, Johnson Atelier.

PARKMAN PLAZA, 1958–60. Three bronze statues, life-size, to Learning, Religion, and Industry.
On Lafayette Mall, Tremont St. side of Boston Common.
Arcangelo Cascieri and Adio DiBiccari.

Both Cascieri and DiBiccari were Boston artists, the former, dean of Boston Architectural Center.

In 1908 George Francis Parkman (1823–1908) left five million dollars to Boston's public parks, expressing a hope that the Common would always remain one of them. Parkman was the son of the wealthy banker Dr. George F. Parkman, who disappeared in 1849, victim of one of Boston's most sensational murders; the perpetrator was found to be a Harvard professor. Commissioned by the City of Boston.

THE FOUNDERS' MEMORIAL, 1930. Bronze bas-relief.
Near junction of Beacon and Spruce Sts.
John F. Paramino (*see* Fenway: *World War II Memorial*).

Boston's first settler, the recluse William Blackstone (he spelled it Blaxton), is shown greeting John Winthrop and his small band who had found Charlestown unsatisfactory and crossed to Shawmut, the peninsula that is now Boston. Distinguishable in the group are John Wilson, clergyman, and Ann Pollard, first white woman to step upon Boston's soil (who is not to be confused with the allegorical female figure symbolizing Boston). Inscription on the rear of the monument is a quote from Winthrop before the group debarked from the ship *Arabella* in 1630. Commissioned by the City of Boston to mark its 300th anniversary.

BOSTON PUBLIC GARDEN

★ EDWARD EVERETT HALE, 1913. Bronze, larger than life.
Near Charles St.
Bela Lyon Pratt (*see* Malden: *The Flag Defenders*).

Pratt's naturalistic portrait of Hale was something of a departure for the time: a statue out for a stroll in the garden, just like everyone else.

Hale (1822–1909), Unitarian minister (chaplain of the U.S. Senate) and popular author, produced or edited more than sixty books of fiction, biography, history, travel, and sermons. He edited several magazines and contributed copiously to others; he was author of *The Man Without a Country*. His uncle was the orator Edward Everett; his great-uncle, the martyred spy, Nathan Hale. Funded by subscription among citizens.

TRITON BABIES, 1922. Bronze fountain, figures larger than life.
Anna Coleman Watts Ladd (1878–1939).

Born in Bryn Mawr, Pa., Anna Ladd studied in Paris in the studio of Rodin and in Rome. She lived in Beverly Farms.

The title of this group is puzzling; the Triton of Greek mythology is a merman, fish from the waist down. These two, although aquatically inclined, are totally human. Brought from the Panama Pacific Exhibit by Mrs. Boylston Beal, a wealthy Beacon St. resident, this fountain was placed across from her home in the spot now occupied by the George Robert White Memorial. It was moved to this site in 1924.

MAKE WAY FOR DUCKLINGS, 1987. Bronze, h. 40″ × 35′ (approx.)
Near Charles and Beacon Sts.
Nancy Schön (1928–   ).

Born in Boston, Nancy Schön took a bachelor's degree in sociology from Tufts, then an M.F.A. and a fifth fellowship year from the Boston Museum School. She has also held a fellowship from the Virginia Center for the Creative Arts. She lives in Newton.

Make Way for Ducklings, a children's book written by Robert Mc-Closkey in 1941, won the Caldecott Medal (an award given annually for outstanding juvenile literature) in 1942. It quickly became a favorite and a classic, going through seventeen printings and selling more than 700,000 copies. With his own drawings, McCloskey relates the tale of a pair of mallard ducks looking for a nesting site in Boston. They find the perfect place on an island in the Charles River Basin, but they remember the peanuts fed them by visitors to the Public Garden. When the ducklings are old enough, Mrs. Mallard and her progeny take an insouciant stroll up sidewalks and through traffic to the pond in the Garden. One of Boston's newer traditions is a children's parade in the spring, retracing the ducklings' route. Dedicated in the 150th anniversary year of the Public Garden, the sculpture is considered a tribute to McCloskey, whose drawings the sculptor followed closely. Given to the City of Boston by Friends of the Public Garden.

WENDELL PHILLIPS, 1915. Bronze, larger than life.
 Boylston St. mall.
 ★ Daniel Chester French (*see* Concord: *Minuteman*).

 Phillips (1811–1884) is best known as a masterly abolitionist orator; after the Civil War, he worked in other reform causes including women's suffrage, prohibition, and penal reform. Funded by appropriation from the Boston City Council.

THOMAS CASS, 1899. Bronze, larger than life.
 Boylston St. mall.
 Richard E. Brooks (1865–1919).

 The granite industry in Quincy is credited with kindling the sculptural interests of Brooks, a native of nearby Braintree. He first set up shop as a commercial sculptor, modeling terra cotta panels for buildings and private homes. Commissioned to do a bust of Gov. William E. Russell, Brooks was inspired to go to Paris to study; there he achieved some success. He became a follower of the Symbolist movement, which departed from strict realism to convey impressions by suggestion. This work, reverting to realism, was awarded a gold medal at the Paris Exposition of 1900.

A native of Ireland, Col. Cass was killed at Malvern Hill in July, 1862, at the head of his "Fighting Ninth" Massachusetts Regiment, a unit he organized entirely of Irish immigrants. Funded by the Jonathan Phillips Fund.

TADEUSZ KOSCIUSZKO, 1927. Bronze, larger than life.
Boylston St. mall.
Theo Alice Ruggles Kitson (*see* Malden: *The Hiker*).

Rallying to the American cause for idealistic reasons, Kosciuszko, a thirty-year-old Polish army captain, became Washington's adjutant and a colonel of artillery; he distinguished himself at the battles of New York and Yorktown. He had less success defending his home-land against Russian and Prussian invaders, but is remembered as a statesman advocating absolute liberty and equality before the law. Commissioned by Boston Polish organizations to commemorate the 150th anniversary of Kosciuszko's joining the Continental Army.

CHARLES SUMNER, 1878. Bronze, larger than life.
Boylston St. mall.
★ Thomas Ball (*see* Downtown: *Josiah Quincy*).

When Anne Whitney's proposal for a Sumner statue was rejected because of her gender (*see* Cambridge [Harvard Square]: *Sumner*), Thomas Ball was the sculptor given the commission. This work is the result.

Uncompromising advocate of emancipation and free speech, Sum-ner (1811–1874) served in the U.S. Senate for twenty-two years. His oratory opposing the Compromise of 1850 (which allowed slavery to expand into new territories) provoked an attack on the Senate floor from a cane-wielding Southern Congressman, who injured Sumner se-verely. During the three years it took Sumner to recover, Massachu-setts re-elected him and let his vacant seat speak for him. Commissioned by the Commonwealth.

GEORGE WASHINGTON, 1869. Bronze, equestrian, larger than life.
★ Thomas Ball (*see* Downtown: *Josiah Quincy*).

On horseback at the west end of the Public Garden, Washington (1732–1798), Revolutionary commander-in-chief and first President, looks down Commonwealth Avenue. The plaster study for this work is

at the Boston Athenæum. Washington's sword has been broken so often by vandals that he is now equipped with a weapon of replaceable fiberglass. Funds raised by the sculptor's friends and an appropriation from the city.

BOY AND BIRD, 1934, recast 1977. Bronze fountain, life-size.
   On *Washington*'s (see above) left.
   Bashka Paeff (1893–1979).

   Paeff was born in Russia; she studied in Paris and at the Boston Museum School under Bela Pratt.

SMALL CHILD. Bronze fountain, life-size.
   On *Washington*'s (see above) right.
   Mary E. Moore (1887–1967).

   Another of Bela Pratt's students, Moore taught at Beaver Country Day School in Brookline. She was born in Taunton. Given to the City of Boston by Mrs. Alfred Tozzer.

GEORGE ROBERT WHITE MEMORIAL, 1924. Bronze, larger than life.
   Beacon and Arlington Sts.
   ★ Daniel Chester French (*see* Concord: *The Minuteman*).

   In his day, French was famous for his sculpted angels. As a boy on his father's farm in Concord he became interested in animals and birds; his biographer daughter recounts that he had a collection of birds' wings that must have inspired his winged figures. French's original title for this statue was *The Spirit of Giving*; the allegorical figure is casting bread upon the waters.
   Having accumulated a fortune in the wholesale drug business, White (1847–1922) became one of Boston's foremost philanthropists. His five-million-dollar legacy to the city provided funds for clinics and for art, including $50,000 for his own memorial.

THE ETHER MONUMENT, 1867. Granite and red marble.
   Near Arlington St.
   ★ John Quincy Adams Ward (*see* Newburyport: *George Washington*).

   The miracle of pain-free surgery was first realized at Massachusetts General Hospital in Boston in 1846: Dr. William G. Morton, a dentist who found ether useful in his practice, assisted Dr. J. C. Warren in removing a tumor from the neck of a patient named Gilbert Abbot. Claim to the discovery was disputed by Dr. Charles T. Jackson, and Ward resolved the dilemma by neither depicting nor naming the pioneers of anesthesia; the solicitous figure he carved is meant to be the Good Samaritan. (Oliver Wendell Holmes quipped that the monument was a memorial "to ether—or either.")

WILLIAM ELLERY CHANNING, 1902. Bronze, life-size.
   Opposite Arlington St. Church, Arlington and Boylston Sts.
   Herbert Adams (*see* Woburn: *Col. Loammi Baldwin*).

   A gentle and much-loved clergyman, advocate of spiritual and intellectual freedom, Channing (1780–1842) was minister of the Federal

Street Congregational Church in Boston from 1803 until his death. Following a sermon in 1819 he became known as "the apostle of Unitarianism," although he objected to the term. He wrote and spoke in opposition to slavery, but rejected enforced abolition as too radical; he thought an enlightened public conscience would end slavery. His thinking on war and peace, the education of children, and separation of church and state would be liberal in our own day. Funded by legacy of John Foster.

COMMONWEALTH AVENUE

ALEXANDER HAMILTON, 1865. Granite, larger than life.
On the mall between Arlington and Berkeley Sts.
Dr. William Rimmer (1816–1879).

William Rimmer's father, spirited out of France as a boy and raised genteelly in England, had reason to believe he was Louis XVII, the lost Dauphin of France. There were some forty other contenders, so for his own safety Thomas Rimmer emigrated to the New World and altered his name. Although the father worked as a cobbler, William was raised in an intellectual and culture-conscious home and encouraged in his pursuit of art as a profession. He had little success, pursuing a variety of odd trades until, in his thirties, his interest in anatomy led to self-taught medical study; he practiced in Randolph and East Milton for a few years. At the age of forty-five he turned to sculpture full-time, with mixed results; this statue was controversial. Rimmer knew so little about technique (he failed to use an armature) that parts kept falling off; nevertheless, powered by creative energy, he completed the clay model for *Hamilton* in eleven days. He later taught art anatomy at Cooper Union in New York and in Boston, and wrote a comprehensive book on the subject.

A native of the West Indies, Hamilton (1757–1804) emigrated to the colonial mainland and threw himself into the American rebellion, becoming General Washington's aide and private secretary. His financial genius (he had been in charge of a counting-house on St. Croix at the age of thirteen) mandated his appointment as first Secretary of the Treasury. His political thought was strongly Federalist, advocating a propertied oligarchy and an elected monarch who would rule for life. Hamilton's brilliance was marred by his penchant for intrigue; he schemed against John Adams, hoping to deprive him of the Presidency. Another feud with Aaron Burr brought about the duel that cost him his life. Gift of Thomas Lee.

GEN. JOHN GLOVER, 1875. Bronze, larger than life.
Between Berkeley and Clarendon Sts.
Martin Milmore (*see* Framingham: *Civil War Memorial*).

Glover (1732–1797) led perhaps the most unusual regiment of the American Revolution, an "amphibious" regiment composed largely of Marblehead fishermen who supplied aquatic transportation for Washington's army. Born in Salem, Glover became one of the "codfish aristocracy"; he was a fish merchant and owner of a fishing fleet. His regiment of small boats saved Washington's army after the Battle of

Long Island, ferrying 9,000 men to New York, and it was he and his men who rowed the general and 2,400 troops across the Delaware on Christmas night, 1776, braving snowstorm and river ice, to attack and rout the Hessian mercenaries at Trenton.

ANGELS FRIEZE, 1872. Carved stone.
Bell tower, First Baptist Church, Clarendon St. and Commonwealth Ave.
Frederic Auguste Bartholdi (1834–1904).

It has been said that if Bartholdi had not created the Statue of Liberty, he would be totally forgotten today. Architect H. H. Richardson, famed for his brownstone Romanesque public buildings, designed this as the Brattle Square Church in 1872. He commissioned the French sculptor Bartholdi to cut the decorative frieze to terminate its flat-topped Italianate bell tower. The bas-reliefs on the four sides represent baptism, communion, matrimony, and death. Thanks to the angels sounding trumpets on the four corners, the building was nicknamed the Church of the Holy Bean Blowers.

PATRICK ANDREW COLLINS, 1908. Bronze bust and supporting figures.
Commonwealth Ave. between Clarendon and Dartmouth Sts.
Henry Hudson Kitson (*see* Lexington: *The Minuteman*), and Theo Alice Ruggles Kitson (*see* Malden: *The Hiker*).

Mayor of Boston from 1902 to 1905, Collins (1844–1905) died suddenly in office. By trade an upholsterer, he became a lawyer, state legislator, member of Congress, and consul general in London. Originally farther down Commonwealth Ave. at Charlesgate West, Collins' monument was relocated in 1968. The figures represent Columbia and Erin. Funded by public subscription.

WILLIAM LLOYD GARRISON, 1886. Bronze, larger than life.
Between Dartmouth and Exeter Sts.
★   Olin Levi Warner (*see* Charles River Esplanade: *General Devens*).

The Garrison family hated this likeness and commissioned Anne Whitney to do a small, more personable one. (For Garrison's biography, *see* Newburyport: *William Lloyd Garrison*.) Funded by public subscription.

★ SAMUEL ELIOT MORISON, 1982. Bronze, larger than life. (*see* cover photo).
    On the mall between Exeter and Fairfield Sts.
    Penelope Jencks (*see* Chelsea: *Chelsea Conversation*).

    One of America's foremost maritime historians, Morison (1887–1976) twice won the Pulitzer Prize, for *Admiral of the Ocean Sea* and for *John Paul Jones*. An able sailor, Morison researched Columbus' life in the libraries of Spain and then personally retraced the great explorer's route in a sailboat, following the entries in his log. He also wrote the definitive *History of U.S. Naval Operations in World War II*. Commissioned by the Back Bay Federation with funds from the George B. Henderson Foundation.

DOMINGO FAUSTINO SARMIENTO, 1973. Bronze, heroic size.
    Commonwealth Ave. between Gloucester and Hereford Sts.
    Ivette Compagnion.

    Compagnion is an Argentine sculptor.
    The bulky, brooding figure of Domingo Sarmiento (1811–1888) seems misplaced on Commonwealth Mall; it is hard to guess that the subject was a famed political leader: writer, legislator, founder of his country's educational system, minister to the United States, and president of Argentina. He stands here because his admiration for Horace Mann led him to model Argentine educational programs on Boston's school system. A monument to Sarmiento in Boston was first proposed in 1913, but not realized until 1973. Gift of the Argentine Republic.

LEIF ERIKSSON, 1887. Bronze, life-size.
    Commonwealth Ave. at Charlesgate.
    ★ Anne Whitney (*see* Quincy Market: *Samuel Adams*).

    The legendary Norse explorer was memorialized here at the behest of Eben N. Horsford, a patent medicine maker, who believed that Vineland was located on the Charles River. This statue once overlooked the river; filling and highway-building have left Leif with a view of nothing much but traffic. Gift of Eben N. Horsford.

BACK BAY

EMANCIPATION GROUP, 1877. Bronze, larger than life.
    Park Square, Charles and Stuart Sts.
    ★ Thomas Ball (*see* Boston Public Garden: *Washington*).

    Commissioned by the Freedman's Memorial Society, the original version of this work stands in Lincoln Park in Washington, D.C. Charlotte Scott, a freedwoman from Virginia, originated the idea for this statue the day after Lincoln was shot, and its $17,000 cost was paid entirely by freed slaves. The head of the slave is modeled on that of Archer Alexander, the last person recaptured under the Fugitive Slave Act. This duplicate casting was given to the city by Moses Kimball in 1877.

GALLERY: Artists Foundation Gallery, in Transportation Bldg., Charles and
Stuart Sts. Exhibitions featuring contemporary regional artists,
particularly winners of Artists Foundation Fellowships.

MURAL, early 1970s.
Top facade of Josiah Quincy School, visible from east end of Mass. Pike.
Maria Termini.

Termini, a maker of serigraph prints and teacher at Brookline Arts
Center, designed this mural with input from students at Quincy
School. She earned her B.A. and M.F.A. at Catholic University in
Washington; she has taught at the Art Institute of Boston and at the
Cambridge Center for Adult Education. Executed by The Architects
Collaborative.

GREEK KEY, 1969-70. Cor-ten steel, h. 6′ × 40′.
Howard Johnson Complex, 200 Stuart St.
Alfred Duca (see Back Bay: Boston Tapestry).

This welded sculpture weighs eight tons. Funded by 1% for Art.

JOHN WINTHROP, 1880. Bronze, life-size.
At First and Second Church, 66 Marlborough St.
★ Richard Saltonstall Greenough (see Cambridge [Harvard University]:
Governor John Winthrop).

Greenough's marble Winthrop is one of the state's two allotted statues in Statuary Hall in the U.S. Capitol in Washington. This bronze
replica was placed in Scollay Square (now the site of Government
Center) in 1880, moved here in 1903, and damaged in a 1968 fire
that gutted the church.
Winthrop (1588–1649), English lawyer and strict Puritan, was first
governor of the Massachusetts Bay Colony, later Boston. Between the
settling in 1630 and his death he was elected governor a dozen times
and is credited with staving off Parliamentary interference with the colony more than once. It was his re-election as governor, opposing the
more tolerant Sir Henry Vane, that initiated the expulsion of Anne
Hutchinson and subsequent persecution of non-Puritans.

SUSPENDED SCULPTURE, 1985. Brass, gold-plating, h. 7′ × 3′ × 2½′.
Interior, First and Second Church, 66 Marlborough St.
Michio Ihara (see Lowell: Pawtucket Prism).

★ SALADA TEA DOORS, 1927. Bronze, marble doorframe, h. 12′.
330 Stuart St.
Henry Wilson (1864–1934).

Architect, sculptor, metalworker, and jeweller, British artist Henry
Wilson taught at the Royal College of Art. These doors, which cost
half a million dollars to produce, won a silver medal at the Paris Salon
in 1927. A generation ago, when possibilities for juvenile entertain-
ment were less spectacular than they are today, parents used to bring
their children into Boston to see the exotic bronze and marble carved

(DETAIL)

reliefs depicting the growing and shipping of tea. The building is no longer occupied by the tea company.

JOHN HANCOCK, 1950. Bronze with gold patina, heroic size.
   Lobby of old John Hancock Bldg. (the Berkeley Bldg.), 200 Berkeley St.
   ★ Paul Manship (*see* Andover: *Armillary Sphere*).

   For Hancock biography, *see* Quincy: *John Hancock*.

THE DAY OF DECISION, 1950. Ceiling mural.
   Lobby, old John Hancock Bldg.
   Barry Faulkner (b. 1881).

   A native of Keene, N.H., Faulkner became associated with the Monadnock School of painting grouped around Abbott Thayer in nearby Dublin, N.H. He went on to work in New York and study at the Art Students League and at the American Academy in Rome. His murals at the National Archives in Washington illustrate the signing of the Declaration of Independence and the Constitution.

   Here Faulkner depicts the moment on July 2, 1776, when Benjamin Harrison of Virginia has resolved "that these United Colonies are, and of right ought to be, free and independent states." John Hancock, president of the Congress, sits in the president's chair.

PHILLIPS BROOKS, 1910. Bronze, larger than life.
   North of Trinity Church, Copley Sq., Boylston and Clarendon Sts.
   ★ Augustus Saint-Gaudens (*see* Boston Common: *Shaw Memorial*) and Francis Grimes. Canopy by Stanford White.

   Completed by Saint-Gaudens' students during the sculptor's final illness, this work falls short of the sculptor's best. The Brooks head was among partially completed clay works saved from a disastrous fire in the Cornish, N.H., studio, in 1903. Saint-Gaudens' first version of a Christ head, bare, its eyes closed, exists in Cornish; the final hooded version here, its hand on Brooks' shoulder, was done by Grimes under the master's supervision. It inspired a comment from a contemporary wit that the group ought to be called "The boys want to talk to you down at the station." Saint-Gaudens did not live to see the work unveiled.

Brooks (1835–1893), former rector of Trinity Church and briefly Episcopal bishop of Massachusetts, is depicted preaching. A century ago his sermons were widely read; he is now best remembered as author of "O Little Town of Bethlehem." Funded by Trinity Church congregation.

At Boston Public Library:

More detailed descriptions may be found in the Handbook to the Art and Architecture of Boston Public Library, *for sale at the library's business office. A partial listing follows:*

★ ART and SCIENCE, 1911. Bronze, larger than life.
Dartmouth St. entrance, facing Copley Sq.
Bela Lyon Pratt (*see* Malden: *The Flag Defenders*).

Architect Charles McKim specified lavish use of art and sculpture for the 1895 Boston Public Library. Saint-Gaudens was commissioned to do the exterior sculpture but, a procrastinator, he had only preliminary models at the time of his death in 1907. Pratt completed these allegorical female figures, and the master's brother, Louis Saint-Gaudens, carved the Sienna marble lions on the main staircase inside. The three heraldic seals above the entrance are by Saint-Gaudens.

KNOWLEDGE AND WISDOM, TRUTH AND ROMANCE, MUSIC AND
   POETRY, 1902. Paired bronze doors.
   Dartmouth St. entrance.
   ★ Daniel Chester French (*see* Concord: *Minuteman*).

Commissioned by the library's architect, Charles McKim, French's doors embodied a new idea in bronze door-making: instead of many narrative panels, there is one low-relief allegorical figure on each. The sculptor's daughter relates that she asked him the difference between wisdom and knowledge; French said, "Knowledge is proud that she hath learned so much—Wisdom is humble that she knows no more."

SIR HENRY VANE, 1893. Bronze, life-size.
   Dartmouth St. entry.
   ★ Frederic MacMonnies (1863–1937).

Although he was born in New York City and died there, MacMonnies spent much of his career working in Paris. While studying at the Art Students League and at the National Academy of Design in New York, he assisted Augustus Saint-Gaudens. After winning the Prix d'Atelier, MacMonnies found commissions from America flowing into his studio and subsequently did important sculpture for the cities of New York and Denver, the Library of Congress, and the Columbian Exposition of 1893. World War I forced his return to this country.

Son of an English secretary of state, Vane the younger (1613–1662) emigrated in 1635 to Massachusetts in order to practice his strong Puritan views. A spokesman for toleration, he served one year as governor in 1636 but was defeated in 1637 by Winthrop; under the latter, Anne Hutchinson and her free-thinking followers were expelled from the Bay Colony, and Vane returned to England in disgust. Although he opposed the execution of King Charles I, Vane served Cromwell until the Puritan dictator forcibly dissolved Parliament. After the king's restoration Vane, despite his advocacy of tolerance, negotiation, and compromise, was accused of high treason and executed. Gift of Dr. Charles Goddard Weld.

THE MUSES OF INSPIRATION WELCOMING THE SPIRIT OF LIGHT, and eight allegorical murals, 1895–6. Oil on canvas, large mural, h. 20' × 40'. Main staircase.
> ★ Pierre Puvis de Chavannes (1824–1898).

The paintings in the stairwell are by France's greatest muralist, who did them immediately after completing acclaimed work at the Hotel de Ville in Paris. The eight panels in the upper arches represent science, poetry, and philosophy, subdivided into categories similar to library catalogue classifications: on the right are pastoral, dramatic, and epic poetry; on the left, history, astronomy, and philosophy, and on either side of the window, chemistry and physics. The City has recently allocated funds to clean this and other murals in the library.

QUEST OF THE HOLY GRAIL, 1895. h. 8'.
Delivery room (research circulation desk).
Edwin Austin Abbey (1852–1911).

An outstanding Victorian-era illustrator, Philadelphia-born Abbey was obsessed with the romance of English medieval legend. In this narrative set of scenes Sir Galahad is always clad in red; the Biblical figure in white is Joseph of Arimethea, from whom Galahad was traditionally descended. Abbey lived in England at this time and was a member of the Royal Academy.

JUDAISM AND CHRISTIANITY, 1893–1919.
Third floor corridor, atop main staircase.
> ★ John Singer Sargent (1856–1925).

Enormously celebrated in his day, Sargent fell into eclipse as twentieth-century modernism flourished. Descended from a Gloucester family, the painter was born in Italy, where his cosmopolitan parents had gone for a change of scene. Although he traveled often to this country, his was a continental life; he lived for forty years in London. Tall, handsome, socially well-connected, Sargent never in his career had to seek a commission; he painted English nobility and American nouveau-riche with equal honesty and facility. In 1910, at the height of his fame, he found himself bored and renounced what he called "paughtraits," turning to watercolor and to commissions such as this one, which he considered the crowning achievement of his life work. Biographers describe Sargent as an omnivorous reader, a passionate musician, an excellent host, and an artist oblivious to critical comment, generous to students and fellow artists. He is buried in St. Paul's Cathedral, London.

Although Sargent traveled to Egypt and Palestine to absorb authenticity, and spent thirty years on the project, this series looks embarrassingly dogmatic today. On the north "pagan" wall are the children of Israel under their oppressors and a frieze of prophets; on the south, the Christian dogma of redemption. On the west wall seven swords representing the seven sorrows pierce the heart of the Virgin, and opposite are the Synagogue, represented as blind and dethroned, and the Church, triumphant. The chauvinistic attitude of these works is an enigma; Sargent's biographers present him as a man who neither evidenced nor practiced any particular religious convictions.

★ PAINT and HENRY, 1987. Welded sheet copper on cast bronze armature, h. 86″ and 89″.
Exterior plaza, Copley Place, Dartmouth and Stuart Sts.
Deborah Butterfield (1949–   ).

Butterfield's horse sculptures are portraits, in a style that has earned her widespread recognition, of the animals she and her husband raise on their ranch in Montana. A Californian, Butterfield received a B.F.A. and an M.F.A. from the University of California at Davis. Her work is owned by such museums as the Hirschhorn, Whitney, and Metropolitan in New York, by museums in Chicago, Cincinnati, and Jerusalem, and by several corporations.

The artist is also a dedicated dressage rider; her love of her animals and knowledge of their forms and postures enable her to create the unmistakable concept, "horse," in an abstract way (she always leaves the interior armature showing) and with unlikely mediums. For interior spaces, she constructs horses of such found materials as branches, burlap, straw, mud, and corrugated iron. Purchase of Urban Investment and Development Co.

FOUNTAIN, 1985. Granite, travertines, marble, h. three stories by 140′.
Second-floor atrium, Copley Place.
Dimitri Hadzi (*see* Brookline: *Primavera*).

The verticals here form "symbolic welcoming gates," the artist says. Color and forms were inspired by local architecture such as nearby Trinity Church.

PEOPLE IN THE PARK, 1983. Bronze, six pieces, h. 4'.
In Boylston Park Cafe, Sheraton Boston Hotel, 39 Dalton St.
Richard Duca (*see* Cambridge [Mount Auburn Cemetery]: *Knoll Garden Sculpture*).

★   BOSTON TAPESTRY, 1962. Cast iron and stained glass, h. 20' × 60', weight five tons.
South Lobby of Prudential Bldg.
Alfred Duca (1920–   ).

A native of Milton, Duca was trained at Pratt Institute and the Boston Museum School and became active on the Boston art scene during the years of Boston Expressionism, the 1950s. As a young painter, he evolved a new artists' medium by hand-grinding pigments into polyvinyl acetate solvents; he is considered the inventor of polymer tempera paint. Invited to M.I.T. to experiment with new casting methods, Duca used them in producing this sculpture for the then-new Prudential Center, at that time the tallest building in New England.

Sand-casting, a traditional means of reproducing forms in metal, ordinarily requires a master object made in some other material, such as plaster, clay, or wood. The master is packed into a mold filled with hardened foundry sand (sodium silicate stabilized with carbon dioxide gas); the object is then removed, and molten metal is poured into the negative hollows, reproducing the original faithfully. For this work Duca omitted what appears to be the essential step, the original object. Working at an ordinary industrial foundry in Waltham (a firm that customarily cast stoves and manhole covers), he pioneered an innovative method: from full-scale drawings, he carved negatives directly into the sand-packed molds. The pouring then produced an object that had not existed before. To install the eighty-three components, he camped out in the lobby of the unfinished building, casting the Sandwich glass "jewels" and installing them on the spot. Vandals have pried out and stolen many of these over the years. The huge screen with its variety of images evokes, the sculptor says, the multiplicity of Boston, its historic three hills, "the vitality of its people, the boldness of their lives, their culture and artifacts."

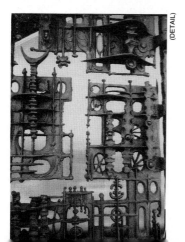

(DETAIL)

QUEST ETERNAL, 1967. Bronze, heroic size.
Boylston St. side of Prudential Center.
Donald De Lue (*see* Lexington: *George Washington*).

GALACIDALACIDESOXIRIBUNUCLEICACID, 1963. Painting, h. 11′ × 14′.
Bank of New England, Prudential Center branch, 800 Boylston St.
★ Salvadore Dali (1904–).

The most flamboyant ego in art of our (or perhaps any) time, Dali was born in Figueras, Spain, and studied at the Fernando Academia of Fine Arts, 1921–25. He worked briefly as a book and magazine illustrator, then spent the decade of the 1930s in Paris as one of the New Surrealist group. His images of limp watches and enigmatic landscapes, beautifully painted in a perfectly controlled old-master style, linger as his best known. After a period in California Dali returned in 1948 to Spain, painting images of Christ in severely difficult perspective intended to awe the viewer. Termed "one of the great manipulators of myth of our time," Dali is credited with originating the concept of artist-as-media-star; one of his autobiographic works is titled *My Life as a Genius*. He is quoted as saying, "I want people to talk about me even if they say nice things."

Four themes important to Dali are interwoven in this painting: Christianity, modern science, the painter's wife Gala, and his Spanish heritage. The work is subtitled *Homage to Crick and Watson*—the two researchers who analyzed the helix structure of DNA (deoxyribonucleic acid, a term interwoven with Gala's name in the title). The tiny riflemen represent the molecular structure of minerals; God, the dead Christ, and the prophet Isaiah can be found in the landscape. The figure with her back to the viewer represents Dali's wife Gala. Purchase of Bank of New England.

THE STORY OF MOSES, ca. 1700. Tapestries, three units, two approx. 15′ × 10′, one 20′ × 10′.
Bank of New England, Prudential Center branch.

Woven at the Royal Gobelins Manufactory in Paris, these three tapestries were designed by Nicolas Poussin (1594–1665) and Charles Le Brun (1619–1690), who in turn were inspired by Raphael's frescoes in the Vatican. The episodes are the gathering of manna, Moses striking the rocks, and worship of the golden calf.

★ WEST FACADE, 1977. Mural, h. seven stories × one block wide.
Boston Architectural Center, 320 Newbury St.
Richard Haas (1936–).

Wisconsin-born, Haas was inspired by Frank Lloyd Wright's work there and thought of becoming an architect. He studied art instead, taught printmaking at Bennington College, Vermont for eleven years, then moved on to New York. After some printmaking (a series of New York's cast iron buildings), Haas painted his first huge tongue-in-cheek mural in 1976 on a facade at Prince and Green Streets in Soho. Perhaps his best-known work is a re-creation of the 1905 New York Times building, demolished in 1965, on the blank shaft of a structure that replaced it. More recently Haas has produced spatial illusions for the underground corridors at the new Smithsonian museums in Washington.

Haas' command of architectural concepts is evident in this trompe l'oeil cutaway drawing of a classic dome-and-buttress structure. Visible from the Massachusetts Turnpike Extension as cars approach the Prudential/Copley exit, Haas' sophisticated satire occupies the entire west wall of the Boston Architectural Center's contemporary concrete structure. Funded by City Walls, New York, and the New York and Boston Architectural Centers.

TRAMONT, 1981. Mural on steel panels, h. 18′ × 45′.
354 Newbury St.
Morgan Bulkeley (1944–   ).

Morgan Bulkeley grew up in the remote Berkshires mountain town of Mount Washington, population thirty-two. Educated at Yale, he still summers in Mount Washington, carving wooden sculptures from trees he personally has felled. In winter he occupies a studio in Boston, painting. Considered by some curators one of the region's more

(DETAIL)

important younger artists, Bulkeley employs a personal imagery that flirts with surrealism, yet has something in common with the dreamlike concepts of Henri Rousseau and René Magritte. Here, on a building that was once a trolley turn-around station, his iconography mingles with images from Boston history.

ANGEL, 1983. Bronze, h. 5′9″.
    At Church Court condominiums, Mass. Ave. and Beacon St.
    Gene Cauthen (*see* Cambridge: *Four Figures*).

BEETHOVEN, 1855. Bronze, larger than life.
    Corridor to Brown Hall, New England Conservatory, 290 Huntington Ave.
    Thomas Crawford (*see* Cambridge [Harvard University]: *James Otis*, and Peabody: *Soldiers and Sailors Monument*).

FENWAY

This green park, created by the eminent landscape designer Frederick Law Olmsted, is part of the ''Emerald Necklace'' of greenery linking Boston Common with Franklin Park.

JOHN BOYLE O'REILLY MEMORIAL, 1896. Bronze and stone.
    East end of Fenway and Boylston St.
    ★ Daniel Chester French (*see* Concord: *Minuteman*).

    O'Reilly (1844–1890), Irish-born but a naturalized Bostonian, poet, and editor of the Catholic publication *The Pilot*, faces the city, back-to-back with an allegorical Erin flanked by her sons Courage and Poetry. Carvings on the background stone are Celtic calligraphy.

JAPANESE TEMPLE BELL, 1675. Bronze, h. 3′.
    Cast under supervision of Suzuki Magoemon.

    This bell was thought to have been donated to the Japanese war effort during World War II but somehow spared. It was ''liberated'' from a scrap heap in Yokosuku, Japan, in 1945 by sailors from the *U.S.S. Boston* and presented to the city. In the 1950s a group of Bostonians asked whether Japan might like the antique bell back; in reply, the former enemy country donated the bell to Boston as a symbol of world peace. The inscription declares ''Priest Koyu states that the bell was dedicated to the Bishamondo at Sendai by Priests Yusho and Sonsai in 1675.''

WORLD WAR II MEMORIAL, 1947–49. Bronze and granite, heroic size.
    Between Agassiz Rd. and Fenway rose garden.
    John Paramino (1889–1856).

    Boston native John Paramino attended North Bennett Street Industrial School; later he was a pupil of Bela Pratt and assisted both Pratt and Saint-Gaudens. Beginning as a designer of commemorative medals and plaques, Paramino cornered the market on plaque production in Boston under Mayor Curley. In 1931 he was accused by a city councilor of running a monopoly and of charging twice the going rate, but his supporters defended him successfully. Many of the city's historical bronze markers are signed with his name.

This granite ellipse with a winged victory commemorates Boston's World War II dead. Redesign of the memorial to include the fallen of Korea and Vietnam is planned by the Boston Art Commission.

JOHN ENDECOTT, 1937. Stone, larger than life.
Forsythe Way, near the Museum of Fine Arts.
C. P. Jennewein (*see* Plymouth: *The Pilgrim Mother*).

One of the six "joint adventurers" who purchased a strip of land (sixty miles wide and extending westward to the Pacific Ocean) from the Plymouth Company, Endecott led settlers of the Massachusetts Bay Colony to join Roger Conat in Salem. He was governor until the arrival of John Winthrop and again after Winthrop's death. Oddly, although he was a member of Roger Williams' congregation at Salem and defended Williams in his difficulties with the colony, Endecott displayed great bigotry and harshness toward Quakers; he was governor at the time Mary Dyer (*see* Beacon Hill/State House: *Mary Dyer*) and others were executed in Boston.

At Boston Museum of Fine Arts (465 Huntington Ave.):

Boston's Museum of Fine Arts, the grande dame of New England art museums, dating from 1870, is said to be second in this country only to the Metropolitan Museum in New York. Superlatives are commonly applied to its collections: finest collection of Chinese and Japanese art in the Western world, examples of Indian painting greater than any in India, Old Kingdom Egyptian sculpture second only to that in Cairo, dozens of renowned "household-word" Impressionist works. Its weakness has been twentieth-century work, a lack for which it has been criticized and which it has tried, by fits and starts, to rectify.

★ APPEAL TO THE GREAT SPIRIT, 1908. Bronze, heroic size.
Huntington Ave. entrance.
Cyrus E. Dallin (*see* Arlington: *Indian Hunter*).

This emotional, perhaps sentimental, work won a gold medal for Dallin at the 1909 Paris Salon. Visitors sometimes express surprise at its presence here; the subject is clearly a Plains Indian. Although he was born in Utah, Dallin lived and taught here, principally at what is now Massachusetts College of Art, for forty years.

JAPANESE GARDEN, 1987. 100′ × 120′.
  Fenway side of Museum.
  Kinsaku Nikane.

  Because of its extensive Asiatic collections, the MFA has a long-standing interest in bringing to Boston examples of Japanese art and culture. This garden is a *karensansui*, or "dry mountain water landscape." Its creator, Prof. Kinsaku Nikane, is considered Japan's leading landscape architect, having built more than 300 gardens throughout the world. Funded by Yosoji Kobayashi, former president of Nippon Television Network.

RHINOCEROS, installed 1987. Polyester resin, bronze powders, life-size.
  Courtyard, Boston Museum School, 230 The Fenway.
  Katherine Ward Lane Weems (1899–   ).

  A graduate of the Boston Museum School, Weems has animal sculptures at other sites in Greater Boston, including a school of dolphins at the Aquarium and a pair of rhinos at Harvard. Her father was Gardiner Martin Lane, president of the Museum of Fine Arts during construction of the Huntington Avenue building in the early 1900s. She lives in Manchester.

GALLERY: Grossman Gallery, west wing, Museum School.

GALLERY: Massachusetts College of Art, North Hall Gallery, 621 Huntington Ave., entrance on Tetlow St.

GALLERY: Simmons College, 300 The Fenway. Rotating exhibits of Boston-area painters and photographers.

MUSEUM: Isabella Stewart Gardner Museum, 280 The Fenway. Completed in 1903, this Venetian-style palace houses the collection of the nouveau-riche and socially controversial Mrs. Jack Gardner (1840–1924). It is worth visiting simply for the ambience of the atrium courtyard, but it also houses Mrs. Jack's personal collection, acquired with the guidance of Bernard Berenson, which ranges from Greco-Roman through the portraits of John Singer Sargent, not omitting Reubens, Rembrandt, Raphael, Titian, Holbein, Botticelli, Piero della Francesca, Fra Lippo Lippi, Vermeer, Whistler, and early Matisse.

SKY COVENANT, Louise Nevelson, Cor-ten steel facade; ETERNAL LIGHT, George Arons, bronze candelabra and sculpture; ETERNAL LIGHT, Harris Barron, wooden arc door and brass sculpture; STAINED GLASS WINDOWS, Jack Duvas; all 1973. FOUNTAIN, Fayette Taylor, 1976. At Temple Israel, 260 The Riverway.
Commissioned by the congregation.

At Northeastern University (360 Huntington Ave):

GLENN PIKE PHOTO COURTESY NORTHEASTERN UNIVERSITY

GALAXY, 1985. Brass on steel frame, h. 64″ × 78″.
Chapel.
C. Fayette Taylor (see Government Center and Environs: Upward Bound).

Taylor exploits carefully controlled "accidental" effects in this work, melting brass on brass to produce ragged forms.

MOTHER AND CHILD, 1931. Bronze, h. 40″.
Mugar Life Sciences Bldg.
Amelia Peabody (1890–1984).

Peabody maintained a studio in Dover.

HUSKY, no date. Bronze, larger than life.
Ell Bldg., outside Alumni Auditorium.
Arcangelo Cascieri (see Boston Common: Parkman Plaza).

CIRCULAR FOUNTAIN, 1984. Granite, h. 9′.
School of Law.
Edward P. Monti (see Quincy: Constitution Common Sculpture).

GALLERIES: Northeastern University Art Gallery, 213 Dodge Library; African American Master Artists in Residency Program (AAMARP) Gallery, 4th floor, Ruggles Bldg.

At Children's Hospital Medical Center (300 Longwood Ave.):

SUNDIAL, 1976. Bronze.
   In Prouty Garden.
   Lu Stubbs (*see* Brookline: *Three Women*).

FOUR SEASONS, 1987. Ceramic mosaic bench, length 126'.
   Winter garden.
   Joan Wye (see MBTA [Davis Station]: *Children's Tile Mural*).

A GARDEN, 1987. Painted silk, twenty-five banners, each h. 6', various
   widths from 1' to 8'.
   Lobby, new wing.
   Norman Laliberte (1925–   ).

   Laliberte's work is owned by some sixty corporate, public, and museum collections in this country and Canada. Designer, teacher, muralist, banner-maker, painter, printmaker, he was born in Worcester of
French-Canadian parents, and grew up in Montreal. He studied at Illinois Institute of Technology, Chicago Institute of Design (B.S., 1951;
M.S. in art education, 1954), the Montreal Museum of Fine Arts, and
Cranbrook Academy. As either author, designer, or illustrator, Laliberte has been involved in the production of thirty-five books. His
teaching stints include Notre Dame in Indiana and the Rhode Island
School of Design.

FOLK TALES FROM THE FOUR CORNERS OF THE EARTH, 1987. Fabric,
   h. 6' × 10'.
   Entrance, new wing.
   Clara Wainwright (1936–   ).

   Wainwright is originator of two of Boston's favorite festivals, First
Night—the New Year's Eve city-wide arts festival—and the Great
Boston Kite Festival. She attended Winsor School and the University
of North Carolina; in 1986 she was a Bunting Fellow.

MURALS, 1976–1987. Mosaic, four units, various sizes.
   Judge Baker Clinic, 295 Longwood Ave., exterior and first and second
   floors.
   Lilli Ann Killen Rosenberg (*see* Newton: *Five Concrete Mosaic Sculp-
   tures*).
   Commissioned by Judge Baker Clinic.

BRIGHAM TRIPTYCH. Wall hangings, three quilts, each approx. 2½' × 3½'.
   Lobby, Hematology-Oncology Division, third floor, Brigham and Wom-
   en's Hospital, 75 Francis St.
   Rhoda Cohen (*see* Natick: *Fiber Revival*).

BANNER, 1982. Appliqued felt, 6' sq.
   Lobby, Dana Farber Institute, 44 Binney St.
   Norman Laliberte (*see* Fenway [Children's Hospital]: *A Garden*).

At Boston University:

★ FREE AT LAST, 1975. Cor-ten steel, h. 20′.
  Marsh Plaza, 740 Commonwealth Ave.
  Sergio Castillo (1925–   ).

    A distinguished Chilean artist, Castillo was visiting professor of sculpture at B.U. in 1975, at which time he produced this memorial to Martin Luther King. He has more recently been an adjunct professor here (see *Explosion* below), as well as a visiting professor at the University of California at Berkeley. Although he maintains a home and studio in Spain, he has been a professor of sculpture at the University of Chile for twenty years. Among his forty-five or more public works world-wide are seven in the United States.

    The Rev. Martin Luther King, Jr. (1929–1968) was the charismatic spokesman for the Civil Rights movement in the late 1960s, seeking equality for blacks. He was assassinated by a sniper in Memphis, Tenn., in 1968.

FOUNTAIN, 1976. Granite, h. 15′.
  Hearst Plaza, in front of B.U. School of Communications.
  Edward P. Monti (*see* Quincy: *Constitution Common Sculpture*).

    Funded by the Hearst Foundation and Robert Bergenheim, alumni trustee.

EXPLOSION, 1987. Welded stainless steel, h. 24′.
  In front of Metcalf Science Center, 590 Commonwealth Ave.
  Sergio Castillo (*see Free at Last* above).

    Called "the big bang" by the student body, this work was created on site by Castillo while teaching here. A campus story relates that architects and engineers who saw Castillo's model said it wouldn't work; the sculpture would have to be held up by guy wires. But the physics department said it could, and the physics faculty has worked with the sculptor on the project. Commissioned by Dr. Arthur G. B. Metcalf, chairman of B.U. board of trustees.

COUNTERPOINT, 1983. Stainless steel, h. 12' × 14' × 9'.
    Storrow Dr., behind Marsh Chapel (735 Commonwealth Ave.).
    Russell Jacques (1943–   ).

    Vermont-born, Jacques is a Boston University alumnus who now lives in Northampton. He describes this work as "an interplay of lyrical and energetic rhythms."
    Placed on the embankment overlooking the Charles River that is often called "B.U. Beach," this work was intended for the courtyard of the George Sherman Union. On the day of installation, the crane operators opined that it was too risky to place it there; this site, perhaps temporary, is a substitute. The material is surgical-quality stainless steel.

UNTITLED, 1974. Epoxy over ferrocement, h. 8'.
    140 Bay State Rd.
    Gregg LeFevre (1946–   ).

    Gregg LeFevre's parents opposed his boyhood choice of art as a profession, so he took pre-medical courses at St. Lawrence University, then philosophy at Columbia and B.U., from which he graduated cum laude. As an alternative to military service he taught in a tough South Bronx school. He and his students combed the streets for materials to make assemblage sculpture, a project so successful he wrote a classroom manual, *Junk Sculpture*. Since 1974 LeFevre has lived in Boston and pursued art full-time; he has created some thirty large-scale works for public and corporate spaces, including NASA, the U.S. State Department, the cities of Boston, Chicago, and Richmond, Va., and the town of Brookline.

PROVINCETOWN WHEELS. Steel, h. 7' × 12' × 20".
    121 Bay State Rd.
    George Greenamyer (*see* Marshfield: *Webster, The Farmer of Marshfield*).

UNTITLED, 1974. Epoxy and urethane paint over ferrocement, h. 10'.
    Behind Student Union and Mugar Library.
    Gregg LeFevre (*see Untitled* above).

ALLSTON/BRIGHTON

BOSTON SKYLINE, 1982. Exterior mural.
  Cambridge-Lee Industries, 510 Lincoln St. Visible from Mass.
  Pike, just west of Cambridge-Allston interchange.
  Charles Trainer.
  Commissioned by Cambridge-Lee Industries.

MURAL, 1971.
  MBTA power station, Washington St. at Oak Sq.
  Maria Termini (*see* Back Bay: *Mural*).
  Funded by Summerthing.

WALK IT DOWN, 1985. Varnished Okawara paper, bamboo, leather lacing,
cotton cord, h. 12 stories.
  Atrium wall, Embassy Suites, 400 Soldiers Field Rd.
  Susan Singleton.

SFERA, 1983. Bronze, h. 3'.
  Lobby, Embassy Suites, 400 Soldiers Field Rd.
  ★ Arnaldo Pomodoro (*see* Downtown [Hotel Meridien]: *Awakening City*).

At Harvard Business School: **see** *Cambridge [Harvard University].*

KING'S CHAPEL AND OLD CITY HALL

At King's Chapel (Tremont and School Sts.):

SHIRLEY MONUMENT, 1754. Marble.
  Peter Scheemakers (1691–1781).

  Scheemakers was a native of Antwerp working in London between
  1716 and 1771; fourteen of his portrait busts adorn Westminister Abbey. This is his only work in North America, and is likely the first public sculpture erected in Boston.
  Shirley, royal governor of Massachusetts Bay Colony 1741–56,
  erected this plaque alongside his pew in memory of his wife Frances
  and their married daughter, Frances Bollan, both of whom had died in
  the previous decade. It is not known which Frances is depicted, but
  the fulsome Latin inscription extolls the virtues of both.

APTHORP MEMORIAL, 1758. Marble.
  Henry Cheere (1703–1781).

  A London portrait sculptor, Cheere executed works for William III
  and Queen Caroline, and was eventually knighted and created a bar-
  onet.
  The cherub, urn, and plaque commemorate Charles Apthorp (1698–
  1758), a prosperous merchant and provisioner of the army, who with
  Governor Shirley was one of the donors who made possible the building of King's Chapel in 1750–54.

SAMUEL VASSALL, 1766. Marble.
    William Tyler (d. 1801), member of the Royal Academy.

    This portrait bust was sent by Vassall's great-grandson Florentius,
who had contributed ten guineas toward the construction of King's
Chapel. Jamaican settler Vassall (1586–1667) refused to pay royal
mercantile taxes in 1628 and was imprisoned and ruined financially.
He was later elected to Parliament and awarded damages by that
body. Seeing his ancestor as a predecessor of American colonial protest, Florentius paid to have a pew removed so the bulky memorial
could fit here.

At Old City Hall (School St. near Tremont St.):

★ BENJAMIN FRANKLIN, 1856. Bronze, larger than life.
    In front of Old City Hall.
    Richard Saltonstall Greenough (*see* Cambridge [Harvard University]:
    Governor John Winthrop).

    This may be Richard Greenough's finest work; here he understood
that Bostonians wanted their "very own" Franklin, not an abstraction.
The Massachusetts Historical Society provided a suit of Franklin's
clothes, and the sculptor labored to render Franklin, he said, as
"thoughtful, dignified, of kindly expression, and un(self)conscious."
Two of the bas-reliefs on the pedestal (scenes from Franklin's life) are
by Greenough; the other two, the signing of the Declaration of Independence and the Treaty of Paris, were Thomas Ball's first public
commission.
    Franklin (1706–1790), most famous scientist, inventor, journalist,
philosopher, and ambassador of Colonial America and the young Republic, was born on Milk St. in Boston. He apprenticed here to his
brother James, publisher of *The New England Courant*, sometimes
called "the first sensational newspaper in America." At age seventeen
he left for Philadelphia. Funded by public subscription.

★ JOSIAH QUINCY, 1879. Bronze, larger than life.
    In front of Old City Hall.
    Thomas Ball (1819–1911).

    Son of a Charlestown house and sign painter, Ball began his career
as a self-taught portrait painter. It did not go well, and he found other

income as a church choir soloist. Turning to portrait busts, Ball found success with images of Jenny Lind and Daniel Webster, later mass-duplicated for public sale. At age thirty-five Ball went to study sculpture in Florence, returned to Boston for eight years during which he constructed the equestrian *Washington* for the Public Garden and other works, then settled in Florence for the next thirty years, dean of the expatriate American artistic community.

Josiah Quincy (1772–1864), third of at least six generations to bear that name, lawyer and author, served in the Massachusetts Senate, the U. S. Congress, as mayor of Boston 1823–29, and finally as president of Harvard College. Before the century was out his son and great-grandson, also Josiah Quincys, served as mayors of Boston.

CITY CARPET, 1983. Ceramic, brass and stained concrete, 25' sq.
    In front of Old City Hall.
    Lilli Ann Killen Rosenberg (*see* Newton: *Five Concrete Mosaic Sculptures*).

It was on School St. that Boston Latin School, with its unique concept of free education (for boys only, however) was established in 1635. Although it has long since moved, Boston Latin remains a prestigious public school and the oldest educational institution in the country, antedating Harvard by a year. Rosenberg's "carpet" is a hopscotch diagram, but details within its borders recall old-fashioned games and Boston traditions. Latin's motto, beneath its image, translates "Work conquers all—Opportunity for all." Commissioned by Townscape Institute.

OLD CITY HALL ENTRANCE MURAL, 1984. Acrylic on canvas, 16' × 16'.
    Vestibule of Old City Hall.
    Joshua Winer and Campari Knoepffler (*see* Cambridge [Harvard Square]: *Harvard Square Theater Mural*).

Built in 1865 in elaborate Second Empire style, Old City Hall served the city until the development of Government Center in 1968. In rehabilitating the structure, the new owners were required by city fire codes to gut the interior. This fool-the-eye mural was designed to restore some of the architectural detail. At both sides the names of Boston's mayors are inscribed in typestyles reflecting the era in which they served.

MURAL.
    Inside Old City Hall.
    Elizabeth Carter (*see* Cambridge [Central Square]: *Floating Down Mass. Avenue*).

DOWNTOWN

TAPESTRIES, 1979.
    Boston Five-Cent Savings Bank, 10 School St.
    Jane Bell, Fritz Stewart, and Edward Fields.
    Commissioned by Boston Five-Cent Savings Bank.

COURTYARD GATE, 1987. Wrought iron, h. 9½′ × 10′.
 Washington and Milk Sts., entrance to Orange Line State St. Station.
 Albert Paley (1944–   ).

 Born in Philadelphia, Paley lives in Rochester, N.Y., where he is a professor at New York State University College at Brockport. He received a B.F.A. (1966) and an M.F.A. (1969) from Tyler School of Art, Temple University. His interest in the handmade object, both wood and metal, has led to film and video documentaries. Before coming to Brockport in 1972, he taught at the School for American Craftsmen at Rochester Institute of Technology. Paley has styled this one-of-a-kind gate in the Art Nouveau tradition of the early twentieth century.

VIEW OF BOSTON HARBOR FROM PEMBERTON HILL, 1829. Tempera
 on canvas, 95″ × 180″.
 Lobby, One Boston Place, Washington and State Sts.
 ★ Robert Salmon (ca. 1775–ca. 1846).

 Probably self-taught, Robert Salomon exhibited his marine paintings in England and Scotland until 1828, when he emigrated to Boston and simplified his name. To establish his reputation here, he began work on several large-scale panoramic views, exhibiting this and eighty other works in 1829 in the newly built Quincy Market. He gained the patronage of collectors and philanthropists (a number of his works are at the Boston Museum of Fine Arts and at Peabody Museum, Salem) and worked here for fourteen years. At one time he exhibited alongside Gilbert Stuart, Asher Durand, and John James Audubon; he is considered an important influence on what is now called the Luminist School, painters of light-in-landscape. He returned to Europe and died, possibly in Italy; his last works are dated 1845.
 The painting is on long-term loan from its owner, the Society for Preservation of New England Antiquities, to Equitable Real Estate, which donated funds for its restoration.

PHOTO COURTESY EQUITABLE REAL ESTATE INVESTMENT MANAGEMENT, INC.   (DETAIL)

GALLERY: The Vault Gallery, 1 Boston Place, at Washington and State
 Sts. An exhibition space new in mid-1987, this gallery is located at
 The Boston Company/Boston Safe Deposit and Trust. It focuses on
 new regional talent. Open business days only.

THE BOSTON MASSACRE, 1966. Painting, h. approx. 10′ × 12′.
Lobby, Bank of New England, 28 State St.
★   Larry Rivers (1923–   ).

Born Larry Grossberg in the Bronx, Rivers is a man of multiple talents. Becoming a jazz saxophonist in his teens, he played New York gigs before serving in the U.S. Army in World War II. After the war he studied music at the Julliard School, then painting with Hans Hofmann. He began painting full-time in 1950 (graduating from New York University in 1951), but has since found time to try his hand at welded sculpture, Broadway set and costume design, poetry, and video. He has collaborated with the French kinetic sculptor Jean Tinguely, whose performance sculptures self-destruct; he has been artist-in-residence at the Slade School, London, and an instructor at the University of California at Santa Barbara. His work is widely held by museums including the Whitney, the Hirschhorn, the Corcoran in Washington, D.C., the Tate Gallery in London, and the Rose Art Museum at Brandeis.

Beginning with banal "Pop" images such as Washington crossing the Delaware or Rembrandt groups from cigar box tops, Rivers builds on them a free and expressive style, transforming the all-too-common into images both playful and painterly. Commissioned by Bank of New England.

MILK STREET MURALS, 1986. Painted wall, h. two stories × approx. 12′.
31 Milk St., near Broad St.
Richard Haas (see Back Bay: West Facade).
Commissioned by Windsor Building Associates.

HUNGARIAN MONUMENT, to be installed 1988. Bronze, h. approx. 20′.
Liberty Square, Milk and Kilby Sts.
E. Gyuri Hollosy (1946–   ).

Hungarian artist Gyuri Hollosy is associate professor of sculpture and drawing at Bethany College, Lindsborg, Kan. He received a B.F.A. from Ohio University and a master's from Tulane University. He has done three other major memorials, in Ohio and Louisiana.

In 1956 a student-led anti-Communist uprising in Hungary gave that iron-curtained nation an illusive week of freedom. Soviet tanks crushed the revolt and reimposed the repressive regime, and 200,000 refugees fled the country, many to the Boston area. The thirtieth anniversary of the short-lived revolt was marked in Boston by the dedication of this sculpture. Sponsored by the Hungarian Society of Massachusetts, with funding from the Browne Fund, Liberty Square Park Associates, and private donations.

GALLERY: Concourse Gallery, 225 Franklin St., at State Street Bank and Trust Co. Rotating exhibits; open business hours.

THE CREATURE POND, 1982. Bronze, granite, diam. 14′.
Post Office Sq., Congress and Milk Sts.
Collaboration: Lowry Burgess, Donald Burgy, John Cataldo, Carlos Dorrien, Robert Guillemin, David Phillips, Sydney Roberts Rockefeller, William and Clara Wainwright.

Site of the first post office in America in 1639, this square had been occupied by a horse fountain and memorial to Dr. George Thorndike Angell, founder of Massachusetts Society for the Prevention of Cruelty to Animals. By 1975 it was severely neglected. Citizen advocates raised funds and recruited artists to revive the square in a collaborative effort. The artists wanted to continue the animal theme set by the Angell memorial; to forestall vandalism, they tried to make the work as "lovable" as possible. Funded by the Browne Fund.

At Hotel Meridien (250 Franklin St.):

AWAKENING CITY, 1962. Brass, h. 6'.
★ Arnaldo Pomodoro (1926–).

Pomodoro's feel for intricacy and detail is attributed to his early career with his brother Gio as a jewelry-maker, largely self-taught. Arnaldo later worked in Milan as a stage designer, a profession that added a sense of drama to his art. He has taught in California.

Pomodoro's gleaming forms, their flawless exterior skins eroded to reveal complex inner detail, gained international popularity a quarter-century ago. In 1964 Pomodoro won the grand prize for sculpture at the Venice Biennial. Commissioned by The Beacon Companies.

HAGAR IN THE DESERT, 1947–57. Bronze, h. 30".
★ Jacques Lipchitz (see Cambridge [M.I.T.]: The Bather).

EXODUS, 1982–84. Mixed media, framed.
Edward Giobbi (1926–).

Giobbi has been a Guggenheim Fellow and Ford Foundation grant recipient. His works are owned by the Boston Museum of Fine Arts, the Whitney, and the Art Institute of Chicago; he has been artist-in-residence at Dartmouth College. A native of Connecticut, he now lives in Katonah, N.Y.

WHITE COLUMN, 1981, sculpture.
Peter Saari (1951–).

New Yorker Peter Saari earlier in his career was known for his tromp l'oeil paintings. A graduate of C. W. Post College (B.F.A., 1974), he studied in Rome and at Yale; his work is at the Hirschhorn Museum. He has taught at Yale.

ABRAHAM LINCOLN AND SALMON P. CHASE; GEORGE WASHINGTON, ALEXANDER HAMILTON, AND ROBERT MORRIS Murals, each 8' × 8'.
N. C. Wyeth (see Needham: Wyeth Paintings).

Done when this building was the Federal Reserve Bank, these two murals depict important figures in United States financial history. (For Hamilton biography, see Commonwealth Avenue: Alexander Hamilton.) Morris (1734–1806) was a prosperous Philadelphian businessman, conservative enough to oppose the Declaration of Independence at first. He did sign it, as a member of the Continental Congress, and became the chief finance officer of the Revolution. Scraping together requisitions from the states, loans from the French, his own private credit, and money from his own pocket, Morris provided the means for Washington's army to move to Yorktown for the decisive final battle of the War. He was offered the office of Secretary of the Treasury by Washington but deferred to Hamilton and was elected to the Senate. Speculation in Western land eroded his fortune, and ironically the man whose credit was once better than the government's spent three years in debtor's prison.

Lincoln's Secretary of the Treasury during the early years of the Civil War, Chase accomplished two great innovations: establishment of a national banking system, and issue of legal tender paper currency. A lawyer and early opponent of slavery, he argued that slavery laws were local and could not be established by the Constitution; he became known in Ohio as "attorney general of fugitive slaves." He served in the Senate, failed to secure the Republican nomination for President in 1860, and in 1864 was appointed Chief Justice of the Supreme Court, an office he held until the end of his life.

MARITIME SCENES, 1924. Oil on canvas, four units, each h. 15′ × 12′.
Lobby, Bank of Boston, 100 Federal St.
N. C. Wyeth (*see* Needham: Wyeth Paintings).

Although he spent most of his career in Pennsylvania, Wyeth returned to his birthplace, Needham, for two years and painted this series at about that time for the original First National Bank building. A pictorial marine history, these four paintings depict important eras: the first maritime traders of the Mediterranean, the age of galleons, the age of clippers, and the age of steam. A fifth work from the series is at the Peabody Museum.

GALLERY, 36th floor, Bank of Boston. Open to the public during business hours, this corridor displays changing exhibitions from Bank of Boston's collection. It is closed at the noon hour because the area doubles as an executive dining room.

CROSSING, 1975. Painting on canvas, h. 12½′ × 15′.
Lobby, Shawmut Bank, 1 Federal St.
Friedel Dzubas (1915–   ).

Teacher of painting at the Boston Museum School, Dzubas was born in Berlin but fled Germany in 1939. In the 1960s he held two Guggenheim fellowships and another from the National Council on the Arts. He has been visiting artist at Cornell, New York University, Dartmouth, Sarah Lawrence, and University of Pennsylvania. Widely collected, his work is owned by two dozen museums, including the Metropolitan, Guggenheim, and Whitney Museums in New York, Boston Museum of Fine Arts, the Phillips Collection in Washington, and Yale, Brandeis, and Cornell Universities.

This painting is representative of Friedel's "staining" technique, an innovation of the 1950s. The painter leaves the canvas unprimed and thins his paint to a stain, so the fibers absorb the pigment; instead of resting on the surface, the color becomes visually part of the canvas.

(DETAIL)

★ ART DECO PANELS, 1930. Bronze.
75 Federal St., surrounding exterior of the building.
Paul Fjelde (b. 1892).

When H. N. Gorin Associates renovated this building in 1987,
cleaning the decorative exterior bronze panels was not part of the
original plan. Someone decided to do it anyway, and the results were
stunning; the bronze looked like gold leaf. The metal has been sealed
and the owners say they plan to maintain it. The panels are grouped
into six themes: Finance, with a beehive representing thrift, an owl for
wisdom watching a clerk record investment in a ledger, and a family
receiving the benefits; Architecture and Sculpture (the sculptor carves
a griffin, which represents the arts); Trades essential to building (car-
penter, mason, blacksmith); Transportation; Power (horse, water, and
electric); and the three basic industries, agriculture, manufacturing,
and mining.

Of Norwegian extraction, Fjelde was born in Minnesota, attended
Minneapolis School of Art and the Art Students League in New York,
then taught at Pratt Institute. He was a member of the Society of
Beaux-Arts Architects, dedicated to promoting the traditional Beaux-
Arts principles. His architectural sculpture was commissioned in Nor-
way as well as in this country.

ROBERT BURNS, 1917. Bronze, larger than life.
Winthrop Sq., junction Otis and Devonshire Sts.
Henry Hudson Kitson (*see* Lexington: *The Minuteman*).

Burns (1759–1796), considered the greatest of Scottish poets,
author of "Auld Lang Syne," among hundreds of other songs and
poems, is depicted walking with his collie dog. Originally intended for
the Public Garden, this statue was shunted to the Fens and stood
there in obscurity for fifty years; it was relocated downtown in 1975.
Presented to the city by Burns Memorial Association.

BOSTON BRICKS, 1985. Bronze, more than 100 brick-sized units.
Winthrop Lane, off Winthrop Sq. between Arch and Otis Sts.
Gregg LeFevre (*see* Boston University: *Untitled*) and Kate Burke
(1952–   ).

A sculptor/painter who divides her time between Boston and Provincetown, Kate Burke studied at the Art Institute of Boston. This collaboration is her first public work; she is completing another in Brighton with a grant from the Browne Fund.

HELION, 1975. Molded polyethylene, aluminum, h. 26′, diam. 16½′.
Cabot, Cabot & Forbes Bldg., 100 Summer St.
Robert Amory (*see* Burlington: *Windhover*).

This work is from a series that Amory calls "windflowers"; mounted on ball bearings, the twenty-four orange disks move in the wind, as does the entire "flower head." It is popularly called the Lollipop Sculpture. Funded by 1% for Art.

MURAL, 1973. Plaster, carved and painted, h. approx 8′ × 10′.
At Provident Institution for Savings, 30 Winter St.
Constantino Nivola (1911–   ).

Born in Sardinia, Nivola learned such skills as masonry, plastering, stucco work, and woodcarving from his father. He studied art in Milan, worked as art director for the Olivetti Co., then migrated to the United States in 1939. His work draws upon the terra cotta traditions of his birthplace. After a stint at *Interiors* magazine, he became director of the Design Workshop, then a visiting professor at Harvard and at Harvard Graduate School of Design. He has taught at Columbia, International University of Art in Florence, the University of California at Berkeley, and has been artist in residence at the American Academy in Rome. Commissioned by the Provident Institution for Savings.

At Federal Reserve Bldg. (Atlantic Ave. and Summer St.):

★ THREE ELEMENTS, 1978. Steel, h. 12'.
Ronald Bladen (1918–   ).

Born in Vancouver, Bladen emigrated to California to study painting. Working in an abstract expressionist style, he found his paint application becoming thicker and thicker, assuming the quality of bas-reliefs. In the 1950s he moved to New York and "without premeditation" turned to three-dimensional works and became a sculptor. Although he is associated with the Minimalists, his work contains an uncharacteristic drama, such as the instability implied by these *Elements*. On permanent loan from the artist.

ZAG FOUR, 1968. Stainless steel.
Lobby.
Beverly Pepper (*see* Government Center and Environs: *Sudden Presence*).
On indefinite loan.

TIMELESS COLUMN. Marble.
Lobby.
Colette Perazio-Itkin.

OMINOUS IKON SERIES VIII, 1977. Steel h. 8'.
Dennis Kowal (*see* Wellesley [Babson College]: *Ominous Icon #6* and *Yaddo Study*).
Lobby.
Gift of Rita and Samuel Robert.

MURALS, 1968. Acrylic on cotton duck.
Lobby.
Hugh Stubbins.

Stubbins, a Cambridge architect, also designed this building.

CHINATOWN

CHINESE ZODIAC, 1986. Mosaic walkway, twelve floor panels each 2' sq., and wall mural, h. 4' × 5'.
First floor interior, China Trade Center, Washington and Boylston Sts.
Lilli Ann Killen Rosenberg (*see* Newton: *Five Concrete Mosaic Sculptures*).

The Chinese calendar assigns to each year in its twelve-year cycle an animal, whose characteristics determine the traits of those born in that year. The floor panels identify the years of this century associated with each animal; the mural outlines the character traits associated with each sign. Commissioned by the Bay Group.

CHINA TRADE GATE, to be installed winter, 1988. Painted steel tubing, h. 29′ × 22′.
Washington and Boylston Sts.
David Judelson (*see* Cambridge: *Flag Fragments*).

With steel tubing, Judelson creates at the entrance to Chinatown a line drawing in space of a ceremonial Ming arch. Commissioned by China Trade Center.

CHINA GATES, 1982. Ceramic.
Beach St.
Jun-Brannen Associates.
Funded by the Browne Fund.

MURAL, 1970.
Chinese Merchants' Association Bldg., Hudson and Beech Sts.
Dan Hueng and Bob Uyeda.
Funded by Summerthing.

LOVE CONQUERS FIRE AND THE DRAGON, 1970. Mural on masonry, h. three stories.
Chinese Christian Church, Harvard and Tyler Sts.
Pietro Ferri.
Funded by Summerthing and Project '70.

CONFUCIUS, ca. 1984. Bronze, h. approx. 30″.
At Chinese-American Civic Association, Tyler St., near Oak.
Taiwanese artist, name unknown.

The sage whose thinking permeates China's cultural traditions,
Confucius (551–479 B.C.) was born to an impoverished noble family.
His clan name was K'ung; the boy was called Ch'in, meaning hill, because of the prominent bump on his forehead. His literary name is
Chung-ni, but he is referred to as K'ung Fu-tzu, or Grand Master
K'ung. He was supervisor of parks and herds for another noble clan;
then at the age of twenty-two began a school for those who wished to
be instructed in the principles of right conduct and government. For a
time he was influential in the government of Lu. Centuries before
Christianity, he expressed the Golden Rule in negative form: "What
you do not like when done to yourself, do not do to others." Gift to the
Chinese Consolidated Benevolent Association of Boston from the government of Taiwan.

UNITY-COMMUNITY, 1986. Paint on masonry, h. 40′.
34–36 Oak St.
David Fichter (see Lawrence: Bread and Roses Mural) and Wen-ti Tsen
(1936–   ).

Wen-ti Tsen grew up in China, moved to Europe, and now lives and
works in Cambridge. After art studies in London and Paris, he earned
a diploma at the Boston Museum School and was awarded a traveling
scholarship to study in Pakistan. He has taught at the Museum School

and, for three years, in Lebanon. Interested in using art for progressive purposes, he has created comic-strip books about social problems, in addition to a sophisticated body of painting and installation work.

Community residents, children, and adults alike were invited to help paint this mural depicting the history of Chinese immigration into Boston. The story begins with laborers brought here as contract workers for the construction of the old telephone exchange building; it continues through other trades and segues into contemporary life in Chinatown. Funded by Massachusetts Council on the Arts and Humanities; sponsored by Quincy School Community Council.

SOUTH END/ROXBURY

THREE FIGURES, 1965. Cor-ten steel, h. 8'.
    Courtyard, Castle Square Project, 438 Tremont St.
    Alfred M. Duca (see Back Bay: *Boston Tapestry*).

    This work is cut entirely from 1" steel plate.

GROUND RELIEF, 1982. Stone and concrete.
    Roxbury Youthworks, 135 Dudley St.
    Susan Hoenig.

THE UNITED STATES OF MIND, 1970. Acrylic on masonry, h. 15' × 50'.
    Roxbury Comprehensive Clinic, Tremont and Lenox Sts.
    Collaboration: Paul Chin, Paul Goodnight (see MBTA [Ruggles Station]:
    Mural), Periwinkle, Gary Rickson (1942–   ).

    Rickson says his philosophy about art is, "put it outside, where the people are. It's like music on the radio; they'll absorb it, and it will come back out of them, like music." A life-long Roxburian, Rickson was an active organizer of neighborhood mural production in Roxbury in the early 1970s. He was a minister at twenty-one, then for ten years a radio personality on WHRB, Harvard University radio. Rickson studied painting technique with Don Berry of Roxbury; he has held a National Endowment for the Arts fellowship. More recently he has become a landscape contractor and is in charge of campus maintenance at Roxbury Community College. Of the other muralists, Periwinkle is a Gay Head Indian; Chin was simply a young man living in the neighborhood at the time.

THE BRIDGE, INC., 1972. Acrylic mural, 5' × 8'.
    At The Bridge (community center), 537 Mass. Ave., interior.
    Gary Rickson (see *The United States of Mind* above).
    Gift of the artist.

AFRICA IS THE BEGINNING, 1969, and AMERICA IS OUR BEGINNING
    THRU MEDITATION, 1975. Exterior murals, each approx. 30' × 50'.
    Roxbury YMCA, 401 Warren St. at Martin Luther King Blvd.
    Gary Rickson (see *The United States of Mind* above).
    Funded by Summerthing.

BETANCES MURAL, 1977–78. Ceramic, h. 14' × 45'.
  Courtyard, Villa Victoria housing project, Aguadilla St.
  (formerly West Newton St.), south of Tremont St.
  Lilli Ann Killen Rosenberg (see Newton: *Five Concrete Mosaic Sculptures*).

When Villa Victoria project was built, a pre-existing electric power station remained like a sore thumb in one of the courtyards. An activist group at the project thought its wall would be a prime site for a mural and sought out Rosenberg, who was teaching at the South End Settlement House. Together they wrote a funding proposal that Boston Edison accepted. More than 300 children and residents made clay pieces which Rosenberg organized into this colorful collective statement. The portrait of Betances was sculpted in cement by Rosenberg, a process calling for speed and a sure hand. Into the wet concrete she mixed additives including iron oxide, which gives the work its reddish color plus greater plasticity; nevertheless, she had to complete the sculpture in less than three hours.

Dr. Ramon E. Betances (1827–1898) is called "the Abraham Lincoln of Puerto Rico"; he freed his own slaves and was exiled after causing several abortive uprisings against the Spanish colonial government. The inscriptions read, "Let us know how to fight for our honor and our liberty," "The clay in this mural was made by neighbors and groups from Villa Victoria," and "a gift from the Hispanic community to this and future generations." Sponsored by Casa del Sol and the Emergency Tenants Council; funded by Boston Edison Co.

IN PRAISE OF HANDS, 1976. Ceramic mural, h. 7' × 4'.
  Exterior, Charles E. Mackey Middle School, 90 Warren St.
  Mackey students and Lilli Ann Killen Rosenberg (see Newton: *Five Concrete Mosaic Sculptures*).

I'VE BEEN TO THE MOUNTAIN TOP, 1982. Acrylic on plywood.
  Martin Luther King School, Laurence Ave.
  Dana Chandler (see *Knowledge is Power* below).
  Funded by Martin Luther King School.

KNOWLEDGE IS POWER/STAY IN SCHOOL, 1972.
    Warren Ave. and Zeigler St.
    Dana Chandler (1941–   ).

    A graduate of Massachusetts College of Art, Chandler was born in
Lynn, lives in Newton, and now is a professor at Simmons College.
He was founder and is director of the African American Master Artists
in Residency Program at Northeastern.

VALUE LIFE, 1974. Acrylic on masonry, h. three stories.
    Braddock Park, West Newton and Carleton Sts.
    Gary Rickson (*see The United States of Mind* above) and VALUE stu-
    dents.
    Funded by ICA VALUE program.

BLACK WOMEN, 1970. Mural, acrylic on masonry, h. three stories.
    Columbus Ave. and Yarmouth St.
    Sharon Dunn.

    Although the mural itself is in fair condition, the upper courses of
brick are deteriorating. Funded by Project '70 and Summerthing.

FREDERIC DOUGLASS, 1976.
　　1002 Tremont St.
　　Arnold Hurley and Gary Rickson (*see The United States of Mind* above).

　　Rickson painted the background for this mural, but to do the figure
he recruited Hurley, a portrait painter in the African American Master
Artists in Residency Program at Northeastern.
　　Douglas (1817–1895), born into slavery as Frederick A. W. Bailey,
was secretly taught to read and write by the wife of a family he served
in Baltimore. Apprenticed as a ship caulker, he made his escape to
New York masquerading as a sailor. For greater safety he went on to
New Bedford, Mass., and changed his name to Douglass. In 1841 he
created a sensation with an extemporaneous speech in Nantucket,
was appointed an agent of the Massachusetts Anti-Slavery Society,
and began to speak extensively for the cause of abolition. Accused of
being an imposter, he responded by writing his autobiography, *Narrative of the Life of Frederick Douglass, an American Slave*. Fearing his
recapture, his friends sent him to England on a two-year lecture tour,
and during his absence raised funds to buy his legal freedom. He
published an anti-slavery weekly, *The North Star*, continued to lecture
even after the Civil War, and late in life served as consul-general to
the Republic of Haiti.

BEAUTIFUL PEOPLE COMING TOGETHER IS TRUTH, 1971. Mural, 8′ × 10′.
　　William Monroe Trotter School, 135 Humbolt Ave.
　　Gary Rickson (*see The United States of Mind* above).

SELF DISCIPLINE/FAMILY DISCIPLINE, 1971. Mural, 60′ × 50′.
　　Interior, Lena Park Community Center, 150 American Legion Highway.
　　Gary Rickson (*see The United States of Mind* above).

　　The fifteen-foot figure here is Jubal, in African myth the first story-
teller.

CITYSCAPE III, 1984. Painted steel h. 7½′ × 7′ × 2½′.
　　West Concord St. Park, at Shawmut and West Concord Sts.
　　Miriam Knapp (1934–　　).

　　Brookline sculptor Miriam Knapp was born in France, educated at
Bennington College, Columbia University, and the Boston Museum

PHOTO COURTESY HOME, INC.

School. Her steel sculpture appears minimalist but is not; it is a landscape (or cityscape) drawing in space. Knapp calls this series of works "landscapes of the mind." Sited by HOME, Inc., Rutland Housing Associates, and West Concord Street Homeowner's Association with funding from the City of Boston and the Browne Fund.

MARCUS GARVEY, 1980. Acrylic on masonry.
Exterior, Marcus Garvey Center, Roxbury and Shawmut Sts.
Bra Sharihed and James E. Newton.

Garvey (1887–1940), born in Jamaica, was founder of a black nationalist movement advocating self-help, race purity, and social separation. He founded the Universal Negro Improvement Association, a militant newspaper, *Negro World*, and the Black Star steamship line intended to link black communities in the United States and the Caribbean. In dealings with its stock, he was accused of mail fraud and was convicted and jailed. Deported to Jamaica, Garvey never regained his effectiveness as a leader, but his concept of race pride persists.

MURAL, 1984. Exterior paint, h. 12½′ × 100′.
Beulah Pilgrim Holiness Church, 455 Blue Hill Ave.
Elizabeth Carter (*see* Cambridge [Central Square]: *Floating Down Mass. Avenue*).

Populating the mural are figures from the neighborhood and from Boston black history, including Judge George Ruffin, singer Roland Haynes, and sculptor Meta Fuller.

★ ETERNAL PRESENCE, 1987. Bronze, h. 8′.
In front of National Center for Afro-American Artists, 300 Walnut Ave.
John Wilson. (1922–   ).

Professor emeritus of sculpture and drawing at Boston University, Wilson was born in Boston and studied art at the Boston Museum School. He worked under painter Fernand Léger in France and later worked in Mexico, where muralists had a profound influence on his work. There Wilson turned toward what he calls "democratic" forms of expression, public art and printmaking. He worked for a time in Chicago and New York before coming to B.U. in 1964. In 1986 he was commissioned to create the portrait bust of Martin Luther King Jr. for the U.S. Capitol. This monumental head is, the artist says, "a symbolic black presence infused with a sense of universal humanity." It memorializes the 350-year history of black people in Massachusetts. Commissioned by Elma Lewis.

ROSIE, 1984–85. Fiberglass and wood, h. 5′ × 8′ × 8′.
At NCAAA, 300 Walnut Ave.
Robert Tinch, Jr.

Born in Roxbury, Robert Tinch, Jr., studied at the University of Hawaii, Hunter College, the New York Studio School, and New York University. He has taught at Wesleyan University, Sacred Heart University, and the Silvermine School of Art.

At Boston City Hospital (818 Harrison Ave.):

YES AND NO, 1977. Two mobiles, bronze. Lobby.
Artist unknown.
Gift of Mrs. Benjamin Jeffries.

GEN. LEONARD WOOD, 1931. Bronze plaque, h. 4′.
Entryway, Administration Bldg.
Bruce Wilder Saville (see Quincy: The Doughboy).

ABRAHAM SHUMAN, 1920. Bronze plaque, h. 4′.
Entryway, Administration Bldg.
Fred K. W. Allen.

SOUTH BOSTON

CYBELE, 1889. Bronze., h. 64″.
In front of Boston Design Center, Marine Industrial Park, Summer St.
★ Auguste Rodin (see Wellesley [Wellesley College]: Walking Man).

A contemporary casting (1986) from a plaster original by the great French master, this Cybele is one of three in the U.S. It is said to be a study for Rodin's Gates of Hell series, bas-relief doors based on Dante's Divine Comedy. In the religion of Phrygia (an ancient country occupying what is now northwest Turkey), Cybele, the Great Mother, was a principal deity. Her cult competed with those of Greek and Roman gods until the second or third century A.D. Casting commissioned by Lucy Billingsly and Trammell Crow Co.

ADMIRAL DAVID GLASGOW FARRAGUT, 1893. Bronze, larger than life.
Marine Park, William J. Day Blvd. and Broadway.
Henry Hudson Kitson (see Lexington: The Minuteman).

Foremost naval hero of the Civil War, Tennesseean Farragut (1801–1870) entered the U.S. Navy at the age of nine, and was competent enough to command a prize ship when he was twelve. His bold seamanship enabled Federal ships to blockade the South, capture New

Orleans, cut off Vicksburg during Grant's siege, and control the Mississippi. It was while his fleet was penetrating the heavily mined and fortified Mobile Bay (mines were called torpedoes at the time) that the admiral uttered his famed "Damn the torpedoes! Full speed ahead!" Commissioned by the city on petition of South Boston Citizens Association.

ICESKATES, 1982.
Warming room, Francis L. Murphy Rink, Day Blvd.
Elizabeth Carter (*see* Cambridge [Central Square]: *Floating Down Mass. Avenue*).
Funded by 1% for Art.

CERAMIC TILE PANELS, 1983. Two units, h. 30″ × 18″.
Exterior walls, Marine Park sanitary.
Joan Wye (*see* MBTA [Davis Sq. Station]: *Children's Tile Mural*).

Wye's small murals echo the marine theme of this area: dolphins (outside the men's room) and four species of food fish (outside the women's room). Funded by 1% for Art.

DORCHESTER

EDWARD EVERETT, 1867. Bronze, larger than life.
Richardson Park (just east of Edward Everett Sq.), Columbia Rd. and East Cottage.
William Wetmore Story (1819–1895).

Son of a jurist, W. W. Story took a law degree from Harvard, published both poetry and legal textbooks, and dabbled in art as a hobby. When his father died in 1846, he was commissioned (although he had never done anything remotely so ambitious) to create a memorial statue, and promptly sailed to Italy to study sculpture. He and his wife settled more or less permanently in Rome, center of an expatriate literary circle; Story was the model for the protagonist of Hawthorne's novel *The Marble Faun*. Something of a dilettante, Story did achieve a reputation as a sculptor and completed the marble statue of his father, although it is not considered a strong work. The same may be said of this statue, with its trite declamatory gesture. So ill was it received that it has been moved three times before ending up on this spot.

A Unitarian minister before he was twenty, Everett (1794–1865) abandoned the pulpit to become a professor of Greek at Harvard and editor of *North American Review*. Elected to Congress at thirty and governor of Massachusetts at forty-one, Everett subsequently became ambassador to Great Britain, president of Harvard College, and Secretary of State. Capitalizing on his power as an orator, he toured the nation in an effort to avert the Civil War. He failed, of course, but he donated proceeds of the speaking tour toward the purchase for the nation of Mount Vernon, George Washington's home. Everett was the now-forgotten "other" orator who shared the platform when Lincoln delivered the Gettysburg Address. Funded by public subscription following Everett's death.

COURTYARD, installation planned 1988. Granite, area 35' × 45'.
At Massachusetts State Archives bldg., Columbia Point.
Carlos Dorrien (*see* Waltham [Bentley College]: *Portal*).

Dorrien's expressive stone work here takes the form of a portal eleven feet high and a fourteen-inch stone slab, seven by eleven feet.

★ GAS TANK RAINBOWS, 1971. Painted graphic, h. 150'.
Victory Rd.; visible from Southeast Expressway.
Corita Kent (1919–1986).

This rainbow is the largest and perhaps now the best-known work of the printmaker who gained fame in the 1960s as Sister Corita. Born in Fort Dodge, Iowa, and reared in Los Angeles, Corita Kent became a Roman Catholic nun of the Sisters of the Immaculate Heart of Mary at the age of seventeen. She graduated from Immaculate Heart College in Los Angeles, became a grade school teacher in British Columbia, and in 1946 returned to her alma mater to teach art, later becoming head of the art department. In 1951 she earned a master's degree from the University of Southern California. Gaining fame as a printmaker, she exhibited for years at the Botolph Group Gallery (no longer extant) on Newbury St. Her splashy silkscreened work, laced with humanistic quotations from poets, philosophers, and Scripture, gained such popularity that she was chosen to design the 1985

PHOTO COURTESY BOSTON GAS CO.

"LOVE" stamp. She resigned from her Catholic order in 1968, saying, "You should be true to your own conscience. That's a . . . way of saying you know what God's will is." She settled in Boston and contributed her commissions to those causes that support the downtrodden, world-wide.

The idea of having Kent invent a megadesign for the gas storage tanks originated with Eli Goldston (d. 1975), chief executive officer of Eastern Gas and Fuel Co. This design is the largest object ever copyrighted by the U.S. Copyright Office. Commissioned by Project '70 and Boston Gas. Co.

JAMAICA PLAIN

PARKMAN MEMORIAL, 1906. Granite, h. approx. 18'.
On Parkman Dr., west side of Jamaica Pond.
★ Daniel Chester French (*see* Concord: *Minuteman*).

Francis Parkman (1823–1893), first great American historian, chronicled the English and French settlement of North America and the conflicts of those two nations on this continent. He was the first historian to understand the character and motives of the native American.

Parkman's contorted visage, his eyes closed to the beauties of Jamaica Pond, is puzzling unless something is known of the man. Victim of a neurological disorder that made him hypersensitive to light, Parkman spent much of his adult life in a darkened room. He had books read to him, and invented a mechanism that helped him take notes and write his manuscripts with his eyes shut. Although of delicate health as a boy, in his teens he undertook a wilderness trip to New Hampshire that fired his ambition to chronicle the French and Indian wars. He became a proficient woodsman; he had a gift for handling horses, both tame and wild—skills that aided him when he and a Harvard classmate spent some months among the Ogillalah Sioux. These rugged experiences failed to save him from decades as an invalid, through which he persisted with his life work, *France and England in the New World*, twenty-seven years in the writing. A horticulturist by avocation, developer of some new species, he rallied enough to spend his fiftieth year teaching horticulture at Harvard. This monument is on the site of his house in Jamaica Plain.

FISH MURAL, no date. Paint on masonry.
Seaverns Ave. side of Hailer's Rexall Pharmacy, 674 Centre St.
Joseph Scanlon and Christine Cooper.

VIVA MOZART PARK, 1987. Mural on masonry, h. 7' × 180'.
Mozart Park, Mozart and Bolster Sts.
Bayardo Gamez (1951–) and Baltazar Gutierrez (1959–   ).

As part of a cultural exchange program, these two Nicaraguan artists, chosen by the National Center for Popular Culture in that country, were brought to Boston to paint this community-participation mural. Sponsored by Arts for a New Nicaragua.

In Forest Hills Cemetery:

Mount Auburn Cemetery in Cambridge pioneered the concept of the parklike "garden cemetery," with landscaping, sculpture, and architect-designed monuments. Forest Hills, consecrated in 1848, followed close behind. There is room here to list only the most prominent works. The cemetery offices will provide maps and a booklet for visitors interested in more detail.

★ DEATH STAYING THE HAND OF THE SCULPTOR, 1892. Bronze relief, larger than life.
Grave of Martin Milmore, just inside entrance.
Daniel Chester French (*see* Concord: *Minuteman*).

The sculptors French and Milmore had neighboring studios in the Studio Building in Boston; when Milmore died at the age of thirty-seven, his family approached French for a memorial. French's concept of the Angel of Death as a woman, dignified, tender, almost maternal, created a sensation; it was hailed as the noblest and most sublime conception ever produced by an American artist. People wrote poems and letters to French about it; clergymen preached sermons. In Paris, where it was cast, it won a gold medal in the spring salon, although the artist was unknown in Europe. French here indulges the popular concept of the sculptor attacking his stone directly with chisel, although sculptors of the era, Milmore and French included, actually worked in clay and hired skilled artisans to transfer the model to stone. Milmore is depicted working on his *Sphinx*, now at Mt. Auburn Cemetery, Cambridge.

SOLDIERS' MONUMENT, 1867. Bronze, larger than life.
Martin Milmore (*see* Framingham: *Civil War Memorial*).

Although it sometimes seems that a successful monument salesman traveled New England selling Civil War soldiers leaning on their rifles, the fact is that many of them are by the same artist, Martin Milmore. This one was the first.

(DETAIL FROM BASE)

FIREMEN'S MONUMENT, 1906. Bronze, larger than life.
John A. Wilson (b. 1878).

Not to be confused with the contemporary John W. Wilson, this John Wilson was born in Nova Scotia and was a student of H. H. Kitson and Bela Pratt. Commissioned by the Boston Fire Department in memory of fallen comrades.

ROSLINDALE

STAR POOL, 1987. Stone pavement, 16′ diam. circle.
Adams Park, Washington St. and Cummins Hwy.
Be Allen (*see* Somerville: *Flag*).

Allen here translates her conceptual star patterns, done as a set of mobile screens in the Somerville police department lobby, into granite, bluestone, and puddingstone. Commissioned by Townscape Institute.

WEST ROXBURY

DR. JOSEPH WARREN, 1904. Bronze, larger than life.
At Roxbury Latin School, Centre and St. Theresa Sts.
★ Paul Wayland Bartlett (1865–1925).

A native of New Haven, Conn., son of sculptor Truman Howe Bartlett, Bartlett was sent to France as a schoolboy at the age of nine and spent most of his life there. He studied at the Ecole des Beaux Arts and became a skilled animal sculptor, often collaborating with other sculptors who did not do animals well. His interest lay in historical and symbolic figures; his Columbus and Michelangelo stand in the U.S. Library of Congress, his equestrian Lafayette is in Paris.

Dr. Warren (1741–1775) was born in Roxbury and was a graduate and at one time school master of this second oldest secondary school in the country, dating from 1645. A graduate of Harvard and a respected physician, he drafted the Suffolk Resolves urging opposition, by force if necessary, to British taxes. He was president of the third provincial congress. Commissioned a major general in the Colonial forces, he was killed in the battle of Bunker Hill (a statue of him by Henry Dexter stands there).

After sixty years on Warren Street in Roxbury, the statue was displaced by new traffic designs, moved to storage at Franklin Park, and subsequently rescued by Warren's alma mater in 1969.

THEODORE PARKER, 1887. Bronze, larger than life.
At Theodore Parker Unitarian Church, Centre St.
Robert Kraus (*see* Boston Common: *Boston Massacre Monument*).

Born in Lexington, Parker (1810–1860) was a grandson of Captain John Parker, who commanded the militiamen at the Battle of Lexington. A schoolmaster at seventeen, he enrolled in Harvard but pursued his studies while still working at his family's farm, traveling to Cambridge for exams. Entering the theology school, he found himself extremely antagonistic to the popular Calvinist religion of the day. Preacher and reformer rather than thinker/philosopher, Parker was a fearless advocate of emancipation, active in the Underground Railroad, and a friend and supporter of John Brown. Parker's admirers intended this likeness for Boston Common, but the Boston Art Commission refused it. It was stored until 1902, when it was retrieved by members of the First Church in West Roxbury, where Parker had held his first pulpit, 1837–1845. Funded by public subscription.

HYDE PARK

UNTITLED, 1987. Bronze, h. 4′ × 9′ × 4′.
Outside Bajko Rink.
Mark Cooper (*see* Brockton: *Political Trilogy*).
Funded by 1½% for Art.

CELEBRATION OF THE FIGURE EIGHT, installation planned 1988.
   Stainless steel wall relief, h. 5′ × 20′ × 4′.
   Interior, Bajko Rink.
   Peter Lipsitt (1940–   ).

   After earning a B.A. from Brandeis, then a B.F.A. and an M.F.A.
(1965) from Yale, Lipsitt spent two years in the Peace Corps teaching
at Haile Selassie University Laboratory School. He has also taught at
Brandeis, Wheaton, Concord Academy, and at the University of Wisconsin, and has held a fellowship from Triangle Artists' Workshop,
New York, and a Brookline arts council grant. Funded by 1½% for Art.

MBTA (Mass. Bay Transportation Authority)

*The oldest subway system in the United States (1897), Boston's "T"
during the 1980s has undergone a modernization program incorporating art as each station is renovated.*

ON THE RED LINE: ⟶

*This section of the "T," dating to 1912, was extended in both directions between 1978 and 1985. Arts on the Line, a collaboration between Cambridge Arts Council and the MBTA, placed a rich set of
installations both under and above ground. Most of the artists live and
work in Massachusetts. Community participation encouraged art indicative of each place.*

Alewife Station:

*The architecture of this end-of-the-line parking garage is sculptural in
itself. It contains six works, all so thoroughly integrated they may not
be recognized as art.*

END OF THE RED LINE, 1985. Neon.
   Above outbound subway platform.
   Alejandro and Moira Sina.

   The Sinas' pun, a series of red neon tubes hanging at the terminus
of the northbound track, is typical of the whimsy found in a good deal
of "T" art.
   Alejandro Sina was born in Santiago, received a master's degree
and then taught at the Universidad de Chile. He held a Fulbright
Scholarship in 1973–75, and since 1973 has been a fellow at the
Center for Advanced Visual Studies at M.I.T. He works with neon, argon, and mercury gasses, sometimes incorporating optoelectronics
and computer technology. His wife collaborates with him.

TWO SCULPTURAL BENCHES, 1985. Wood.
   Park-and-ride waiting area.
   William Keyser, Jr.

   Keyser is a Rochester, N.Y., woodworker.

DECORATIVE BRONZE FLOOR TILES, 1985.
Scattered throughout mezzanine.
Nancy Webb.

Fish and other aquatic creatures hint at the source for the name of this station, Alewife Brook. (Alewives are a species of herring that, swimming up freshwater streams to spawn, were once an important food source on the New England coast.)

PORCELAIN TILE WALL MURAL, 1985. Ceramic panels.
Rindge Ave. ramp.
David Davison.

ALEWIFE COWS, 1985. Painted panels.
Bus waiting area.
Joel Janowitz.

This fool-the-eye painting evokes the rural scene that once existed here at Alewife Brook.

ABOVE GROUND at Alewife Station: *see* Cambridge: *Environmental Site Work*.

Davis Station:

POETRY, 1985. Incised brick. Eleven sections, varying sizes.
Platform, underfoot.
Richard C. Shaner.

These works may be the hardest of all to find and the most pleasing. Unexpected intellectual fodder beneath the feet of the waiting commuter, they materialize almost as if in answer to the idle thought, "I wish I had something to read." The poems, each about ten bricks long and five wide, quote Walt Whitman, Emily Dickinson, and lesserknowns, including Shaner himself.

SCULPTURE WITH A 'D,' 1985. Painted aluminum.
Wall, outbound platform.
Sam Gilliam.

Variations on the letter "D" form the design for this wall sculpture.

CHILDREN'S TILE MURAL, 1985. Ceramic tiles.
Mezzanine wall.
Jack Gregory and Joan Wye.

Ceramicists Wye and Gregory are partners in the Belfast Bay Tile Works in Somerville, founded by Wye in 1974. Gregory studied graphic arts and has taught at the Boston Museum School. Wye focused on painting at the Art Students League, New York, and worked in bronze and wood sculpture in Provincetown.
Drawn by children in nearby schools and fired at the tile works, these signed tiles provide an amazing ethnic census.

ABOVE GROUND at Davis Station: *see* Somerville: *Untitled*.

Porter Station:

THE GLOVE CYCLE, 1985. Bronze, life-size gloves.
  Placed throughout the station.
  Mags Harries (*see* Chelsea: *Bellingham Square*).

★ THE LIGHTS AT THE END OF THE TUNNEL, 1985. Aluminum and mylar mobile sculpture.
  Above exit stairs.
  William Wainwright (*see* East Boston/Logan Airport: *Windwheels*).

  In Wainwright's current work, he uses diffraction gratings—tiny grooves that break up light and create rainbows in the same way a prism does. These forms, crafted to imply three-dimensionality, are in actuality single planes. This work was awarded a Massachusetts Council on the Arts Regional Governors' Design Award in 1986.

ABOVE GROUND at Porter Station: *see* Cambridge [Porter Sq.]: *Gift of the Wind, Ondas, Embroidered Bollards, Porter Square Megaliths*.

Harvard Station:

STAINED GLASS WALL, 1985.
  Bus station.
  ★ Gyorgy Kepes (1906–   ).

  The "red line" pun runs through Kepes' glowing blue wall, whose colors evoke the stained glass of the great cathedrals of Europe. Kepes, Hungarian-born, was nurtured among the *wunderkind* in the academy at Budapest until he began to paint in the cubist style. Expelled, he went to Berlin, London, and finally to Chicago to teach at the New Bauhaus (now the Institute of Design). He taught a course on light, which included photography and much more. He came to the department of architecture at M.I.T. in 1946. Kepes has had a long and distinguished career as a particularly lyrical abstract expressionist painter. In 1967 he founded the Center for Advanced Visual Studies at M.I.T., committed to closing the gap between art and technology by using technological media for aesthetic purposes.

NEW ENGLAND DECORATIVE ARTS, 1985. Ceramic tile.
  Bus ramp.
  Joyce Kozloff.

  Designed to mimic quilt patterns, Kozloff's colorful wall mural refers to such regional folk art as weathervanes, ship figureheads, nautical etchings, stenciling, and gravestone carving.

ABOVE GROUND at Harvard Station; *see* Cambridge [Harvard Sq.]: *Omphalos* and [Brattle Sq.] *Gateway to Knowledge*.

Central Station:

MURAL, 1987. Ceramic, fused glass, and enamel tiles, seven sections, each 4′ × 12′.

Seating bay areas.
Elizabeth Mapelli (1949–   ).

Oregonian Liz Mapelli earned her B.F.A. and M.F.A. at the University of Colorado and followed with post-graduate study at U.C.L.A. and the University of Washington. She is a regular exhibitor at international exhibitions of art glass and has executed a dozen commissions like this in the West.

MEDALLIONS, 1986. Ceramic tile, 100 units, each 12″ square.
At top of columns.
Dennis Cunningham and Anne Storrs (1953–   ).

Ceramicist Storrs attended the Art Institute of Chicago and the University of Oregon; she has held a fellowship from the Oregon Arts Commission. Cunningham, a printmaker, is a graduate (B.F.A.) of Pacific Northwest College of Art and has been recognized with three Art in Public Places awards.

Kendall/MIT Station:

★ THE KENDALL BAND, 1987. Audiokinetic sculptures, aluminum, stainless steel, teak, three parts: *Pythagoras*, h. 14′ × 48′, *Johan Kepler* and *Galileo* each h. 11′ × 5′.
Paul Matisse.

Designed for riders to play as they wait, these three musical works are tuned to the same key so their sounds will be harmonious, however randomly they ring. The sixteen aluminum chimes, titled *Pythagoras*, may be played by pulling levers that activate teak hammers; the aluminum ring, *Johann Kepler*, will resonate for five minutes; the sheet steel, *Galileo*, provides what the artist calls "musical thunder." Matisse, grandson of French painter Henri Matisse, lives and works in Groton.

Park Street Station:

★ CELEBRATION OF THE UNDERGROUND (see Green Line: *Celebration of the Underground*).

HANDS, to be installed 1988. Bronze, two units, each h. 5′.
Ralph Helmick (*see* Charles River Esplanade: *Arthur Fiedler*).

These forms are constructed of seventy to eighty stacked layers (Helmick's characteristic work style) but, unlike the Fiedler portrait, are then cast in bronze. The artist says these hands "should imply 'safe passage' and 'peaceful welcome,' functioning as generic St. Christopher images."

Downtown Crossing Station:

GRANITE BENCHES, 1987. Forty units, h. 18″ or 25″.
Randomly placed on platform.
Lewis C. (Buster) Simpson.

Seattle artist Buster Simpson majored in sculpture at the University of Michigan (B.F.A.; M.F.A. 1969), has participated in many collaborative and sound-installation projects, and has worked as consultant and advisor to artistic and historic projects in Seattle.

South Station:

WHEELS IN MOTION, 1971. Aluminum.
Silvana Cenci.
Funded by ICA and MBTA.

Installations planned between 1988 and 1990:

INSTALLATION. Granite, h. 10½' × 75' × 26.
Main concourse.
Jeffrey Schiff (*see* Charlestown: *Untitled*).

Schiff's granite environment is intended "to restate the condition of the journey, dramatize the act of passage," the sculptor says. An inlaid path will lead to a low-walled enclosure with columns both within and outside it. The split-granite columns are to be set at the angle of the tracks. Funded by MBTA, the Federal Railroad Administration, and the National Endowment for the Arts.

(1,2) (3,4) 5. Cast iron, h. 7'.
Mayer Spivack. (*see* Newton: *(1,2) (3,4) 5*).

NEON INSTALLATION. Red neon, 96' × 48'.
Suspended from ceiling, Red Line level.
Christopher Sproat (1945–   ).

Educated at Boston University, the Boston Museum School, and Skowhegan, Sproat has worked in a variety of media, from light to art-as-furniture. He has held grants from the National Endowment for the Arts and the Massachusetts Arts and Humanities Foundation.

MURAL.
Todd McKie (*see* Government Center: *Mr. Bignose Comes to Boston*).

Broadway Station:

UNTITLED. Painted aluminum, sixty forms, h. each 2'–3' on 16' × 40' wall.
Stairway to platform level.
Jay Coogan.

Coogan's black-and-white forms are abstracted from the shapes of tools and functional objects.

Ashmont Station:

TWO INTERSECTING SIXTEEN-CELLED POLYTOPES IN A HYPERCUBE.
Stainless steel wire, eight units, 4' × 12' × 20'.
Overhead .
David Brisson (d. 1982).

PHOTOMURALS. Ten 4′ × 8′ porcelain enamel panels.
    Eugene Richards, Ken Robert Buck, and John Heymann.

Quincy Adams Station:

CIRRUS CLOUDS. Stainless steel and diffraction mylar. Three sections, each
    6′ × 24′ × 10′.
    Overhead .
    Elaine Calzolari.

    Calzolari sought to enhance the airiness of the station with sculp-
ture that would react to wind and light, offering different aspects to
changes in the hour and the season.

BRIAN DOWLEY PHOTO

FOSSIL, 1982. Aluminum, h. 7′ × 2′.
    Red Line car no. 1506.
    Mags Harries (see Chelsea: *Bellingham Square*).

    This work is a handprint sculpted into a standard aluminum standee
pole in a subway car, as if a rider had stood and held onto it so long
the metal softened. One critic has written that Harries is interested in
forms "indicative of recurrent human situations." A playful (if frustrat-
ing) aspect of this work is, as the artist says, "You can never go to
find it—it finds you."

ORANGE LINE: ————————————————➤

State Street Station:

ABOVE GROUND at State Street Station: *see* Downtown: *Courtyard Gate*.

Chinatown (formerly Essex Street) Station:

LOCOMOTIVE, 1976–79. Welded steel, h. 9′4″ × 18′ × 18″.
    George Greenamyer (see Marshfield: *Webster, Farmer of Marshfield*).
    Funded by MBTA and 1% for Art.

COLORS ON THE LINE, 1987. Painted sheet steel, 9′ × 360′.
Safety niches, wall, inbound side.
Toshihiro Katayama (1928–   ).

Printmaker, environmental artist, and graphic designer, Katayama has been a teacher of graphics and visual design at Harvard since 1966. He describes himself as self-taught. Born in Osaka, Japan, he became a free-lance designer, was recruited by Geigy AG to work as a designer for that company in Switzerland, and subsequently was invited to teach at Harvard. His work is included in the collection of the Museum of Modern Art, New York, which also published his collaboration with Octavio Paz, *Visual Poetry*. He is the designer of the Alewife Station "T" sign and the State Street "star" sign.

Reflecting the activities of the subway platform, Katayama's bars are clustered where crowds are dense, sparser where the population of riders thins out. His colors are chosen to set up a tension and dynamism which will appear different from the platform and from the moving train.

New England Medical Center Station:

CARAVANS, installation planned 1988. Painted aluminum, four units averaging 17′ × 27′.
Stairway walls.
Richard Gubernick (1933–   ).

A graduate of the State University of New York at Buffalo, Gubernick is currently professor of fine arts there. He also holds degrees from the Yale University School of Music and Art and from the University of Massachusetts at Amherst (M.F.A.). Gubernick has constructed a similar wall relief for a transit station in Buffalo.

Back Bay Station:

NEON FOR THE BACK BAY/SOUTH END STATION, installation planned 1988. Neon, four units, varied sizes.
In arched windows over both entrances to station lobby, at subway entrance, and on ceiling of transit headhouse.
Stephen Antonakos (*see* Waltham [Brandeis University]: *Neon for the Rose Art Museum*).

Mass. Ave. Station:

KINETIC SCULPTURE, installation planned 1988. Carbon steel, slotted and textured. Three units, each h. 12′ × 2′ diam.
Suspended over staircase.
Bruce Taylor (1950–   ).

Coloradoan Bruce Taylor has done works for corporate and public sites in Denver and northern Colorado. He holds a B.F.A. from the University of Denver.

Ruggles Station:

MURAL, installation planned 1988. Painted masonry, h. 18′ × 50′.
  Exterior staircase wall.
  Paul Goodnight (1946–   ).

A former Artists Foundation fellow, Paul Goodnight attended Vesper George School of Art, Roxbury Community College, and Massachusetts College of Art, taking a B.F.A. in 1975. He has exhibited in China and Africa and has done murals in Nicaragua and Russia, as well as in Boston. Among owners of his work are the Smithsonian Institution and Howard University. Goodnight lives in Roxbury.

STONY BROOK DANCE, installation planned 1988. Painted aluminum, thirty units suspended from three 36′ cables.
  Overhead, concourse.
  John T. Scott (1940–   ).

An alumnus of Xavier University (B.F.A., 1962), John Scott is now professor of fine arts there. He holds a masters' of fine arts from Michigan State University. His work is in the collections of the Dallas Museum of Art and Fisk University.

Scott's art reaches deep into his African cultural heritage. In this kinetic work the long forms are based on the shape of the diddle-bow, a one-stringed African musical instrument.

Roxbury Crossing Station:

BANNER, installation planned 1988. Sailcloth, five units, one 8′ × 8′, four 8′ × 5′.
  Overhead, lobby.
  Susan Thompson.

A resident of Dorchester, Susan Thompson attended Hunter College. She teaches at Paige Academy and at the Neighborhood Arts Center in Roxbury, and is a member of the African American Master Artists in Residency Program at Northeastern University.

These banners bear images, both historic and present-day, from the surrounding communities of Mission Hill and Highland Park.

Jackson Square Station:

FACES IN A CROWD, installation planned 1988. Reinforced resin, h. 4′ × 7′.
  Wall above outbound track.
  James C. Toatley, Jr. (1941–1986).

James Toatley earned both his B.F.A. and M.F.A. (1977) at Boston University; previously, he studied at the University of California at Los Angeles and at Pennsylvania Academy of the Fine Arts. He was awarded a Cresson Fellowship for European study. Interspersed with his teaching career, Toatley was sculptor/designer for several toy companies, including Mattel and Hasbro. His teaching stints included Carney Academy in New Bedford, Boston University, Southeastern

Massachusetts University, Brockton Art Center, and Philadelphia Art Institute.

Toatley based his design on the "glimpses and short impressions" subway riders get of one another. Following the artist's untimely death, this work is being completed by UrbanArts in collaboration with Toatley's widow.

Stony Brook Station:

MURAL, installation planned 1988. Ceramic tile, h. 8'9" × 40'.
Lobby.
Malou Flato (1953–   ).

Texan Malou Flato completed her bachelor's degree in theater arts at Middlebury College in 1975. She has executed public and corporate commissions in Texas, California, and Washington. This work will depict people and scenes from the surrounding neighborhood.

Green Street Station:

COLOR PASSAGE, installation planned 1988. Stained glass, wire cloth. Three units all 5' deep; 10' × 50', 10' × 20', 20' × 20'.
Suspended from ceiling, station interior.
Virgina Gunter (*see* Needham: *Color Sweep*).

Gunter's work exploits the light entering the station's windows and floor-to-ceiling glass wall.

Forest Hills Station:

SERIAL SCULPTURE, installation planned 1988. Aluminum, seventeen units approx. 14' × 12'.
Lobby and exterior walkway.
Dan George (1949–   ).

A former artist-in-residence at Bennington College, Dan George has done site projects for Poughkeepsie and Lake George, N.Y. He was educated at Academie v. Shönekunsten in Antwerp, Belgium, and at the Art Students League in New York, and has been awarded grants from the New York Foundation for the Arts, New York State Council on the Arts Works in Public Places, and Collaborations in Art, Science and Technology.

George's leaf forms, attached to concrete columns, evoke the nearby open space of Franklin Park and Arnold Arboretum.

ON THE GREEN LINE: ⟶

PHOTOMURALS, 1975.
North Station.
Col. H. S. Bingham Associates.
Funded by MBTA.

★ CELEBRATION OF THE UNDERGROUND, 1976–78. Ceramic and found objects, h. 10′ × 110′.
Park St. Station.
Lilli Ann Killen Rosenberg (see Newton: *Five Concrete Mosaic Sculptures*).

This mural is located at the site of the initial excavation for the oldest subway system in America, opened in 1897; the braces seen between the panels are the original supports for the first tunnel. Alongside the turn-of-the-century trolley, the artist has incorporated antique trolley parts, tools, gears, bones, horseshoes, shells, fossils, Italian glass, marbles, and rail spikes into the work.

PHOTOMURALS, 1967.
Arilngton Station.
Bill Goodwin.
Funded by MBTA.

PHOTOMURALS, 1970.
Copley Station.
Beder & Alpers Inc.
Funded by MBTA.

PHOTOMURALS, 1970.
Kenmore Square Station.
Alonzo Reid.
Funded by MBTA.

ON THE BLUE LINE: ⟶

PHOTOMURALS, 1968.
Bowdoin Station.
Sert-Jackson and Associates.
Funded by MBTA.

DIAGONAL STRIPES ON A SPECTRUM, 1971.
State St. Station.
Robert V. Kennedy.
Funded by ICA and MBTA.

GEOMETRICS, 1968. Photomural.
Aquarium Station.
Funded by MBTA.

PHOTOMURALS, 1966.
MBTA Airport and Maverick Stations.
Arthur Hoener.
Funded by MBTA.

Cambridge

WAINWRIGHT, NEVERGREEN TREE

LECHMERE AREA

For photographs of new work and more detail, see the pamphlets "Public Art in Cambridge" and "Red Line Northwest Extension," both available from Cambridge Arts Council, City Hall, Cambridge 02139. CAC has sponsored some eighty works in the city; the listing below is partial. (CDBG is the acronym of Community Development Block Grant).

★ NEVERGREEN TREE, 1987. Windsculpture, diffraction grating on stainless steel, h. 35'.
Lechmere Canal Park.
William Wainwright (*see* East Boston/Logan Airport: *Windwheels*).

BUBBLE CHAMBER SERIES, 1987. Bronze, six splash pavers, five each 16" sq., one 30" sq.
Lechmere Canal Park.
David Phillips (*see* Cambridge [Porter Sq.]: *Porter Square Megaliths*).

Phillips has used the abstract graffiti drawn in a bubble chamber by subatomic particles as an overlay for actual castings of beach fragments. The work is a comment on this area's history, the marine detritus recalling the days when the Charles River Basin was the Back Bay, a tidal flat open to the sea.

THE FACES OF CAMBRIDGE, 1986. Bronze, life-size, h. 9'.
Lechmere Canal Park.
James Tyler (*see* Somerville: *Untitled*).

THE BRITISH ARE COMING, THE BRITISH ARE COMING, to be installed, 1988. Enamel paint on steel panels, two sections each h. 8' × 13'4".
Bridge over Lechmere Canal.
David Judelson (*see* Flag Fragments below).

When General Gage's men rowed across from Boston to Cambridge to begin their ill-fated march to Lexington and Concord in April, 1775, they landed near this spot.

FLAG FRAGMENTS, 1987. Ceramic, forty elements, varying sizes.
East Cambridge Parking Facility, First St. between Spring and Thorndike Sts.
David Judelson (1941–   ).

Artist/architect David Judelson holds degrees in architecture and city planning from M.I.T. He has received grants from the Massachusetts Council for the Arts and Humanities and in 1986 was among winners of the Governor's Design Award. In recent years Judelson has turned to three-dimensional architectural constructions.

The flags of the world are here, but largest are the major nationalities of East Cambridge: Italian, Irish, Polish, Portuguese, and Lithuanian.

EAGLE, circa 1870. Bronze, h. approx. 15'.
Bulfinch Sq., Thorndike and 2nd Sts.
Artist unknown.

This bronze eagle was made for the facade of the old post office building in Boston and salvaged when it was demolished. From the collection of Graham Gund.

GATE HOUSE, 1987. Three painted steel arches.
Cambridge Pkwy. near Rogers St.
Lloyd Hamrol.

Hamrol is an artist from Venice, Cal. Funded by CAC.

LUPUS, 1985. Cor-ten steel, h. 41'.
55 Cambridge Pkwy., in front of Lotus Development.
John Raimondi (1949–   ).

Raimondi grew up in East Boston and Winthrop, attended the Portland (Me.) School of Art and Massachusetts College of Art. After graduation he was artist-in-residence at Quincy Vocational Technical School, introducing sculptural concepts to welding classes. Purchased by Cabot, Cabot & Forbes, owners of the building.

At Royal Sonesta Hotel (5 Cambridge Pkwy):

Sonesta International Hotels, under the guidance of chairman Roger Sonnabend and his wife Joan, an art dealer, has achieved some fame for its policy of placing original works of art, rather than reproductions and decor items, in its hotels. In this building, every guest room contains an original print, and the public spaces boast forty-six other works by both international and local artists. A partial listing follows.

UNTITLED, 1984. Painted metal sculpture, h. 13'4".
Outside entrance.
Dennis Croteau (1948–   ).

Croteau is a Fitchburg, Mass., native who has studied at a number of institutions including the Boston Museum School, Tufts University, Emerson College, the San Francisco Art Institute, and the New School for Social Research in New York. He now lives and works in Charlestown, S.C.

I DREAMED I WAS HAVING MY PHOTO TAKEN, 1982. Silkscreen with unique painting, h. 78" × 98".
FLYING MAN WITH BRIEFCASE NO. 28169, 1983. Hanging sculpture, painted gatorfoam, h. 24" × 94" × 1".

MOLECULE MAN, 1982. Lithograph, h. 96″ × 80″.
All in Toff's restaurant.
Jonathan Borofsky (1942–   ).

Born in Boston, Borofsky graduated from Carnegie Mellon University and took a master's degree from the School of Fine Arts at Yale University. Having taught at the School of Visual Arts in New York and at California Institute of the Arts, he now lives in Venice, Cal. His work has been widely exhibited in major museums both in this country and in Europe.

DIGGING KIDS, 1982. Etching, h. 38″ × 52″.
BEACH BALLS, 1982. Etching, h. 38″ × 52″.
Opposite entrance to Toff's restaurant.
Eric Fischl (1948–   ).

New Yorker Fischl earned his B.F.A. at California Institute of the Arts. Fischl has received a good deal of critical attention in recent years, including a retrospective at the Whitney.

FLOWERS, 1970. Silkscreen, eight prints, h. 36″ × 36″.
Facing first-floor elevators.
★ Andy Warhol (1930–1987).

Andy Warhol is remembered for the statement that in the future "everyone will be world-famous for fifteen minutes." Jet-setter Warhol was the object of media attention for much longer than that, beginning with his Pop Art prints of huge Campbell soup cans in the early 1960s. Son of Czech immigrants, he was born Andrew Warhola in McKeesport, Pa., near Pittsburgh. He studied design at Carnegie Institute of Technology, moved to New York, and was a successful commercial artist for about a decade before his work began to receive international acclaim. His art is a commentary on the boredom and banality of mass-produced objects sold by slick packaging and promotion; his career has been said to be an example of same.

THE GLASS WISHES. Print from a series, h. 34″ × 27″.
In lobby lounge.
★ James Rosenquist (1933–   ).

From Grand Forks, N. D., Rosenquist migrated east to the University of Minnesota and then to the Art Students League in New York. A leading Pop Art painter, he produced magnified realistic drawings and prints that sometimes reached billboard size. His work was included in the 1981 Whitney Biennial and frequently earns exhibition throughout America and Europe.

COLOSSAL SCREW IN LANDSCAPE—TYPE 1; SOFT SCREWS TUMBLING #2; ARCH IN THE FORM OF A SCREW FOR TIMES SQUARE, N.Y. Three lithographs, 1976, each 68″ × 41″.
In Charles Bar.
★ Claes Oldenburg (1929–   ).

Born in Stockholm, Oldenberg came to Yale to study art and literature, and later studied at the Art Institute of Chicago. For a time he was a reporter and illustrator for a Chicago newspaper; moving to New York, he took a job in the library of the Cooper Union and met a group of artists who were devising "happenings" instead of making objects. His first giant soft sculpture was exhibited in 1962, challenging the most basic concepts we have about commonplace objects. Turning the everyday into the monumental by vastly enlarging the scale occupied Oldenberg for a number of years and brought him international fame. Some, like Philadelphia's clothespin, were built; others, like the Times Square arch, exist only in Oldenberg's drawings and prints.

INSIGHT, 1980. Steel, h. 76″ × 95″ × 36″.
Lobby.
★ Anthony Caro (1924–   ).

Caro was for two years an assistant to Sir Henry Moore, then went on to build an international career of his own. London-born, he was awarded the CBE (Commander of the British Empire) by the Queen in 1971. Caro has exhibited extensively in Europe and America; an example of his work is owned by most major museums. He now has a studio in New York state.

TWO REALMS WITNESS A CHANGE, 1984. Diptych, acrylic on canvas, 5′ × 7′.
Old lobby, to right of reception desk.
Natalie Alper.

After earning a master's degree in history at Boston University, Alper attended the Boston Museum School. Her drawings and large-scale watercolors have been widely exhibited along the Eastern Seaboard.

CUP, 1983. Oil on canvas, h. 66″ × 72″.
Outside Somerset Room.
Aaron Fink (1955–   ).

Boston-born, Fink was educated at Skowhegan School of Painting and Sculpture, the Maryland Institute College of Art, and Yale University School of Art and Architecture. His works on paper have been exhibited in this country, Europe, and Australia.

STELLER'S ALBATROSS, 1977. Lithograph/silkscreen, h. 34″ × 46″.
In Riverfront Room.
★ Frank Stella (1936–   ).

Now living in New York, Stella is a Boston-area native, born in Malden, educated at Phillips (Andover) Academy and Princeton. One of the stars of the mid-twentieth-century New York School, Stella has produced sculpture, painting, and prints which have been shown throughout Europe, North America, and Japan.

TRIPTYCH C, 1983. Mixed media, paper, h. each 28″ × 20″.
UNTITLED TRIPTYCH, 1983. Mixed media, paper. h. 30″ × 22″.
In Riverfront Room.
Carl Palazzolo (1945–   ).

Born in Torrington, Conn., Palazzo took a degree in 1968 through the combined Boston Museum School/Tufts University program. Shown primarily in Boston, New York, and the Netherlands, his work in 1975 was included in the prestigious Whitney Museum Biennial in New York.

CERAMIC COLUMNS, 1984. Four vases, each h. 25″ × 18″.
In Riverfront Room.
Paul Heroux.

Paul Heroux is a 1970 graduate of the Boston Museum School. His work has been exhibited by galleries in Boston, New York, Portland, Me., and Houston, Tex.

NIGHT SUN, 1984. Ceramic tile, 11′ × 16′3″.
Outside ballroom.
★ Katherine Porter (1941–   ).

Considered a peripheral member of the Boston Expressionist School, Porter worked in a "gestural expressionism" characterized by calligraphic Xs, zigzags, and spirals. Such linear motifs may be seen in this ceramic work, commissioned specifically for this space. An Iowan by birth, Porter studied at Boston University and Colorado College, and now lives in Vinalhaven, Me.

UNTITLED, 1979. Welded steel sculpture, h. 52″ × 50″.
Outside ballroom, second floor.
Jacqueth Hutchinson (1942–   ).

Hutchinson, Boston-born, studied at Bennington College, Vt., and St. Martin's School of Art, London. She has exhibited throughout New England and New York, and in Holland.

MAN IN THE CITY, 1983. Lithograph, diptych, h. 72″ × 36″.
Second floor elevator landing.
Robert Longo (1953–   ).

Brooklyn native Longo earned a B.F.A. at the State University of New York in Buffalo; he lives and works in New York. His enigmatic vignettes often imply a moment of violence, unexplained, a commentary on contemporary life. Longo's work has appeared in major museums throughout this country and in Stockholm, Munich, and London.

JIM HARRISON PHOTO

TWELVE AROUND ONE, 1981. Portfolio of thirteen screen prints, 30″ × 40″ each.
Outside second-floor conference rooms.
★ Buckminster Fuller (1895–1983).

Perhaps the twentieth century's foremost futurist and visionary designer, Buckminster Fuller was born in Milton, graduated from Milton Academy, went on to Harvard but was expelled for cutting classes and (Fuller said) ''general irresponsibility.'' After service in the Navy in World War I Fuller attended the Naval Academy. This series of prints displays some of his ideas, both those that have entered the mainstream (the geodesic dome) and those that failed to gain acceptance (the Dymaxion car). At his death, Fuller was professor emeritus at Southern Illinois University and the University of Pennsylvania, and world fellow in residence at University City Science Center in Philadelphia.

UNTITLED, ca. 1970. Set of four serigraphs, h. 42″ × 40″ each.
Corridor to Lotus bldg.
Neil Welliver (1929–   ).

Welliver's lyrical sylvan paintings and prints are widely held in New England. From Millville, Pa., Welliver went to the Philadelphia Museum College of Art, took a graduate degree at Yale, and taught there for a decade. Since 1966 he has taught at the University of Pennsylvania in Philadelphia.

EAST CAMBRIDGE

FOUR FIGURES, 1987. Bronze, h. approx. 18″ on 6′ support pole.
Sennot Park, Broadway at Tremont St.
Gene Cauthen (1942–   ).

A teacher at Mount Wachusett Community College, Cauthen lives in Royalston. He graduated from the University of Texas in 1964 with a B.F.A., spent a year studying at Cleveland Institute of Art, then earned an M.F.A. at Yale.

SUN ARC, 1981. Stainless steel, five units, h. 3′–6′.
Sennot Park playground.
Beth Galston (1948–   ).

Environmental artist Galston makes sensitive installation art, simple yet stunning in effect, but little of it is permanent—this early piece is an exception. A 1970 graduate of Cornell, she took a B.F.A. from Kansas City Art Institute, a master's in visual studies from M.I.T., and has been a Fellow of the Center for Advanced Visual Studies.

Doing double duty as climbing structures and light sculptures, Galston's Sennot Park frameworks are designed to cast interesting shadows on the sand, their configurations changing as the sun moves.

PARK BENCH GROUP, 1987. Bronze, h. 18″ plus 5′ support pole.
POLE CLIMBERS, 1987. Bronze, h. approx. 7′.
Columbia Park, Columbia and Washington Sts.
Gene Cauthen (*see Four Figures* above).

Pole Climbers depicts the *pola en ceval*, or greased-pole-climbing contest, a traditional competition of Hispanic festivals.

ARBOR, 1987. Bronze, h. approx. 5′.
Park, Harvard St. between Clark and Moore Sts.
Gene Cauthen (*see Four Figures* above).

GROUND MURAL, 1981. Ceramic, 18′ × 37′.
Hurley St. playground.
David Judelson (*see* Cambridge [Lechmere]: *Flag Fragments* above) and Elee Koplow.

Koplow is a graduate of the Boston Museum School; she also studied at San Miguel School of Art, Mexico.

INNER CITY TOTEM, 1983. Steel and landscape timber, 10′ × 30″ × 10″.
Margaret Fuller House, 71 Cherry St.
Dennis Didley (1940–   ).

Cambridge native and Boston Museum School alumnus, Didley draws profoundly on his African heritage. Most recently curator of exhibitions at Harriet Tubman House in Boston's South End, he has exhibited extensively. Funded by CDBG.

PLAY IS CHILD'S WORK, 1983. Ceramic tile, h. 7′ × 12′.
Roberts School, Harvard and Windsor Sts.
Judith Inglese (*see* Cambridge [Central Sq.]: *I'd Hammer Out Love*).
Funded by 1% for Art.

ANIMAL WEATHER VANES, 1981. Painted steel, four pieces.
Main St. at Bishop Allen Dr.
Joseph Barbieri.

Barbieri is known for his fanciful paintings of animals impeccably garbed. He studied at Pennsylvania Academy of Fine Arts and in Florence; he has taught at Harvard Graduate School of Design and at children's workshops at the Fogg Museum. Funded by CDBG and NEA.

ENGINE COMPANY 5, 1976. Exterior enamel paint on brick, h. 15′ × 25′.
Inman Sq. firehouse, Hampshire and Cambridge Sts.
Ellery Eddy.

Eddy, a young artist living near Inman Square, concluded that the most unifying element in her diverse neighborhood was the firehouse; her reasoning won her the commission for this work. To the portraits of the men in the engine company, Eddy whimsically added George Washington, once a volunteer fireman, and Benjamin Franklin, founder of America's first fire insurance company. Funded by CETA.

BUTTER IN THE BATTER, 1982. Acrylic on masonry, $13' \times 45'$.
Rosie's Bakery, Inman Sq.
Heddi Siebel.
Funded by CDBG.

TREES AND FLOWERS, 1979–80. Mosaic murals, various sizes.
Interior and exterior, Miller's River Houses for elderly and handicapped, Cambridge and Lambert Sts.
Lilli Ann Killen Rosenberg (see Newton: *Five Concrete Mosaic Sculptures*), with participation of tenants and neighborhood schoolchildren.

At M.I.T.:

For a complete listing and discussion of the 1000 or more works owned by Massachusetts Institute of Technology, consult the paperback Art and Architecture at MIT: A Walking Tour of the Campus, *available at the List Arts Center (Wiesner Bldg.) on Ames St. Only the most visible works will be listed here.*

FOR MARJORIE, 1961. Red-painted steel, h. 18'.
West end of campus, off Memorial Dr. between Audrey St. and Amherst St.
★ Tony Smith (1912–1980).

Minimalist sculptor Tony Smith is known for his "cubes," works ordered by telephone from steel fabricators, to exemplify the interrelationship between art and contemporary technology. Born in New Jersey, Smith studied architecture at the New Bauhaus in Chicago, was briefly an assistant to Frank Lloyd Wright, worked initially as a toolmaker and draftsman, spent twenty years as a practicing architect and then another twenty as a sculptor. He taught at New York University, Cooper Union, Pratt Institute, Bennington, and Hunter College. Many of his large works are sliced from geometric forms; *For Marjorie* would fit within a tetrahedron.

BELLTOWER FOR MIT CHAPEL, 1953–55. Aluminum, h. 45'.
★ Theodore Roszak.

M.I.T. also owns the drawings and models for this functional sculpture, developed in collaboration with the architect Eero Saarinen. Springing from richly encrusted arches, the three vertical elements symbolize the three major Western religions intended to be served by the interdenominational chapel.

ALTARPIECE SCREEN, 1955. Brass, h. 20'.
Inside chapel.
★ Harry Bertoia (1915–   ).

Italian-born, Bertoia came here as a teenager and studied at Cranbrook Academy of Art in Michigan. Like the narrow reflecting moat, the screen is designed to scatter light inside the chapel.

THREE PIECE RECLINING FIGURE, DRAPED, 1976. Bronze,
h. 8′8″ × 15′7″ × 8′8″.
Killian Ct., main bldg., Memorial Dr.
★ Henry Moore (1898–1986).

Widely acknowledged as the greatest sculptor of the twentieth century, Moore has worked with the figure throughout his career. His drawings of families sheltering in London subways during the German air raids of World War II inspired many of the *Reclining Figure* pieces. An earlier and smaller reclining figure is in the courtyard near M.I.T.'s Wiesner Building on Ames Street, and another is at Harvard University.

Moore's earliest figure drawings display a tendency toward bulk and monumentality. His distinctive organic forms, with their references to bones and beach pebbles, are universally familiar now. The negative spaces—hollows and holes in the sculpture—are as important visually as the positive forms. When Moore first pierced the figure, however, his style became the subject of caricature on a par with Picasso's cubist faces.

GUENNETTE, 1977. Granite, eleven pieces.
Killian Ct.
★ Michael Heizer (1944–).

Heizer is an environmental artist best known for his *Double Negative*, a trench 1500 feet long by fifty feet deep cut across the flanks of a gorge in the Nevada desert. *Guennette*, forty-six tons of pink Canadian granite from the town of Guennette, is a set of variations on circles and circle fragments. M.I.T. does not discourage tactile enjoyment of its public sculpture, and this work is a popular spot for readers, sunbathers, and occasional musicians. On long-term loan from the Metropolitan Museum of Art, New York.

CALVIN CAMPBELL PHOTO COURTESY M.I.T.

ANGOLA, 1968. Cor-ten steel, $7' \times 8\frac{1}{2}' \times 6'$.
On Memorial Dr., in front of Hayden Memorial Library.
Isaac Witkin.

Born in South Africa, Witkin emigrated to England in the mid-1950s, where he studied with Anthony Caro and became an assistant to Sir Henry Moore. In 1965 he served as artist-in-residence at Bennington College, Vt.

ELMO-MIT, 1963. Bronze, h. $65'' \times 56''$.
Outside Hayden Library.
Dimitri Hadzi (*see* Brookline: *Primavera*).

The first work commissioned for M.I.T.'s outdoor collection, *Elmo-MIT* presages Hadzi's much larger *Thermopylae* in City Hall Plaza, Boston. A Hadzi work in radically different style (*Omphalos*) stands in Harvard Square.

THE BATHER, 1923–25. Bronze, h. $76'' \times 29'' \times 28''$.
Courtyard, Hayden Library.
★ Jacques Lipchitz (1891–1973).

Lipchitz was born in Lithuania, but before he was twenty went to study sculpture in Paris, where he was intimate with such innovators as Brancusi, Modigliani, Picasso, and Gris. He escaped to New York in 1941 and continued working there, his style becoming less abstract, more emotional, and more dramatic. Many of his late works reflect Biblical texts.

Of the collection of familiar Lipchitz works in the Hayden courtyard, only this one is permanent; the others are on long-term loan from the sculptor's widow. This, Lipchitz' first life-size sculpture, reflects his involvement in the Cubist movement in Paris. The other works here mirror important changes in the sculptor's style up to 1957. Gift of Yulla Lipchitz.

★ THE BIG SAIL, 1965. Painted steel, h. $40'$.
McDermott Ct., in front of Green Bldg., M.I.T.'s tallest.
Alexander Calder (1898–1977).

Third-generation of a family of Philadelphia sculptors, Calder is famed as the inventor of the "mobile," free-hanging sculpture that is

CALVIN CAMPBELL PHOTO COURTESY M.I.T.

moved by currents of air. By contrast, *The Big Sail* is one of a series of "stabiles," related in their planar construction to the mobiles but unmoving. Calder studied mechanical engineering at Stevens Institute of Technology before becoming an art student in New York and, later, in Paris. This work was fabricated under Calder's direction in an ironworks. A small preliminary version of the piece stands at the entrance of Building 9 on Massachusetts Ave.

TRANSPARENT HORIZON, 1975. Painted Cor-ten steel, h. 20′ × 21′ × 18′.
Near Landau Bldg., Ames St.
★   Louise Nevelson (1899–1988).

Nevelson was well known for her all-black (or, later, all-white) assemblages of wooden "found objects" such as newel posts, lintels, and other architectural scraps, carefully placed in compartments of wall-sized cases. Although born in Russia, Nevelson was brought to Maine at an early age and lived and worked in New York from the 1920s until her death.

CALVIN CAMPBELL PHOTO COURTESY M.I.T.

M.I.T. students have never liked this work, and one winter buried it completely in snow. It tends to be a natural "bulletin board" for posters, as well.

NIAGARA, 1973. Cor-ten steel, h. 9′ × 22′ × 18′.
Compton Ct., near Alumuni Pool.
Michael Steiner (1945–   ).

Steiner's study in the interrelationships of steel slabs has puzzled M.I.T. students even more than the Nevelson. From time to time it contains a chair or two, as if it were a ramshackle kids' clubhouse; when the work was first installed, pranksters tried to equip it as an outhouse.

★ RECLINING FIGURE: WORKING MODEL FOR LINCOLN CENTER
SCULPTURE, 1963. Bronze, h. 5′.
Upper courtyard, Wiesner Bldg.
Henry Moore (*see Three Piece Reclining Figure, Draped* above).

Gift of Albert and Vera List in memory of Mrs. List's brother, Samuel
Glasner, a 1925 graduate of M.I.T.'s School of Architecture and Planning.

UNTITLED COLLABORATION, 1985.
At the Wiesner Bldg. (List Arts Ctr.).
BANQUETTES, BALCONY and RAILINGS: Scott Burton (1939–   ).
SCULPTURE GARDEN: Richard Fleischner (1944–   ).
EXTERIOR and ATRIUM WALL PATTERN.
★ Kenneth Noland (1924–   ).

Designs by these three artists, in collaboration with architect I. M.
Pei (an M.I.T. graduate), were integrated into the planning and construction of the arts center and its surrounding plaza. Acknowledged
one of the most powerful practitioners of Minimalism, Noland is best
known for his series of color studies in target and chevron patterns.
He was born in Asheville, N.C., attended Black Mountain College and
the Institute of Contemporary Art in Washington, D.C. During World
War II he served in the U.S. Air Force as a glider pilot and cryptogra-
pher. He has taught at the ICA, at Catholic University in Washington,
and at Bennington College, Vt. Burton, a maker of sculptural furniture
in stone and wood, studied literature and art history at Columbia and
New York University (M.A., 1963), and then studied art with Hans
Hoffman at Provincetown. Fleischner earned a master's degree in
sculpture at Rhode Island School of Design in 1968 and has taught at
Brown and at RISD. For a time he made large-scale earthworks; now
Fleischner builds big sculptured forms using groups of blocks of uni-
form size as a common denominator (*see* Cambridge [Alewife station]:
Environmental Site Work). He has designed environments at the Dal-
las Museum of Fine Arts and at the University of California, San
Diego.

Whether in sarcasm or in genuine constructive criticism, college
pranksters for the first year of this building's existence repeatedly altered colorist Noland's color scheme by painting one tile near the entrance a sickly green. The Institute gamely kept cleaning it off, and the
critics now seem to have graduated.

FIGURE DÉCOUPÉE, 1958–63. Cast concrete, h. 11′6″.
Wadsworth and Amherst Sts.
★ Pablo Picasso (1881–1973) and Carl Nesjar.

Less a sculpture than a drawing, this work was cast, using a process called "bétongravure" (concrete-engraving), by the Norwegian artist Nesjar from a wooden maquette by Picasso. *Figure Découpée* translates, "Cut-Out Figure," one of a series of such planar cut-outs made by Picasso in the 1950s and 60s. This one represents a bird with wings outstretched above.

Picasso, probably the best-known painter of our century, worked in a number of styles as he addressed the formal problems of art in the modern day. What is less commonly known is that Picasso was a consummate draftsman. He learned his craft from his father, a Spanish painter specializing in realistic pictures of doves; when the boy was twelve, the father recognized that the son had surpassed him and turned his brushes and palette over to Pablo. Picasso's experiments with an expressionist form of Cubism have led to a popular cliché, the profile portrait with both eyes visible. Later in life Picasso experimented with ceramics and sculpture of vast creative verve and lack of inhibition.

CALVIN CAMPBELL PHOTO COURTESY M.I.T.

Not part of the official M.I.T. collection (thus not listed in the catalog of Art and Architecture*) are five wall hangings of C. Fayette Taylor, professor of engineering who logged a twenty-year career as a professional sculptor after his retirement from M.I.T. (see Government Center and Environs:* Upward Bound*). His works at M.I.T. are:*

UNTITLED, 1966. Stainless steel, 34″ × 60″.
Faculty Club.
PENDULAR, 1970. Brass and steel, 48″ × 66″.
Chemistry Department.
RECTANGULAR, 1979. Brass and steel, 3′ × 5′.
Mechanical Engineering Department.
WATER MILL, 1971. Brass, stainless steel, plastic, h. 2½′ × 5′.
Hydraulic Laboratory.
AIR MILL, 1982. Brass, stainless steel, plastic, 2′ × 3′.
Sloan Automotive Laboratory.

CENTRAL SQUARE

FLOATING DOWN MASS. AVENUE, 1978. Acrylic on masonry wall, 20' × 28½'.
Putnam Furniture Leasing Bldg., 614 Mass. Ave., Central Sq.
Elizabeth Carter (1950–   ) and Michael Stanton.

Carter and Stanton both studied at Antioch College and began doing murals in Ohio. Carter later studied at Massachusetts College of Art and is now seeking a graduate degree at Boston Museum School. She has received Artists Foundation grants for teaching, serving as artist-in-residence at elementary and high schools in Boston-area communities.

Carter's river murals (see *Magazine Street Beach Scene* below) are meant to comment on nostalgic uses of the Charles River, before pollution was a factor. Working at night, Carter and Stanton projected a pair of slides on the wall and traced the outlines, combining a "reflection" of the neighborhood with an old-fashioned boating scene. Funded by CAC and Art Army.

CENTRAL SQUARE WINDSCULPTURE, 1977. Gold-plated stainless steel and steel, h. 26' × 4' × 4'.
Central Sq.
Michio Ihara (see Lowell: *Pawtucket Prism*).
Funded by CDD, private donations, and by the artist.

CENTRAL SQUARE NEWS, 1984. Trompe l'oeil architectural perspectives on newsstand kiosk. Acrylic on plywood, three panels, each 4' × 7'.
Central Sq. (removed during subway construction; to be replaced 1988).
Joshua Winer (see Cambridge [Harvard Sq.]: *Harvard Square Theater Mural*).
Funded by CAC and private donations.

MAGAZINE STREET BEACH SCENE, 1979. Exterior paint on clapboard, 15' × 22'.
Putnam Ave. and Brookline St.
Elizabeth Carter (see *Floating Down Mass. Avenue* above) and Jean Broughton.

Although members of the Charles River Watershed Council occasionally take a dip upriver to demonstrate the increasing cleanliness of this once-foul waterway, scenes like this one are long since gone from the river. Carter's mural recalls nearby Magazine Beach about 1900. The difficulty of restoring this mural on clapboard may mean that it will be destroyed. Funded by CAC and Cambridge River Festival.

FLOOR MURAL, 1979. Three parts, 3½' × 3½' and 2' × 4'.
Central Sq. Library, Green St.
David Judelson (see Cambridge [Lechmere]: *Flag Fragments*).
Funded by CAC.

UNTITLED, 1980. Stained glass, $7' \times 3'$.
Central Sq. Library, Green St.
Linda Lichtman (1942–   ).

Now working full-time as a stained glass specialist, Lichtman has been on the staff at the Museum School and at Hayden Gallery, M.I.T.; she has taught at Tufts University and at Middlesex and Bunker Hill Community Colleges. After taking degrees in psychology and social work at Simmons College, Lichtman returned to Massachusetts College of Art for an M.F.A. She also attended the Boston Museum School, and has traveled to England, Ontario, and Washington state for apprenticeships and workshops. Funded by CDBG.

I'D HAMMER OUT LOVE, 1984. Ceramic tile, $4'6'' \times 22'$.
Saundra Graham and Rosa Parks Alternative School, Upton St.
Judith Inglese.

Inglese's many murals include a forty-foot-long work for the National Zoo in Washington, D.C. Her style imitates in clay the techniques of stained glass, cutting shapes that follow the patterns of color. She studied at Sarah Lawrence College, the Boston Museum School, and at the Accademia di Belle Arti in Rome. The title here is taken from a folk song, and some of the lyrics are stamped into the mural. Funded by CDBG and 1% for Art.

BEAT THE BELT, 1980. Acrylic on masonry wall, $13' \times 75'$.
Back of Stop & Shop supermarket, Memorial Dr.
Bernard LaCasse.

This mural celebrates the triumph of people over bureaucracies: the successful effort in the 1970s by residents to block the construction of the Inner Belt, Interstate 95, through the city. Funded by CAC, neighborhood donations, and the artist.

MEMORIAL TO MARTIN LUTHER KING, JR., 1986. Ceramic, mosaic, h. $7' \times 3'$.
Martin Luther King Plaza, Franklin St. entrance to Central Sq. Library.
Lilli Ann Killen Rosenberg (*see* Newton: *Five Concrete Mosaic Sculptures*).
Commissioned by CAC.

REMEMBRANCES, 1982. Mosaic, h. $5' \times 7'$.
Left side, Pearl St. entrance, Central Sq. Library.
Lilli Ann Killen Rosenberg (*see* Newton: *Five Concrete Mosaic Sculptures*).

The aquatic motifs here remind that sections of Cambridge were once marsh areas. Commissioned by CAC.

At Hyatt Regency Hotel (575 Memorial Dr.):

In guest rooms and suites here are fine-art prints by Vasarely, Josef Albers, Jergens Peters, and Mark Rothko, and original oils by Hector

Leonardi. The following is a partial listing from the forty works placed in public spaces:

WINDWHEELS (see Logan Airport: *Windwheels*)
Outside entrance (temporary location).

VENETIAN WALL. Trompe l'oeil mural, h. 21' × 36'.
Atrium.
Richard Haas (*see* Back Bay: *West Facade*).

MERCURY ARGON CLUSTER. Neon, h. ten stories.
Atrium.
Alejandro Sina (*see* MBTA [Alewife Station]: *End of the Red Line*).

GREEN TURBULENCE, 1968. Acrylic on canvas, 94" × 157".
Atrium.
★ Adolph Gottlieb.
On loan from Graham Gund.

LOOKING FOR AN ISLAND, 1976. Fabric collage.
Entry lobby.
Clara Wainwright (*see* Fenway [Children's Hospital]: *Folk Tales From the Four Corners of the Earth*).

EDGES #1, 1979. Textile relief collage, 49" × 45".
Diana D. Filippi.

UNTITLED (CYCLAMEN), 1981. Pastel on paper, 95" × 95".
At foot of escalator.
Michael Mazur (1935–   ).

New Yorker Michael Mazur has reversed the customary procedure for artists, leaving New York and establishing himself in Boston. After graduation from Amherst College in 1958, Mazur garnered a B.F.A. and an M.F.A. from Yale and almost immediately found recognition as a printmaker, his works gaining entry to exhibitions at the Museum of Modern Art and the Whitney. Turning to painting, Mazur has become a force on the Boston scene, his painterly realism incorporating increasing quantities of expressionism. Mazur's work is owned by nearly thirty museums, nationwide.

IOS. Watercolor on paper.
Lobby at base of escalator.
Susan Shatter.

SUDDEN, 1976. 52" × 152".
At Pallysadoe Lounge.
Friedel Dzubas (*see* Downtown: *Crossing*).

CROSSROADS, 1987. Mural, h. 28' × 46'.
Pearl St. parking garage, between Green and Franklin Sts.
Daniel Galvez.

From Oakland, Cal., Galvez has organized community mural-painting in other New England localities. This one was painted in connection with the 1987 Cambridge River Festival, enlisting volunteer artists from the neighborhood. It is based on photos of local scenes and people. Funded by CAC.

LEVITATED STONE, 1987. Bronze and granite, h. 8'.
Dana Park, Magazine and Lawrence Sts.
David Phillips (see MBTA [Porter Sq.]: Porter Square Megaliths).

FIVE REVOLUTIONARY FIGURES, 1987. Steel.
Fort Washington Park., Waverly and Talbot Sts.
Madeline Lord.

Lord is an artist working in Bedford.

STONE WORK, 1980. Granite and bronze, h. approx. 4'.
Riverside Press Park, Memorial Dr. east of Western Ave.
David Phillips (see MBTA [Porter Sq.]: Porter Square Megaliths).
Funded by CDBG and NEA.

HARVARD SQUARE

IN CONSIDERATION OF HALF-LIVES AND ATTITUDES, 1979, 1981.
Cement, bronze, clay, stone, enamels, h. $7' \times 7' \times 7'$.
Harris Communications, 80 Trowbridge St.
Mark Cooper (see Brockton: Political Trilogy).

★ OMPHALOS, 1985. Granite, h. 21'.
Harvard Sq.
Dimitri Hadzi (see Brookline: Primavera).

The title translates "navel," and refers to stones used in ancient cults (such as Delphi) to mark the center of the universe; Hadzi correlates this site with the center of the educational universe. The artist

chose his different-colored granites from quarries in Maine, New Hampshire, Rhode Island, Pennsylvania, South Dakota, Missouri, and India. Funded by MBTA and private donations.

★ QUIET STONE, 1986. Marble, h. approx. 3'.
Winthrop Park, Harvard Sq., JFK Blvd. and Eliot St.
Carlos Dorrien (see Waltham [Bentley College]: Portal).

Dorrien likes to make "imaginary remnants" in stone, objects that look as if they have a history. His sculpture here summarizes contemporary thinking about public art: thoroughly melded into its site, full of arcane references to the place, witty, a little puzzling, inviting interaction. New Towne was the first name of Cambridge, and this spot was its marketplace. From Eliot St. the work looks like an authentic ruin, the lintel of the now-vanished market fallen to earth. Its opposite side would look like unworked stone, except that Dorrien has thoughtfully cut steps into it, inviting passers-by to do what they would do anyway —climb, sit, or lie on it.

HARVARD SQUARE THEATRE MURAL, 1983. Paint on masonry; 57' × 20'.
Harvard Sq. Theatre, Church St. at Mass. Ave.
Joshua Winer and Campari Knoepffler.

Members of the First Unitarian Church, an 1833 edifice, were uneasy when Harvard Square's movie house shifted its entrance from Massachusetts Ave. to Church St., directly across from the church. Negotiations between the owner, the church, the city's Historical Commission, and Renata von Tscharner and Ronald Reed of the Townscape Institute resulted in this tromp l'oeil mural. Winer and Knoepffler, graduate architecture students at Harvard, refined and executed Townscape Institute's design ideas (adding their own visages to the masks of Comedy and Tragedy). The muralists used a new color coating based on liquid silicate technology that is guaranteed not to fade for at least a decade.

GATEWAY TO KNOWLEDGE, 1979–83. Brick, 20'6" × 5'6" × 5'.
Brattle Sq., one block west of Harvard Sq.
Ann Norton.

Norton studied at the National Academy of Design, the Art Students League, and Cooper Union. In the 1940s she left New York to teach in West Palm Beach, Fla.; late in life she was rediscovered and her work exhibited to acclaim in New York. She died before this work was completed. This is the seventh in a series of gateways, some constructed in Florida. Funded by MBTA.

SUMNER, 1900. Bronze, larger than life.
Harvard Sq., Mass. Ave. and Garden St.
★ Anne Whitney (see Quincy Market: Samuel Adams).

Anne Whitney, perhaps suspecting the bias of the commission which set out to memorialize Sumner in 1875, submitted her model anonymously. She was right; it was judged one of the three best, but when the commissioners learned it was by a woman it was disqualified. It was, they said, unthinkable for a female to model the male body, even a thoroughly clothed one. (The argument made little sense, because Whitney had already been chosen to sculpt Samuel Adams for Statuary Hall in Washington.) With financial help from her friends, Whitney stubbornly completed the work anyway, finishing it in 1900 when she was almost eighty. It was her last major work.

It is fitting that Sen. Charles Sumner (1811–1874) sits here near Harvard Law School, from which he graduated at the age of twenty-three. Sumner was also a graduate of Harvard College, and lectured there until his election to the U.S. Senate in 1851 (*see* Boston Public Garden: *Charles Sumner*).

At Harvard University:

The following list is partial:

JOHN HARVARD, 1884.
  In front of University Hall, Harvard yard.
  ★ Daniel Chester French (*see* Concord: *Minuteman*).

  At the unveiling of *John Harvard*, a physician complained to French, "You've given John Harvard the legs of a consumptive." The sculptor gently informed his critic that John Harvard died of consumption when he was scarcely thirty. Little else is known of the benefactor of the college. Harvard probably lived 1608–1638; he took bachelor's and master's degrees from Emmanuel College at Cambridge University, came to Charlestown (it is thought) in 1637, died within the year, and is buried in Charlestown. He willed one-half his estate and his library of 302 books to the inhabitants of New Towne (now Cambridge), who had in 1636 founded a college, yet unnamed. In the absence of any record of Harvard's appearance, French's friend Sherman Hoar posed for the head.

CHINESE CH'ING DYNASTY STELE.
  Between Boylston Hall and Widener Library.
  From Yuan-ming garden.

  Harvard's alumni in China gave this stele to commemorate the college's tercentenary in 1936; at that time Yenching Institute, Harvard's center for Far Eastern research, occupied nearby Boylston Hall.

DEATH AND VICTORY and THE COMING OF THE AMERICANS TO EUROPE.
  Widener Library, main staircase.
  ★ John Singer Sargent (*see* Back Bay [Boston Public Library]: *Judaism and Christianity*).

  One critic has described these murals, which record the arrival of American forces in France in World War I, as "probably the very worst works of public art ever done by a major American painter."

ONION, 1965. Steel, h. 6′.
   ★ Alexander Calder (*see* Cambridge [M.I.T.]: *The Big Sail*).
Gift of Susan Morse Hines.

★ LARGE FOUR-PIECE RECLINING FIGURE, 1972–73. Bronze, h. 5′.
Outside Lamont Library, near Quincy St.
Henry Moore (*see* Cambridge [M.I.T.]: *Three Piece Reclining Figure*).
Gift of Sandra and David Bakalar.

TANNER FOUNTAIN, 1984. Environmental work combining stone, steam,
and water mist, diam. 60′.
In front of Science Center, Cambridge St.
Peter Walker and Joan Brigham (*see* Government Center and Environs:
Winterbreath Fountain).

    Peter Walker, designer of the fountain, is a member of SWA Group,
a Boston landscape architecture firm.

WALL SCULPTURE. Sand casting.
  Science Center, first floor, west wing.
  Constantino Nivola (*see* Downtown: *Mural*).

DISCOBOLUS, ca. 5th century B.C. (copy). Bronze, life-size.
  Outside Hemenway Gym.
  ★ Myron, Greek sculptor, 5th century B.C.

  Although the original of this work was lost centuries ago, many copies exist from antiquity; this is a more recent version. The *Discobolus*
is considered transitional between the stylized, somewhat primitive Archaic period and the Classical sculpture usually associated with ancient Greece; capturing the athlete's body in motion was a radical
departure from the usual static Archaic poses.

UNTITLED, 1973. Plexiglass and stainless steel, h. 18′ × 12′.
  Courtyard, Perkins Astrophysical Library, Harvard College Observatory.
  William Reimann (*see* Cambridge [Porter Sq.]: *Embroidered Bollards*).

  Commissioned by Ball Brothers Research Corp. to commemorate
the 500th anniversary of the birth of Copernicus.

SCULPTURE: RED BLUE, 1964. Painted stainless steel.
  Peabody Terrace garage.
  ★ Ellsworth Kelly (1923–   ).

  Initially a painter, Kelly has produced both two- and three-dimensional work of intriguing simplicity. Critics have placed him variously
with Minimalists, Constructivists, hard-edge, and color-field painters,
yet agree that he brings something of his own, an ability to "visualize
essences." Trained at Pratt Institute, the Boston Museum School, and
the Academie des Beaux Arts, Kelly served in World War II before
continuing his art career. Among his teaching stints was one at the
American School in Paris, and another in Roxbury.

JUSTICE JOSEPH STORY, 1853. Marble, larger than life.
  Law School.
  ★ William Wetmore Story (*see* Dorchester: *Edward Everett*).

  Hard as it is to believe when one sees the forest of memorials at
Mount Auburn Cemetery today, considerable controversy attended the
introduction of sculpture there. This statue was the first, proposed as
a memorial when Judge Story, Mount Auburn's first president, died in
1845. His successor, Dr. Jacob Bigelow (a respected physician sometimes described as a frustrated architect and stubborn admirer of
sculpture) persuaded the board of trustees to commission statues of
John Adams, James Otis, and John Winthrop on the same scale.
Money-conscious proprietors—those who owned plots in Mount
Auburn—objected to "lavish expenditures on unworthy objects," but
Bigelow had his way. The four statues initially stood in the Gothic
chapel, then in the rotunda of its adjoining office. When more office
space was needed, the four were offered to Harvard. The other three
(see below) are in Harvard's Memorial Hall.
  For thirty-six years an associate justice of the Supreme Court,

Justice Story (1779–1845) is credited with important contributions toward Chief Justice Marshall's work in establishing the Court's powers. Story also established a body of opinion in admiralty law, patent law, and equity jurisprudence. He was a professor of law at Harvard. Funded by private subscription.

GOVERNOR JOHN WINTHROP, 1856. Marble, larger than life.
Refectory, Memorial Hall.
★ Richard Saltonstall Greenough (1819–1904).

Younger brother of Horatio Greenough, who is considered America's first professional sculptor, Richard Greenough was born into a well-to-do mercantile family. He chose to forego the usual Harvard education and go into business with his family, but at the age of eighteen changed his mind and followed Horatio to Italy. Shuttling between Boston and Rome and between accounting and sculpture, he became established as a competent portrait sculptor. In 1853 he received the first commission awarded by the City of Boston in twenty-five years, this to sculpt a statue of Benjamin Franklin which now stands in front of Old City Hall. This work and the two below are the other three statues involved in the controversy described above under *Justice Joseph Story*. Commissioned by Mount Auburn Cemetery.
For Winthrop biography, *see* Back Bay: *John Winthrop*.

JAMES OTIS, 1857.
Beside Sanders Theatre stage, Memorial Hall.
★ Thomas Crawford (ca. 1813–1857).

First American sculptor to settle permanently in Rome, Crawford was born in New York and apprenticed as a wood carver and gravestone cutter. After studying neoclassical sculpture (and mortuary anatomy) in Italy, Crawford brought to Boston in 1844 an exhibition which established his artistic reputation. He married New York heiress Louisa Ward, thus becoming the brother-in-law of Julia Ward Howe. The figure atop the U.S. Capitol, *Armed Liberty*, is Crawford's, as well as the pediment of the U.S. Senate, the bronze doors of the House and Senate, and colossal statues of History and Justice at the Senate.
Otis (1725–1783) was until 1769 recognized here and abroad as the leader of the rebellious spirit of the New England colonies. Trained in law at Harvard, he was advocate-general of Massachusetts in 1760 when George III decided to issue new writs of assistance, empowering customs officials to search any house for smuggled goods. Rather than represent the King in these matters, Otis resigned and became the principal voice in opposition. He was elected to the General Court (legislature) and served in 1775 as a volunteer at Bunker Hill. However, after 1769 except for brief periods he was harmlessly insane. He was killed by lightning, a death for which he had often expressed a wish. Commissioned by Mount Auburn Cemetery.

JOHN ADAMS, 1857.
>   Refectory, Memorial Hall.
>   ★ Randolph Rogers (1825–1892).

>   Born in frontier Michigan, Rogers ended his schooling by the age of twelve and went to work as a baker and dry goods clerk. After designing several woodcut advertisements, he traveled to New York in 1847 in hopes of learning engraving. Unable to do so, he again took work as a retail clerk, but his enlightened employers discovered his talent for modeling busts, and underwrote a trip to Italy for him. After a year or two of study Rogers established a studio in Rome and remained there for the rest of his life. Among his major works were the bronze *Columbus Doors* of the U.S. Capitol; he also completed works left unfinished by Thomas Crawford's sudden death. This statue was Rogers' first public commission.

>   John Adams (1735–1826), second President of the United States, was born in Quincy, graduated from Harvard, and admitted to the bar in 1755. Inspired by James Otis' arguments for the rights of the Colonials, Adams espoused the crusade for legal rights of the Colonies. His influence was primarily as a constitutional lawyer; Adams lacked any qualities of popular leadership. He was courageous but impetuous, contentious, vain, and often vehement. In the Continental Congress, he was among the first and most persistent to advocate separation from Great Britain, and was instrumental in the acceptance of the Declaration of Independence. As President he suffered from the presence of an opposition vice-president, Thomas Jefferson, and from intrigue by Alexander Hamilton, a leader of his own party. After a single term he was defeated by Jefferson and retired to the family estate in Quincy. Like Jefferson, he died on the 50th anniversary of the Declaration of Independence, July 4, 1826. Commissioned by Mount Auburn Cemetery.

FIGURE—UPRIGHT MOTIVE NO. 8, 1956. Bronze.
>   Lehman Hall.
>   ★ Henry Moore (*see* Cambridge [M.I.T.]: *Three Piece Reclining Figure, Draped*).

RHINOCEROSES, 1937.
>   Biology laboratories.
>   Katherine Ward Lane Weems (*see* Fenway: *Rhinoceros*).

>   The carved brick frieze (1932) and bronze doors (1933) were also designed by Weems.

FISH, 1972. Aluminum.
>   Gund Hall.
>   Alberto Collie.

ASPECT OF THE ORACLE: PORTENTOUS. Bronze, h. 6′.
>   Radcliffe Yard, near Radcliffe Institute.
>   Mariana Pineda (*see* East Boston/Logan Airport: *Twirling*).

★ NIGHT WALL I, 1972. Steel, h. approx. 13'.
   In front of Langdell Hall, Law School.
   Louise Nevelson (*see* Cambridge [M.I.T.]: *Transparent Horizon*).

MURAL.
   Dining room, Harkness Commons.
   ★ Hans Arp (1887–1966).

   Dadaist, then surrealist painter, Arp is best remembered for relief
sculpture of whimsical simplicity.

PAINTING. h. approx. 5' × 25'.
   Mallory Smith room, Harkness Commons.
   ★ Joan Miro (1893–1984).

   The Spaniard Miro claimed to paint in an "automatic writing" mode,
never planning, but simply letting his hand and brush go where they
might. The resultant surrealist works are characterized by flat intersecting forms, often asterisks, moons, and protean animal and human
shapes.

TREE OF LIFE, ca. 1950. Steel.
   Harkness Commons.
   Richard Leopold.

MOUNT VERNON WALL PIECE, 1971. Cor-ten steel.
   Currier House courtyard.
   ★ Beverly Pepper (*see* Government Center and Environs: *Sudden
Presence*).

EULOGY. Sculpture.
   Currier House courtyard.
   ★ William Zorach (1887–1966).

   An American, Zorach pioneered in carving directly in stone, rather
than making clay models to be translated by stonecutters.

ORPHEUS AND EURYDICE XIV½. Bronze.
   Currier House courtyard.
   Marie Zoe Mercier (b. 1912).

   The artist is a 1933 graduate of Radcliffe.

DINING HALL GRAFITTO, 1959. Sand-cast concrete.
   Dining hall, Quincy House.
STONE MURAL. Bas-relief carving.
   Lobby, Quincy House.
   Constantino Nivola (*see* Downtown: *Mural*).

JAMES RUSSELL LOWELL, 1904. Bust.
   Lowell House courtyard.
   ★ Daniel Chester French (*see* Concord: *Minuteman*).

I GIVE YOU A POND: MEDITATION 1 & 2. Pastel, 42″ × 84″.
Kresge Hall, Harvard Business School (Allston).
Judith Berman (1946–   ).

   Somerville artist Judith Berman draws on her fascination with natural history and on an intimate knowledge of biology. As a graduate student at the University of New Mexico she explored the desert and mountains around Albuquerque; she toured the Galapagos Islands to study the fauna there, canoed on the Amazon River, and became a certified scuba diver so she could study the undersea world of the Caribbean.

WALL SCULPTURE, 1986. Stainless steel, gold-plated brass, four elements, h. 9′ × 18′, 10′ × 12′, 11′ × 12′, 9′ × 20′.
Burden Hall, Harvard Business School.
Michio Ihara (*see* Lowell: *Pawtucket Prism*).

MUSEUM: Busch Reisinger Museum, Kirkland St. and Divinity Ave.
   Founded in 1902 for the study of Germanic culture and bolstered by the addition of Netherlandish work, this collection provides a thorough survey of north-central European art. In addition to medieval treasures, it is strong in materials related to the Bauhaus movement.

MUSEUM: Arthur M. Sackler Museum, 45 Broadway.

MUSEUM: Fogg Art Museum, Quincy St. at Broadway. The epitome of the academic museum, the Fogg is said to have the most extensive collection of any university museum in the world, barring England. Particular strengths are drawings and prints, Far Eastern art, and European work around 1800. The Sackler, opened in 1985, has taken over the public exhibition functions of the Fogg.

JOHN BRIDGE, 1882. Bronze.
Cambridge Common, Mass. Ave. and Waterhouse St.
Thomas Gould (1818–1881) and M. S. Gould.

   A successful dry-goods merchant who practiced drawing and modeling as a hobby, Gould turned to portrait sculpture for a living when his business went sour during the Civil War. He went to Florence in 1868 and was modeling this work at the time of his death; his son finished it.
   Bridge (1578–1665) came to Cambridge with the Rev. Thomas Hooker and remained when Hooker and followers went off to settle Hartford, Conn. Deacon Bridge is memorialized as founder of Cambridge's grammar school in 1635. Given to the City of Cambridge by Samuel Bridge, sixth-generation descendent of John Bridge.

CIVIL WAR MEMORIAL, 1869–70. Granite and bronze.
Cambridge Common.

   A Cambridge police officer wounded in the Civil War, Samuel E. Chamberlain was the model for the heroic-size granite soldier atop the monument. The eleven-foot bronze figure of Lincoln within is a casting of Augustus Saint-Gaudens' Lincoln done for Chicago in 1887; it was added here later. Erected by City of Cambridge.

THE HIKER. Bronze, larger than life.
Garden and Concord Sts.
Theo Alice Ruggles Kitson (*see* Malden: *The Hiker*).
Erected by the City of Cambridge.

BUTTERCUP, 1984. Painted steel wall relief, h. 4½' × 9' × 2'.
At University Pl., 124 Mt. Auburn St.
Peter Lipsitt (*see* Hyde Park: *Celebration of the Figure Eight*).

The developer of this office complex asked a curator of the Museum of Fine Arts, Kenworth Moffett, to select for this space a collection of works by emerging artists, worldwide. Almost entirely abstract, the group of forty-one pieces is described by a brochure available at the security desk. Hines plans to display the collection here for five years, then replace it with newer work and offer this selection to the M.F.A. Commissioned by Hines Industrial.

At Charles Hotel, Bennet and Eliot Sts:

LOBBY GALLERY: rotating exhibitions from the collection of the Polaroid Corp. in Cambridge.

The permanent collection here focuses on views of Cambridge, Harvard Square, and the Charles River by contemporary realists. Of more than fifty works, a partial listing follows:

LONGFELLOW HOUSE, 1985. Oil on canvas, h. 6½' × 4'.
Lobby.
George Nick (1927–   ).

A resident of Concord, Nick was graduated from Yale and has long been a teacher of painting at Massachusetts College of Art. His paintings, usually not this meticulously realistic, are included in the collections of the Boston Museum of Fine Arts, the Metropolitan Museum of Art in New York, and many corporate collections.

Now maintained by the National Park Service, the historic Longfellow mansion, a few blocks from here at 105 Brattle St., was for forty-five years the home of Henry Wadsworth Longfellow (1807–1882), Harvard professor and poet. Dating from 1759, the house was Washington's headquarters in 1775 when the fledgling Continental Army was encamped on Cambridge Common.

MASS. AVE., HARVARD SQUARE, 1985, h. 5' × 20'.
Lobby.
Joel Babb.

A graduate of Princeton and the Boston Museum School, Babb is at present an instructor at Harvard University Extension School.

MURAL, 1987, h. 4′ × 23′.
  Bennett Street Cafe
  Carol Acquiland.

MARTINI GLASS, 1985. Oil, h. 62″ × 42″.
  Second floor, outside Rarities Restaurant.
  Aaron Fink (*see* Cambridge [Royal Sonesta Hotel]: *Cup*).

SYCAMORES—CAMBRIDGE VIEW and SYCAMORES—CHARLES RIVER
  VIEW, 1985. Charcoal triptychs, h. 72″ × 45″.
  Third floor lobby.
  Michael Mazur (*see* Cambridge [Hyatt Regency Hotel]: *Untitled*).

BIRCHES, 1982–3. Woodcut, h. 34½″ × 34″.
  Third floor corridor.
  Neil Welliver (*see* Cambridge [Royal Sonesta Hotel]: *Untitled*).

HARVARD STADIUM SERIES, 1986. Three units, each h. 26″ × 25″.
  Third floor corridor.
  Max Mason.

TWO VIEWS OF ANDERSON BRIDGE, 1985. Oil, h. 48″ × 62″; 40″ × 68″.
  Outside Regatta Jazz bar.
LONGFELLOW BRIDGE, 1985. Oil, h. 48″ × 62″.
  In Regatta Jazz bar.
  Emily Eveleth.

  A recent graduate of Smith College, Eveleth now lives in the Boston
  area.

PORTER SQUARE

GIFT OF THE WIND, 1985. Red
  kinetic sculpture, painted steel,
  h. approx. 20′.
  Susumu Shingu (*see*
  Waterfront [New England
  Aquarium]: *Echo of the
  Waves*).
  Funded by MBTA.

ONDAS, 1984. Carved granite wave (vertical ribbon), h. 24'.
On headhouse.
Carlos Dorrien (*see* Waltham [Bentley College]: *Portal*).
Funded by MBTA.

EMBROIDERED BOLLARDS, 1984. Six granite barriers, h. 27″ × 12″ × 12″.
Surrounding headhouse.
William Reimann (1935–   ).

A senior preceptor and head tutor in visual and environmental studies at Harvard, Cambridge sculptor William Reimann graduated from Yale, spent a fellowship year in England studying drawing and plastics technology, and took an M.F.A. from Yale in 1961. He has taught at Yale, Old Dominion University, and the University of Pennsylvania.

Interested in traditional textile patterns, Reimann has researched weaving and embroidery designs unique to various ethnic traditions. The patterns chosen here are based on cultures that have occupied the Porter Square area: Penobscot Indian, French-Canadian, Irish, Polish, Slav, Russian, Spanish, German, Italian, Scandinavian, Portuguese, African, Asian. These delicate motifs are created with a modern tombstone-cutting technique; a cutout rubber sheet is fixed to the stone, and sandblasting removes the exposed stone.

PORTER SQUARE MEGALITHS, 1980–84. Granite and bronze, 24' × 24'.
MBTA Plaza at Porter Station.
David Phillips (1944–   ).

Phillips casts his own bronzes at his studio-foundry in Somerville. Born in Michigan, he took a B.F.A. in painting and an M.A. in sculpture at Cranbrook before coming to Boston in 1970. This work is typical of his style through the 1970s, granite boulders sliced with a stonecutter's saw, duplicated in bronze, and re-assembled mix-and-match style, a commentary on the beauty and mass of unworked stone. Funded by MBTA.

INTERFACE, 1986. Limestone, h. 6', wt. 11 tons.
11 Linnaean St., at Nityanananda Institute.
David Rogers.

Rogers is an Indiana sculptor who has other public work at the Chicago Zoo and at the Dia Foundation at New Harmony, Ind. This sculpture is based on a mathematical concept, the Mobius strip, a loop with a twist in it that produces a geometric plane infinite in two directions. Commissioned by The Nityanananda Institute.

NORTH CAMBRIDGE

PAINTED PAINTER, 1981. Acrylic on masonry, 12' × 50'.
57 Walden St.
Elizabeth Carter (*see* Cambridge [Central Sq.]: *Floating Down Mass. Avenue*).

Photorealist Carter does a little fool-the-eye with her mural of the neighborhood, including the building on which the work is painted and life-sized figures painting the mural. Funded by CDBG.

BRICKWORKER and BALLPLAYER, 1983. Handmade bricks, two figures, 7' × 12' × 6'.
Rindge Field, Pemberton St.
David Judelson (*see* Cambridge: *Flag Fragments*).

The committee overseeing this project decided that the work should be constructed of brick to commemorate the now-defunct brickworking industry of North Cambridge. Judelson made his own bricks and inscribed them with family names of Cambridge brickmakers and brick companies that once operated here. Funded by Vingo Trust and CAC.

SAGINAW AVENUE MURAL, 1977 and 1984. Acrylic on masonry.
Davenport St. at Saginaw Ave.
Jeff Oberdorfer and Elizabeth Carter (*see* Cambridge [Central Sq.]: *Floating Down Mass. Avenue*).

Painted by a Cambridge architect and his neighbors, this work is intended to integrate the blank wall of a shopping center into the neighborhood. Restored, with addition of figures, by Carter in 1984. Funded by CETA and CDBG.

ENVIRONMENTAL SITE WORK, 1985. Granite.
East of Alewife Station garage, at Alewife Brook Pkwy. and Rindge Ave.
Richard Fleishner (*see* Cambridge [M.I.T.]: *Untitled Collaboration*).

This work is an example of Fleischner's penchant for constructing sculpture with basic-common-denominator blocks, all of the same dimension.

ARCH, STRAWBERRY HILL PLAYGROUND, 1983–4. Ceramic tile, concrete, steel, 15' × 15'.
At Haggerty School, 110 Cushing St.
Marsha Wright and Yvonne Troxell.

For this cooperative community project, tiles were designed by children and other residents of the neighborhood and made in ceramics workshops with the artists. The tiles have not weathered well, and reworking is planned by Cambridge Arts Council. Funded by CDBG and City Arts.

CAMBRIDGE AND ITS WATERSHED, 1983. Acrylic on masonite, 8' × 16'.
At Cambridge Water Dept., 250 Fresh Pond Pkwy.
Michele Turre (1953–   ).

Aerial landscapes have been a motif for Michele Turre, a California native who studied at Sonoma State University and at the University of Iowa. She came East to paint at Cummington Community of the Arts, stayed on as assistant director, and now lives in the small

Hampshire Hills town of Goshen. This painting is an aerial view high-lighting the city of Cambridge and its reservoirs in the western sub-urbs. Turre says her work is not usually this literal; this one contains every street and almost every house within a thirty-mile radius. Funded by 1% for Art.

MOUNT AUBURN CEMETERY

A map showing the more interesting graves and memorials may be obtained at the cemetery offices just inside the entrance. Mount Au-burn's records list more than forty carvers and sculptors; hundreds of monuments are not attributed. Only a small sampling can be listed here.

SPHINX, 1872. Granite, h. 10′.
   South of Chapel.
   Martin Milmore (*see* Framingham: *Civil War Memorial*).

   Called the strangest of all Civil War memorials, this work was likely designed to please the cemetery's founder, Dr. Jacob Bigelow, who declared the "timeless" Egyptian style appropriate to cemeteries. Here the sphinx is Americanized, its ureaeus snake replaced by an eagle. Commissioned by Dr. Jacob Bigelow.

NATHANIEL BOWDITCH, 1846. Bronze, life-size.
   Central and Cypress Aves.
   ★ Robert Ball Hughes (1806–1868).

   English-born, the precocious Hughes entered the school of the Royal Academy in London at the age of twelve; one of his works was shown at the Academy's exhibition of 1822. He emigrated to New York in 1829 and came to Boston in 1840.
   Bowditch (1773–1838), mathematician and navigator, was born at Salem. A cooper and apprentice ship-chandler as a boy, he devel-oped a taste for mathematics and learned Latin in order to study New-ton. He made four long sea voyages in his twenties as a clerk and supercargo, proving such an excellent navigator that he commanded his own ship at the age of twenty-nine. He published *New American Practical Navigator*, a work of value to American sailing masters, and translated Laplace's treatise on celestial mechanics. Hughes depicts him with some of the instruments of navigation.

KNOLL GARDEN SCULPTURE, 1981. Cast iron, h. 21′.
   Willow Pond knoll.
   Richard Duca (1955–   ).

   Richard Duca describes himself as largely self-taught, learning his casting techniques as apprentice to his father, Alfred Duca (*see* Back Bay: *Boston Tapestry*). With few exceptions, (this is one) he casts and finishes his work personally. To make this piece, Duca produced a full-scale version in styrofoam, which was cast by a Pennsylvania industrial foundry using the foam vaporization technique pioneered by

Duca senior. The work is a single solid cast in ductile iron; it weighs 23,000 pounds. A departure from the cemetery's traditional stone carvings, Duca's sculpture is at once organic, in its references to plant forms, and mathematical in its logarithmic curve, and, the artist says, "spiritual, with its unfurling, uplifting shape." Duca lives and works on Cape Ann. Commissioned through invitational competition by Mount Auburn Cemetery.

HYGEIA.
Poplar Ave. at Lily Path.
★ Edmonia Mary Lewis (ca. 1843–ca. 1909).

The date and place of Lewis' birth and death are unknown. Daughter of a black father and a Chippewa mother, she was raised by her mother's family and admitted in 1859 to Oberlin College, the first co-educational college to accept women and blacks. In 1862 she was accused of poisoning two fellow students and sent to trial. She was acquitted, but left Ohio for Boston, where abolitionist William Lloyd Garrison arranged for her to study sculpture with Edward Brackett. With proceeds from her first sale she went to Rome, was befriended by Harriet Hosmer, and became a member of the group of women sculptors working there. Departing from classical themes, Lewis often chose Amerindian and African subjects. Some of her work is owned by the National Museum of American Art in Washington.

Hygeia, goddess of health, is in Greek mythology daughter of Aesculapius, god of medicine.

RODIN, WALKING MAN (see page 180)

Other Cities
and Towns

ZUMBUSCH, COUNT RUMFORD (see page 184)

ANDOVER

ARMILLARY SPHERE. Bronze.
   At Phillips Academy, in front of library, on Rte. 28.
   ★ Paul Manship (1885–1966).

   The *Prometheus Fountain* at Rockefeller Center in New York is
   likely Manship's best-known work. In 1909 he won a Prix de Rome;
   his studies in that city left him a master of archaic classicism. Returning to New York, he garnered many commissions, awards, and honors, culminating in twenty-two years as chairman of the Smithsonian
   Art Commission. Commissioned by the John Hancock Mutual Life Insurance Co.

GALLERY: Addison Gallery at Phillips Academy, Rte. 28. Adjudged one of
   the leading museums of American art in this region, the Addison
   contains outstanding examples of American painting and (to some
   extent) of sculpture from the eighteenth century to the present.

ARLINGTON

★ INDIAN HUNTER, 1911. Bronze, larger than life.
   Park east of City Hall, Mass. Ave.
   Cyrus E. Dallin (1861–1944).

   Born in Utah, Dallin as a youngster made friends with Ute Indians
   living nearby; from this background came his portrayals of the dignity

125

of native Americans. At age nineteen he came to Boston to study with Truman Howe Bartlett and opened a studio here. In Paris for two years of study, he saw Buffalo Bill's Wild West Show and was inspired to create his first equestrian Indian, *Signal of Peace*. After returning to Boston, then Utah, he taught briefly in Philadelphia before settling in Arlington for forty years of teaching, 1900–1940, at Massachusetts State Normal Art School (now Massachusetts College of Art). Other well-known works in Greater Boston include *Paul Revere* in the North End and *Appeal to the Great Spirit* in front of the Boston Museum of Fine Arts.

UNCLE SAM, 1976. Bronze, larger than life.
    Mass. Ave. and Mystic St.
    Theodore C. Barbarossa (1906–   ).

    Born in Vermont, Ted Barbarossa earned a B.F.A. from the School of Art and Architecture at Yale. After assisting a New York sculptor for eight years, he came to Boston to launch his own studio. His career was interrupted by a five-year stint in the army in World War II. His carvings in stone decorate the National Cathedral in Washington, D.C., St. Thomas' Cathedral in New York, and the Baltimore Cathedral. He now lives in New Hampshire.
    Samuel Wilson (1766–1854), a native son of Arlington, is thought to be the prototype for the national symbol, Uncle Sam. Gift of Frederick A. Hauck of Cincinnati, Ohio.

BRAINTREE

ATRIUM SCULPTURE. h. 35'.
    Grossman Co., 200 Union St.
    William Wainwright (*see* East Boston/Logan Airport: *Windwheels*).

BROCKTON

POLITICAL TRILOGY, 1978. Bronze, h. 12".
    Outside City Hall.
    Mark Cooper (1950–   ).

    Cooper graduated from Indiana University and the Boston Museum School; he teaches at Boston College and the Boston Museum School. His first public commission, this bronze predates his later work in cement (*see* Burlington: *Catalyst I and II*). Heads Cooper modeled during this early period were distinctively flattened profiles, set at right angles to shoulders or bodies. Vandals have wrenched off and stolen two parts of this three-part work.

ASSAULT ON BATTERY WAGNER and other Civil War scenes, 1895. Oil on canvas.
    City Hall west lobby.
    F. Mortimer Lamb (1861–1936).

Son of a carriage-painter, Lamb was born in Middleborough and lived much of his life in Stoughton. He attended Massachusetts Normal Art School, the Boston Museum School, and Academie Julian in Paris. Lamb both taught and exhibited widely; he liked to take pupils, many of whom were Brockton shoe factory workers, into the fields to sketch. He taught art in Brockton schools and at New England Conservatory of Music, was principal for twenty years of the Evening Drawing School in Taunton and later director of Medfield School of Art. The spandrels *War* and *Peace* in City Hall are also his work.

This work depicts the moment that Col. Robert Gould Shaw was killed leading his black troops against Fort Wagner, S.C. (*see* Boston Common: *Robert Gould Shaw and the 54th Massachusetts Regiment*).

At Brockton Art Museum (Oak St. on Upper Porter's Pond):

Although some of Brockton Museum's outdoor art is visible without entering the museum, most of it is located in courtyards and on a terrace bordering Upper Porter's Pond.

GLACE BAY, 1975. Painted steel, h. 6½' × 20'.
Parking lot.
George Greenamyer (*see* Marshfield: *Webster, the Farmer of Marshfield*).

Brockton Art Museum can be identified by this whimsical steam-engine-like work, typical of Greenamyer's style.

BROOKLINE

THE SOLDIERS MONUMENT, 1915. Equestrian bronze, heroic size.
At Brookline Public Library, Washington and School Sts.
★ Edward Clark Potter (1857–1923).

Potter collaborated frequently with Daniel Chester French on equestrian monuments, Potter sculpting the horse and French the rider. Whereas French seldom portrayed animals, Potter could and did do people; this mounted bugler is entirely his. Potter's first professional training came in French's studio, 1883–85, followed by work in marble quarries in Vermont and study in Paris. Among many other works, Potter created the mounts for French's *General Hooker* at the State House and for *General Devens* in Worcester; he is responsible for the famous lions in front of the New York Public Library and for a portrait statue of Robert Fulton in the Library of Congress. This Civil War memorial was commissioned by the City of Brookline.

TERRA COGNITA, 1974. Brass and gold leaf on steel, diam.
44″ on 24″ base.
At Brookline Town Hall.
C. Fayette Taylor (*see* Government Center and Environs: *Upward Bound*).

SIERRA SLICE, 1975. Cast cement play sculpture, h. 3½' × 14'.
  Amory Park, Amory St. off Beacon.
  Gregg LeFevre (*see* Boston University: *Untitled*).

DRAGON, 1983–85. Wood, h. 9'.
  21 Gorham Ave.
  Douglas Smith (1952–   ).

  A free-lance illustrator trained at Rhode Island School of Design,
  Smith was inspired by the carved trees of Fred Faller in Cambridge,
  and spent some years looking for a stump to convert into sculpture.
  When this elm succumbed to disease, Smith persuaded its owners
  and the neighborhood to let him sculpt it. Sitting at curbside and
  sketching many possibilities, Smith received advice from passersby;
  neighborhood children almost unanimously voted for the dragon. The
  sculptor includes one of them nestled, as if for storytime, in the benevolent beast's forked tail. This new organic folk art form appeals to
  people, Smith says, but "by nature it's doomed." Faller's *Hand* and
  Acrobats in Cambridge have already fallen prey to the forces of bio-
  logical decay. Smith has received a second grant to attempt to pre-
  serve the work. Funded in part by the Brookline Council for the Arts &
  Humanities.

(DETAIL)

THREE WOMEN, 1975. Bronze, h. 8'.
  In Hearthstone Plaza.
  Lu Stubbs (1925–   ).

  A native of New York City, Lu Stubbs graduated from the Boston
  Museum School and studied at L'Accademia di Belle Arti in Perugia,
  Italy. She has taught at the Boston Museum School, Boston Univer-
  sity, and Milton Academy. She maintains a studio in Sharon.

WAVES OF TIME, 1971. Stainless steel, h. 30' × 50'.
  Lobby, The Park School, 171 Goddard Ave.
  Alfred M. Duca. (*see* Back Bay: *Boston Tapestry*).

PULPIT, 1985. Carved cherry, h. 5'.
  In St. Paul's Church, 15 St. Paul St.
  Murray Dewart (1947–   ).

  A self-taught sculptor, Dewart was educated at Harvard College.
The work comprises five panels depicting scenes from the life of St.
Paul.

SCREEN, 1977. Triptych in brass, steel, 72″ × 84″.
  Lobby, Brookline Hospital, 168 Chestnut St.
  C. Fayette Taylor (*see* Government Center and Environs: *Upward Bound*).

★ PRIMAVERA, 1987. Granite, h. 15'.
  Pine Manor College, in front of Annenberg Library and Communications
  Center.
  Dimitri Hadzi (1921–   ).

  Studio professor at Harvard, Hadzi was born in New York City of
Greek immigrant parents. He was interested in art from childhood, but
he at first thought it an avocation and became a chemist. After serving
in the South Pacific in the Air Force during World War II, Hadzi began
to study art part-time, then full-time. He graduated from Cooper Union
with honors and won a Fulbright Fellowship to Greece, where his aesthetic vision began to coalesce with his cultural heritage. Hadzi remained in Europe for fifteen years, garnering a Guggenheim
Fellowship and serving as an artist-in-residence at the American
Academy in Rome, where he designed bronze doors for St. Paul's
Church. His work is held by more than twenty-five museums, including
the Museum of Modern Art in New York, the Whitney, the Hirschhorn,
and the Guggenheim. *Primavera* is one of five Hadzi works in the
Greater Boston area.
  Stylistically, this work is related to Hadzi's *Omphalos* in Harvard
Square. Dedicated in conjunction with Pine Manor's 75th anniversary,
it was funded by Carolyn Mann Caswell and Ruth Barstow Dixon,
alumnae of the college.

SARAH HOOD PHOTO COURTESY PINE MANOR COLLEGE

BURLINGTON

CATALYST I AND II, 1987. Two pieces: outside, granite and aluminum h. $18' \times 20' \times 20'$; hanging in lobby, cast and fabricated aluminum, h. $75' \times 20' \times 20'$.
American Landmark Corp., Bedford Rd.
Mark Cooper (*see* Brockton: *Political Trilogy*).
Commissioned by Bruce Silverman.

LAHEY CLINIC COLLECTION, begun 1978. More than 1000 works on paper.
Hung in all waiting rooms, some hospital rooms.
High school art students.

The idea of acquiring student work to fill the blank walls of this medical center originated with Terry Giggey (d. 1983), a resident of Burlington, who suggested it to a friend on the Lahey staff. Work only by Burlington High School art students was chosen the first year; the scope has now expanded to thirty schools in communities near Route 128. The artists donate their work and the clinic pays for framing; the collection is permanent. About one hundred new works, on the average, are now selected each year.

CONTROL, installed 1987. Bronze, larger than life.
In front of Building 8, New England Office Park, Middlesex Turnpike and Rte. 128.
Victor Salmones, figure; Ed Monti (*see* Quincy: *Constitution Common Sculpture*), granite base.

Salmones, a Mexican sculptor, often does figures in athletic poses that imply physical control. The work is located outside the physical fitness center of the complex.

WINDHOVER, 1972. Kinetic sculpture, aluminum, h. $12' \times 18'$.
New England Office Park.
Robert Amory (1942–   ).

A native of Watertown, N.Y., now living in Watertown, Mass., Robert Amory is a graduate of Harvard. He has turned from kinetic sculpture (*see* Downtown: *Helion*) to painting and drawing.

CHELMSFORD

ON EARTH AS IT IS IN HEAVEN, 1987. Appliquéd tapestry, h. 15′ × 5′.
  Entry lobby, North Building at Drum Hill, Rtes. 3 and 4.
  Linda DeHart (*see* Lexington: *Aerial Sculptures*).
  Commissioned by Drum Hill Realty Trust.

CHELSEA

CHELSEA CONVERSATION, 1977–78. Bronze, life-size.
  Chelsea Sq., Broadway and Park St.
  Penelope Jencks (1936–   ).

Newton resident Penelope Jencks was born in Baltimore, attended
Swarthmore College, and studied painting with Hans Hoffmann at
Provincetown before taking a fine arts degree at Boston University in
1958. She also studied at the Kunstacademie in Stuttgart, Germany,
and has taught at Brandeis, Boston College, and the Art Institute of
Boston. She has been a MacDowell Fellow and a Massachusetts Artists Foundation recipient. Her realistic and informal sculpted groups
are located in London, Toledo, Ohio, and Pittsburgh, as well as in the
Boston area.

Described one hunded years ago as the most desirable location in
the metropolitan area, Chelsea more recently was called the "junk
capital" of New England because of its paper, cloth, and rubber recy-
cling centers. A disastrous fire in 1973 destroyed all that and opened
up the possibility of new uses for 300 acres of commercial district.
The landscaping and art in this square is one result. Two of this group
are based on real citizens of Chelsea, a high school track star and a
retired science teacher (who originally was adjusting his eyeglasses
before vandals made off with them). Jencks' daughter posed for the
young girl. Funded by City of Chelsea.

PENELOPE JENCKS PHOTO

★ BELLINGHAM SQUARE, 1978–79. Bronze, life-size.
Bellingham Sq., Broadway and Washington St.
Mags Harries (1945–   ).

Welsh-born Mags Harries possesses one of public art's most fertile imaginations. Harries took a diploma at Leicester College of Art and Design, England, in 1967, and followed it with a scholarship for graduate study in the U.S. which led to a master's degree from the University of Southern Illinois. After completing this commission she was a Bunting Fellow in 1977–78; she has won a design excellence award from the U.S. Department of Transportation (*see* MBTA [Porter Station]: *The Glove Cycle*) and a Grand Bostonian Award. She is a member of the faculty of the Boston Museum School.

Life-size bronze objects—a pocketbook, a pair of gloves—sit on benches as if forgotten. Would-be scavengers find they are firmly bolted down. Funded by City of Chelsea.

THE HIKER, 1934. Bronze, larger than life.
Broadway, at City Hall.
Theo Alice Ruggles Kitson (*see* Malden: *The Hiker*).
Chelsea's version of *The Hiker* has a time capsule sealed in the base.

SOLDIERS AND SAILORS MONUMENT, 1868. Granite, h. approx. 40′.
Basset Sq., Broadway, across from City Hall.
First erected in Union Park, this monument was moved in 1911 to its present location.

CRAB BRICKS, 1977–78. Bronze, sixty-five units each 8″ square.
Bellingham Sq., Broadway and Bellingham St.
David Phillips (*see* Cambridge [Porter Sq.]: *Porter Square Megaliths*).

Bronze insets into sidewalk and crosswalk remind passersby that this spot was once a fresh seafood market. Funded by City of Chelsea.

CHELSEA WALK, 1977–79. Silkscreened enameled panels.
   Off Broadway near Bellingham Sq.
   Collaboration: Ronald Lee Fleming, Peter Johnson, Thomas Kirvan, Susan Roberts.

   Also called the Memory Wall, this installation depicts Chelsea-connected celebrities—actress Barbara Stanwyck, Chick Corea, and songwriter George M. Cohan—as well as local personalities, such as street photographer Harry Siegel. The wall has suffered from graffiti; there is talk of taking it down, cleaning it, and reinstalling it inside City Hall.

SCHOOL OF ALEWIFE, 1984. Aluminum, h. 15′.
   Chelsea Naval Hospital Park, on the Mystic River under Tobin Bridge.
   William Wainwright (*see* East Boston/Logan Airport: *Windwheels*).
   Commissioned by MDC.

CONCORD

THE MINUTEMAN OF CONCORD, 1874. Bronze, larger than life.
   At Old North Bridge (Minuteman National Park).
   ★   Daniel Chester French (1850–1931).

   With the approach of the United States Centennial in 1876, contention heightened as to where the American Revolution really began. At Lexington, where rebel militia first confronted Redcoats (and were massacred)? Or at Concord, where the Colonials massed, turned back the King's troops, and inflicted the first casualties? Concord decided to press its claim by erecting a statue dedicated to its 1775 militiamen.
   Son of a prominent Concord judge, the twenty-three-year-old French had never made a statue when he applied for the commission. He had not even thought of sculpture as a career until, at seventeen, he had astounded his family by whittling a frog from a turnip. He studied drawing briefly with fellow Concordian May Alcott, anatomy with Dr. Rimmer in Boston, and sculpture for a month in the studio of J. Q. A. Ward in New York. He had cast a few small works by trial and error.
   Nevertheless, the Concord committee accepted his model, agreeing to pay the costs of the work if the young sculptor would donate his services. French accepted those terms. Concord citizens searched barns and attics for authentic costume, plow, musket, and powder horn; the French family's farm hand, Patrick, posed for the minuteman's arms. One Concord citizen with influence in Washington arranged for the government to contribute bronze cannon for casting material and to pay for the casting process. After the dedication of the statue the satisfied town reconsidered and voted French a $1,000 fee. (On the base are the first lines of the commemorative poem written by Emerson for the dedication ceremony.) Funded by bequest of Ebenezer Hubbard, public subscription, the town of Concord, and the United States government.

MOURNING VICTORY, 1909. Granite, life-size.
Sleepy Hollow Cemetery.
★ Daniel Chester French (*see Minuteman* above).

A Concord schoolmate of French's, James Melvin, had watched his three older brothers enlist as privates in the Union Army. One died in battle, one in hospital, one in prison. James, sixteen in the last year of the war, also enlisted, but survived and vowed to become wealthy enough to commission a memorial to his brothers. The grieving figure is French's statement on the price of war, even victorious war.

A. BRONSON ALCOTT, 1882. Bust, life-size.
At Concord Library.
★ Daniel Chester French (*see Minuteman* above).

Known today, if at all, as the father of Louisa May Alcott, or as a dreamer and ne'er-do-well Utopian who couldn't provide for his own family, Bronson Alcott (1799–1888) was in his day one of the most famous men in America. A self-educated country boy, he became an iconoclastic educator, pioneering the idea that gentleness and thoughtful conversation were more conducive to learning than the birch rod. The Alcotts lived at Orchard House (now a Concord museum) on Lexington Rd. Here Bronson founded his School of Philosophy, an early Chatauqua; the building still stands and is used for lectures in summer.

RALPH WALDO EMERSON, 1879. Bust.
At Concord Library.
★ Daniel Chester French (*see Minuteman* above).

Emerson (1803–1882), poet, essayist, Unitarian minister, and Transcendentalist philosopher, was the most renowned of the Concord intellectuals who were the nucleus of American thinking in the nineteenth century.

In a sense French was a protégé of Emerson, who served on the committee that commissioned the *Minuteman* and was probably instrumental in seeing that the young sculptor was paid at last. After a year of study in Italy, the diffident artist approached Concord's greatest man, then in his seventy-seventh year, to sit for a portrait bust. Always gracious, he did, and is said to have joked, "You know, Dan, the more it resembles me, the worse it looks." The philosopher and his family pronounced it the best likeness ever done of him. A copy of the bust is at Harvard's Memorial Hall.

RALPH WALDO EMERSON, 1914. Seated statue, marble, life-size. Concord Library.
 ★ Daniel Chester French (*see Minuteman* above).

French's daughter Margaret relates that her father knew and loved Emerson so well he was almost afraid to embark on this commission so long after Emerson's death. The philosopher's family sent him Emerson's favorite heavy dressing gown (which the family called his "Gaberlunzey"), a garment he wore in his study on cold mornings. Drawing on his own memories, French portrayed Emerson leaning forward in a characteristic questioning attitude.

At Middlesex School (Lowell Rd):

ABRAXAS, 1972. Cor-ten steel, h. 12'.
VASQUEZ, 1975. Cor-ten steel, h. 16'.
ASPECT #1, 1969. Mild steel painted, h. 12'.
ASPECT #3, 1970. Cor-ten steel, h. 7' (shown below).
 David Lang (1941–   ).

Manhattan native David Lang studied at Paier School of Art in New Haven, earned a B.S. in biology at Fairfield University, then undertook a three-year graduate program at Massachusetts General Hospital in medical illustration. He has taught art at Middlesex since 1972 and been chairman of the art department since 1975. Known also as a watercolorist, Lang lives in Wayland.

DAVID LANG PHOTO

DUXBURY

FIVE SHAKER HOUSES, 1976. Welded steel, painted h. 7½′ × 20′ × 2′ .
    In front of Duxbury Art Complex Museum, 189 Alden St.
    George Greenamyer (*see* Marshfield: *Webster, the Farmer of Marshfield*).

TRILITH, 1982. Granite and bronze h. 3′.
    Outside Duxbury Art Complex Museum.
    David Phillips (*see* Cambridge [Porter Sq.]: *Porter Square Megaliths*).

MILES STANDISH, 1926. Granite, h. 14′, atop 116′ tower.
    Miles Standish State Park, Crescent St., South Duxbury.
    John Horrigan (*see* Holbrook: *Soldiers Monument*).

    On a promontory of Goose Point, the obelisk formed by the Standish tower and statue provides a landmark up and down the coast. Its cornerstone was laid in 1872, but the monument not completed until 1898. Originally bronze, the figure proved attractive to lightning; old clippings recount that the head and arms were knocked off in a thunderstorm in 1903, the head again in 1923. At that point Horrigan proposed to redo Standish in Quincy granite, producing the version that stands atop the tower now. Recently closed for renovation, the tower when open affords magnificent views of Duxbury, Kingston Bay, and Plymouth Harbor.

EAST BRIDGEWATER

MURAL, 1973. Ceramic, h. 6½′ × 68′ long.
    Grounds of East Bridgewater Unitarian Church, Central and Church Sts.
    John C. Moakley (1931–).

    A graduate of the Boston Museum School and former teacher there, ceramicist John Moakley studied for two years in Florence on a Museum of Fine Arts traveling fellowship. Born in Lexington, he now lives

(DETAIL)

and works in Dennis. For this wall Moakley researched town, church, and area history to create the 600 panels meant to be "a series of chapters" in that history. Commissioned by the Rev. John Paul Rich, pastor of the church.

PARKER MEMORIAL FOUNTAIN, 1940. Stone, h. 5½'.
In front of Washburn Library, Bedford St.
Hildegarde Snow.

Snow was a Framingham artist. Bequest of Mary Folson Parker, who died ca. 1910.

EVERETT

THE HIKER, 1927. Bronze, heroic size.
At Parlin Library, Broadway and School Sts.
Theo Alice Ruggles Kitson (*see* Malden: *The Hiker*).

FOXBOROUGH

CIVIL WAR MEMORIAL. h. 10'.
Atop Foxboro library, South and Central Sts.
Charles H. Pizzano (1893–1987).

Born in Italy, Pizzano emigrated at age twelve to Boston, where he attended Bennet Street Industrial School and the Boston Museum School. Primarily a sculptor in wood, he carved works for many churches, including the National Cathedral in Washington.

FRAMINGHAM

CIVIL WAR MEMORIAL, 1872. Bronze, larger than life.
Framingham Center, Oak St.
Martin Milmore (1844–1881).

Brought to Boston from Ireland as a child, Martin Milmore was educated at Latin School and then given art lessons at Lowell Institute. His brother, who had become a cabinetmaker and stonecutter, taught him stone carving; when he was fourteen, Martin persuaded a reluctant Thomas Ball to take him as an apprentice, and he worked under Ball during the years Ball created the equestrian Washington for the Public Garden. Upon returning to Italy, Ball directed some commissions toward Milmore, whose career progressed from the success of the *Soldiers Monument* now in Forest Hills Cemetery to the large and complex Civil War memorial on Boston Common. Milmore is described as the consciously picturesque artistic figure, with dark hair and eyes, affecting a cloak and a broad-brimmed soft hat. His premature death resulted in the famed memorial work by Daniel Chester French, *Death Staying the Hand of the Sculptor* (*see* Forest Hills Cemetery).

The sameness of Civil War monuments on New England town greens leads one to think that they are factory reproductions. Such is not the case; the ubiquitous statues are based on an original work by Milmore, his *Soldiers Monument* in Forest Hills Cemetery. Leaning on his rifle, heroic but pensive, perhaps grieving, Milmore's soldier best expressed the sentiment of the day. A few of the variations are by Milmore himself; this one, later and more mature, is one of his best. Commissioned by George Phipps.

THE MINUTEMAN, 1905. Bronze, larger than life.
Union and Main Sts.
Theo Alice Ruggles Kitson (*see* Malden: *The Hiker*).

The popular theme of Colonial militiamen leaving their daily work to fight the English troops gets yet another variation here. This Kitson *Minuteman* is a blacksmith, complete with apron, forge, hammer, and tongs; he loads his rifle from his powder horn. The statue stands on what was once the drill field of the town's militia. Commissioned by the Town of Framingham and Framingham Chapter, Daughters of the American Revolution.

MUSEUM: Danforth Museum, 123 Union St. Founded in 1975, the Danforth owns a collection of nineteenth and twentieth-century art; hosts bi-monthly contemporary exhibitions.

THE QUESTION IS THE ANSWER, 1977. Cor-ten, stainless steel, h. 14′.
In front of Danforth Museum, 123 Union St.
David Lang (*see* Concord: *Abraxas*, etc.).

At Framingham State College:

DELTA 1-2-3, date unknown. Stainless steel, h. 30″.
between Hemenway Annex and May Hall.
Arthur Mazmurian (d. 1979).

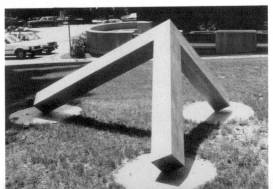

Seldom do the deceased create their own memorials, but such is the case here. Arthur B. Mazmurian, an assistant professor of art, had been teaching at Framingham State for eight years at the time of his unexpected death in 1979. The college dedicated this work of Mazmurian's as a memorial to him.

GLOUCESTER

JOAN OF ARC, 1910. Bronze, larger than life.
Main and Washington Sts.
★ Anna Vaughn Hyatt Huntington (1876–1973).

As a child, Cambridge native Anna Hyatt summered on a Maryland horse farm and there acquired her love of animals. She studied with Henry Hudson Kitson in Boston and at the Art Students League in New York before going to France to pursue her career. At the age of forty-seven she married poet/philanthropist Archer M. Huntington; together they founded Brookgreen Garden in South Carolina, generally acknowledged to be the first outdoor sculpture garden.

The model for this sculpture won an honorable mention at the Paris Salon of 1910; a heroic-scale version was commissioned for New York City and in 1915 won a Purple Rosette from the French government. Because the sculptor lived in Gloucester for a time, the town commissioned this full-scale copy for its World War I memorial.

★ THE FISHERMAN, 1925. Bronze, larger than life.
Western Ave., on Pavilion Beach.
Leonard Craske (1877–1950).

A product of London and London University, Leonard Craske studied anatomy at St. Thomas' hospital and served as a demonstrator in anatomy and pathology. He learned etching, was an actor for a time, and later in life became a color photographer. After studying sculpture

in England, he came to the U.S. in 1910, taking studios in Boston but summering in Gloucester. An enthusiastic sailor, he was engaged in a study of the characteristics of Gloucester fishermen when the town decided, as part of its 1923 tricentennial, to commission a permanent memorial. Craske was chosen. Asked later who his model was, he said that he went out on the *Elizabeth Nunan* one time and was aided by watching Capt. Herbert Thompson in action during a blow.

Twenty years later Craske designed a companion monument: a fisherman's wife, babe in arms, standing on the shore, with the inscription, "They also serve who only stand and wait." He was not able to raise funds to execute it.

HINGHAM

VICTORY, 1922. Equestrian bronze, larger than life.
    Rte. 3A at Hingham harbor.
    Theo Alice Ruggles Kitson (*see* Malden: *The Hiker*).

LINCOLN, 1922. Bronze, larger than life.
    Lincoln and North Sts.
    Charles E. Keck (1875–1951).

The seated Lincoln is a 1939 casting of a work originally done for Wabash, Ind., by Keck, a New York sculptor. Donor Everett E. Whitney conceived the idea of a Lincoln statue here to recognize the

family's roots in Hingham: in 1637, six generations before the sixteenth President was born, a weaver named Samuel Lincoln came to Hingham, Mass., from Hingham, England. Whitney traced the lineage and researched statues done of Lincoln, settling on Keck's as most suitable for this location.

HOLBROOK

SOLDIERS MONUMENT, 1917. Bronze, life-size.
  In Mary Wales Park, jct. Rtes. 37 and 139.
  John Horrigan (1864–1939).

  Largely self-taught, Horrigan grew up in Vermont and from boyhood worked in the Cornish quarries. His only formal education came in Vermont village schools and Quincy night school. Picking up tips in modeling clay from artists for whom he cut stone, Horrigan carved out a career as a sculptor of religious and military works.

HOPKINTON

THE DOUGHBOY, 1931. Bronze, larger than life.
  Junction Rte. 135 and Ash St.
  Theo Alice Ruggles Kitson (*see* Malden: *The Hiker*).

HULL

WORLD WAR I MEMORIAL. Stone, h. approx. 15′.
  Nantasket and Samoset Aves.
  Gerald T. Horrigan (*see* Quincy: *Robert Burns*).

LAWRENCE

BREAD AND ROSES MURAL, 1986. H. 17′ × 50′.
  Exterior, Greater Lawrence Family Health Center, 150 Park St.
  David Fichter (1951–   ).

  A graduate of Harvard College, Fichter has done half-a-dozen murals in this area as a grant recipient from the Massachusetts Council on the Arts and Humanities and arts lottery councils. He also does theater and poster design and paintings. This mural depicts Lawrence's history, including the historic Bread and Roses strike in 1912, which gave lasting impetus to the labor movement. Funded by WBZ Fund for the Arts and the Stevens Foundation.

CIVIL WAR MONUMENT, 1881. Bronze and stone, figures larger than life.
  On the common, Lawrence and Common Sts.
  W. R. O. Donovan.

WORLD WAR II MONUMENT, 1948. Bronze, larger than life.
  On the common, Lawrence and Common Sts.
  Leonard Craske (*see* Gloucester: *The Fisherman*).

WORLD OF THE FUTURE—SPACE, 1973. Steel, h. 23′.
  Haverhill St. side of library.
  Sam Facella.

  When this building was designed, the architect left a space facing
the common for an object to beautify the grounds, without specifying
what it would be. Facella, president of an iron and steel company and
a sculptor by avocation, designed a small model in his studio, and
municipal and private sources provided the funds to build it full-scale.

WORKERS' PLACE, completion planned 1988. Environmental design col-
  laboration using wood, copper, granite, brick.
  Rte. 28 (Broadway) and Rte. 114, next to Pemberton Park.
  Alice Adams (1930–   ) and Carlos Dorrien (*see* Waltham [Bentley
  College]: *Portal*).

  Alice Adams' site-integrated work invites the viewer to walk around
and through an environment; it focuses attention on vistas and elements in the landscape, and builds awareness of the natural sur-
roundings. A native New Yorker, Adams earned a B.F.A. from
Columbia in 1953, then attended L'Ecole Nationale d'Art Décoratif in
France. She has held fellowships from MacDowell Colony, National
Endowment for the Arts, Princeton University, the Guggenheim Foundation, and the French government; she has taught at the School of
Visual Arts, Pratt Institute, California State College, and Manhattan-
ville College. Her outdoor site works are located in New York, Pennsylvania, North Carolina, New Jersey, Ohio, and Washington state.
  Workers' Place, intended to commemorate workers who immigrated
to the mill city of Lawrence, is one of a string of parks being developed in Lawrence. Adams is known for her wood constructions; Carlos Dorrien has done many public works in stone. They will

collaborate closely with landscape designer Sherri Kluesing on a concept of "art as place." Funded by the Art in Public Places program of the NEA.

SYMBOLIC WATER WHEELS, 1976. Steel, diam. 8'.
Massachusetts Commemorative Industrial Park.
William Wainwright (*see* East Boston/Logan Airport: *Windwheels*).

LEXINGTON

★ THE MINUTEMAN, 1899. Bronze, larger than life.
Lexington Green, Mass. and Bedford Rds.
Henry Hudson Kitson (1863–1947).

One of New England's more prolific makers of portrait statues and monuments, H. H. Kitson was English-born and trained in Paris. Shortly after coming to this country to work he took an interest in the career of a young Brookline woman, Theo Alice Ruggles (*see* Malden: *The Hiker*). He encouraged her to go to Paris to study, followed her, and married her in 1893. The Kitsons collaborated on a few works, but later separated and pursued independent careers.

At its inaugural the press of the day, with considerable disregard for historical accuracy, dubbed this statue "Captain Parker," for the commander of the Lexington Minutemen. In 1775 Parker was forty-five years old, described as "a great tall man with a large head and a high, wide brow." Kitson's idealized young militiaman stands on the green where a tiny band of seventy-seven gathered in response to Revere's alarm in the early hours of April 19. Sent from Boston to search for arms and powder and, if possible, to capture Sam Adams and John Hancock, Gen. Gage's men marched through the night and arrived here about sunrise, arrogant and short of patience. Witnesses said that their captain shouted, "Disperse, ye damned rebels!"; no one agrees what happened next. A shot was fired—it is uncertain by whom—and both sides exchanged fire. As the smoke cleared eight Colonials lay dying; the Redcoats, without casualties, marched on toward Concord. Bequest of Francis Brown Hayes.

GEORGE WASHINGTON, 1979. Bronze, h. 4'6".
   At Museum of Our National Heritage, 33 Marrett Rd.
   Donald De Lue (1897–   ).

   One of this country's major living producers of commemorative and
   allegorical sculpture, Donald De Lue created *Quest Eternal* at the Pru-
   dential Center and the bronze doors at the Federal Reserve Bank in
   Boston. Among his dozens of large-scale commissions was *The
   Rocket Thrower*, a gigantic forty-five-foot bronze figure at the 1964–
   65 World's Fair in New York. He was also responsible for the Boy
   Scout memorial on the mall in Washington, D.C., and for bronzes at
   Valley Forge, Gettysburg, the Alamo, and Omaha Beach in Nor-
   mandy, France.
   This depiction of the nation's first President in full Masonic regalia
   was cast from the original half-scale model for a ten-foot statue for
   New Orleans. It is dedicated to the museum's first vice-president, the
   late Wayne E. Stichter (d. 1977), a thirty-third-degree Mason instrumental in the founding of the museum. Gift of the Stichter family.

LEXINGTON: A SENSE OF PLACE, 1987. Photomontage, 54" × 70".
   Lobby, Town Hall.
   Roy Crystal.

   Compiled by Lexington photographer Roy Crystal, this work con-
   sists of fifty-two rear-illuminated transparencies, four large and forty-
   eight small. Commissioned by Lexington Council for the Arts.

AERIAL SCULPTURES, 1983. Two units, fabric, plexiglass, each h. 36'.
   Atriums, Lexington Office Park, 420 and 430 Bedford St.
   Linda DeHart (1939–   ).

   Connecticut-born Linda DeHart studied at Rhode Island School of
   Design, moved to Cambridge, and worked as a fashion designer for a
   dozen years before turning full-time to sculpture. She has taught at
   Boston Architectural Center, and has been recipient of a 1% for Art
   grant. Although these two works are in separate buildings and one
   employs aluminum fabric, the other colored fabric, they are considered a related pair. Commissioned by Boston Properties Inc.

LINCOLN

At DeCordova and Dana Museum and Park:

*Dream house of an eccentric Europhile, the "castle" and its grounds
were given to the town of Lincoln by its owner, Julian DeCordova.
Since 1950 the museum has been a force in the recognition and collection of art by New Englanders. The park, almost thirty-five acres
surrounding the castle and sloping down to Flint's Pond (also called
Sandy Pond), is operated by the museum as an outdoor gallery. Of
the twenty or so sculptures on site at any given time, about a dozen
are actually owned by the museum or are here on extended loan.
Those are listed, with the caveat that there will be others and that the
museum rearranges the display from time to time.*

WHEEL AND STANDING FIGURE, 1983. Wood, cast aluminum, h. (wheel) 10′; (figure) 6′.
★ Magdalena Abakanowicz (1930–).

The work of this Polish artist, much of it in fiber, electrified the Venice Biennial exhibition in 1980. In 1982 the Museum of Contemporary Art in Chicago organized an exhibition of Abakanowicz' work which toured the U.S., including the DeCordova Museum. The artist visited here and was inspired to create a piece for the museum grounds. A major genre for her is grouped "backs" or "fronts," shells of torsos made from a fibrous medium. For outdoors, she has cast a "front" in aluminum, and backed it with another signature form of hers, a primitively built wheel. Although the Museum frowns on the practice, rare is the visitor with a camera who has not posed a friend as the head of Abakanowicz' headless torso.

One of the world's most articulate artists, Abakanowicz has explained her fiber work in terms like this: "That which was soft with a complex tissue became the material of my work. . . . Impermanence is a necessity of all that lives. It is a truth contained in a soft organism . . . [I] give vent to this innate defeat of life by turning a lasting thought into a perishable material." She is a professor at the State College of Art in Poznan, Poland.

X NOTION LIKE AN H, 1978. Steel, h. 12′ × 8′ × 4′.
Lila Katzen (1932–).

Katzen is a New York sculptor.

★ 3 GARDENS, 1981. Shrubs and other media.
Mags Harries (*see* Chelsea: *Bellingham Square*).

Although technically here on loan, Harries' three tiny gardens are literally rooted in place and likely to remain for a while. So small as to seem parodies of the formal English garden, the three areas are meant to contrast with the natural landscape of the museum's acreage. They incorporate on a small scale many horticultural clichés: a sinuous bricked walkway, one wrought iron chair, an archway with yews trained over it, a mergatroid (silver ball on a pedestal). Funded by Massachusetts Council on the The Arts and Humanities.

MASS. ART VEHICLE, 1970. Welded steel, h. 8′3″ × 10′ × 2′.
George Greenamyer (*see* Marshfield: *Webster, the Farmer of Marshfield*).

MIGRATION—SERIES NO. 7, 1976. Steel, h. 7½′ × 5½′ × 6′.
Dennis Kowal (*see* Wellesley [Babson College]: *Ominous Icon #6* and *Yaddo Study*).

CARDINAL POINTS, 1965. Welded steel, h. 9′ × 9½′ × 8′.
★ Alexander Liberman (*see* Waltham [Brandeis University]: *End Free Series XV*).

Unlike most sculptors, Liberman seldom draws or makes a model before he starts a work: "I like to go straight into scale," he says. He often cuts up discarded oil barrels as his medium for rough working concepts.

GROUP OF THREE, 1969. Concrete, h. $9' \times 8' \times 7'$.
Hugh Townley (1923–).

Another version of this work stands in Providence, where Townley teaches at Brown University. The three abstract components can be read as letters which spell "ART."

THORN, 1957. Bronze, h. 64".
Robert Adams (1917–).

An English sculptor, Adams has here attempted to amalgamate in one form the principal ideas of Christianity: the cross, the crown and thorns, and "the spirit of life thrusting ever upwards."

LEANING TORSO, 1969. Forged steel, black marble, concrete, h. $5'2'' \times 3'2'' \times 2'8'$.
Lawrence Fane (1933–).

The contrast of steel and concrete, the sculptor says, suggests the opposition of rigid and soft forms, bone and tissue, in the human figure.

COLLEONI, 1965. Bronze, h. $30'' \times 28'' \times 14''$.
Richard Fishman (1941–).

The title refers to Verrochio's monumental equestrian statue in Venice, a prize of Renaissance art. Fishman's work attempts to deal with animal–human, physical–spiritual metamorphoses, "cohering into a new and powerful presence," the artist says.

THREE LINES, 1964. Stainless steel, h. 18'.
★ George Rickey (1907–).

Minimalist studies in line and balance, Rickey's lines may be seen at such museums as the Hirshhorn in Washington, D.C. Done with calculated engineering skills, the blades are counterbalanced at the base, slender at top to allow a little wind resistance, but not too much. Critics liken their motion to ballet, and to the swaying of grasses and trees in the wind. Rickey says that his works attempt to concentrate movement itself; he thinks of his kinetic wands as "a limited but indeterminate drawing in space."

PHOTO COURTESY OF THE DECORDOVA MUSEUM

CAMPFIRE GIRLS, 1976. Cor-ten steel, h. 7′ × 8′ × 7½′.
David Stromeyer (1946–   ).

Stromeyer fabricates his steel works himself, developing, he says, "a dialogue with my material," and refining his ideas in the process. The intent of his abstraction is to challenge all the viewer's perceptions and concepts of space.

WAR MEMORIAL, 1929. Bronze, larger than life.
Bedford and Trapelo Rds., in front of Lincoln Library.
Anonymous.

Cast by T. F. McGann & Sons Co., Boston, this eagle by an unknown maker has become a town landmark.

LOWELL

★ HOMAGE TO WOMEN, 1984. Bronze, larger than life.
Market Mills Park, Market and Palmer Sts.
Mico Kaufman (1924–   ).

A resident of Tewksbury, Kaufman studied at the Academy of Fine Arts in Rome and Florence, 1947–1951. Much of his work is in the design of commemorative medals and miniatures issued in sets by commercial mints; he designed the official inaugural medals for Presidents Ford and Reagan. He was named sculptor of the year in 1978 by the American Numismatic Association, and his work is owned by its museum in Colorado Springs and by the Smithsonian Museum in Washington.

This work recognizes the role of women, like the mill girls of Lowell, in the industrial revolution, and the changed role of women as a result. Funded by the Lowell Historic Preservation Commission, federal, municipal, and private sources.

THE WORKER, 1985. Bronze, life-size.
    Market and Shattuck Sts.
    Ivan and Elliot Schwartz.

    New Yorkers Ivan and Elliot Schwartz specialize in creating histori-
cally accurate figures for interpretative displays in museums, props for
dance and theater companies, and promotional settings for retail
stores. Among their clients is the National Air and Space Museum in
Washington, D.C.
    Lowell's 5.6 miles of canals, diverting the water which powered the
mills, were dug by hand early in the nineteenth century. This work
honors those laborers.

JACK KEROUAC COMMEMORATIVE PARK, installation planned 1988.
    Granite and stainless steel.
    Eastern Canal Park, Bridge and French Sts.
    Ben Woitena (1942–   ).

    Texan Ben Woitena's sculpture occupies at least a dozen public
sites in Texas, including the Houston and San Antonio Museums of
Fine Arts. Born in San Antonio, he is a graduate of the University of
Texas and a member of the faculty of the Glassell School.
    Controversy surrounded the proposal of this memorial to Lowell na-
tive Jack Kerouac (1922–1969), an iconoclast whose *On the Road* rejected the conformism of the 1950s, spawned the Beat Generation,
and paved the way for the social ferment of the 1960s. Some citizens
felt that Kerouac's life style, particularly the alcoholism that caused his
early death, was not a cause for civic pride. Others argued that the
achievements of this native son far outweighed his personal short-
comings: author of twenty books, he is considered a major influence
in literature and, like Hemingway thirty years before, chronicler of a
generation. Kerouac attended Lowell High School, worked for a time
at the *Lowell Sun*, and is buried in Edson Cemetery. Commissioned
by Lowell Historic Preservation Commission.

HUMAN CONSTRUCTION, 1987. Granite, two units, h. 16′, l. 40′–45′.
    At Central St., in the Pawtucket Canal.
    Carlos Dorrien (*see* Waltham [Bentley College]: *Portal*).

    Placed atop old canal piers, Dorrien's post-and-lintel archways and
stoneworks evoke ancient ways of building. Dorrien's style leaves
large chunks of stone rough-hewn in homage to the material itself; he
then works portions of each stone in ways that define its form.
    Funded by Courrier Citizen Corp., Raytheon Corp., MA/Com Corp.,
and Lowell Historic Preservation Commission.

THE ROUSES MONUMENT, 1979. Bronze, life-size.
    Kennedy Plaza, 50 Arcano Dr., adj. to City Hall.
    Mico Kaufman (*see Homage to Women* above).

    After policeman Christos Rouses was killed in a drug raid, his com-
rades on the Lowell police force raised funds to erect a memorial to
him. Their initial concept was simply a statue of a police officer.

Kaufman advocated enlarging the concept, telling the force, "A cop is a cop, but if you put a child next to him he becomes a policeman."

ITALIA, 1987. Bronze, h. 6'.
Kennedy Plaza.
Mico Kaufman (see *Homage to Women* above).

Commissioned by the Italo-American Cultural Committee of Lowell, this work is meant to commemorate the Italian heritage in Lowell. It incorporates a sample of Italian architecture (the communal palace in Sienna) in the "boot" shape of southern Italy; verso are the mills of Lowell and a pair of immigrants.

PAWTUCKET PRISM, 1987. Gold-plated stainless steel, h. 20' × 19' × 13'.
Junction of the Pawtucket Canal and Concord River, at Lowell Hilton Hotel.
Michio Ihara (1928–   ).

A former fellow of the Center for Advanced Visual Studies at M.I.T., Ihara has produced more than fifty commissioned works in this country, Japan, Australia, New Zealand, Hong Kong, and Singapore. Born in Paris, Ihara grew up in Tokyo. After he earned a degree from the University of Fine Arts, a Fulbright grant allowed him to study art in architecture and to become a research associate at M.I.T. He has taught at Musashino Fine Arts University and has been an artist-in-residence at Newcastle College in Australia. He now lives in Concord.

A number of Ihara's works are kinetically engineered to move in the wind. To illustrate the theme "the power of water" here, Ihara has adapted his design so the fountain's flow will move his kinetic cubes. The Indian word "Pawtucket" is said to mean "falling water." Funded by Arthur Robbins, the Lowell Hilton Hotel, the Lowell Historic Preservation Commission, and the City of Lowell.

CLAUDE DEBUSSY, MUSICIEN FRANCAIS, 1987. Bronze, h. 6' × 8' × 6'.
University of Lowell South Campus.
Mico Kaufman (*see Homage to Women* above).

Debussy (1862–1918), impressionist composer, was born in Paris, trained at the Paris Conservatoire, and won the Prix de Rome at the age of twenty-two. The compositions he submitted while in Rome were judged so formless and unacademic that they were denied the customary public performance. Debussy's originality began to be recognized with *Afternoon of a Faun* in 1894 and with his only opera, *Pelléas and Mélisande*, in 1902. Debussy rejected melody, writing, "Melody is powerless to express the constant change of emotion and life." Developing musical impressionism to a peak of exquisite sensitivity, he was credited with introducing a new system of color into music, and with revealing novel possibilities for the piano. His best-known work today is probably *La Mer* (*The Sea*). Cut into the base are scenes of *Afternoon of a Faun* (on the front) and *Pelléas and Mélisande* (on the back). Privately funded by the Claude Debussy Trust Fund, Inc.

LYNN

CIVIL WAR MEMORIAL, 1873. Bronze, three figures, larger than life.
  Common and Commercial Sts.
  John Adams Jackson (1825–1879).

   Born in Bath, Me., Jackson went to Paris to study in the late 1840s,
one of the first American sculptors to choose that city rather than Italy.
He later settled in Florence and spent the last twenty years of his life
there. Jackson is known primarily as a portraitist. The three figures
represent War, Peace, and the City of Lynn extending the laurel
wreath of victory and honor to her sons.

LYNN WORKS, 1987. Forged and welded steel, h. 22′ × 60′ × 4′.
  At North Shore Community College, Lynnway and Broad St.
  George Greenamyer (see Marshfield: *Webster, the Farmer of Marshfield*).

   Greenamyer's delight in antique toys and Americana is well suited
to this commemoration of Lynn's industrial history, from shoemaking
to aircraft engine manufacture. Funded by 1% for Art.

LYNN HERITAGE MURAL, 1987. Ceramic, mosaic, found objects, h. 6′ × 120′.
  Lynn State Heritage Park, 154 Lynnway, exterior of Seaport Lauding.
  Lilli Ann Killen Rosenberg (see Newton: *Five Concrete Mosaic Sculptures*).

   As part of the package in developing condominiums here, Seaport
Landing Inc. gave this exterior wall to the city of Lynn. The mural celebrates Lynn's heritage and its waterfront. Clay pieces which became
components of the mural were made by an assortment of groups in
Lynn, from children on a playground through senior citizens. Commissioned by Seaport Landing Inc. and the Massachusetts Department of
Environmental Management.

MURALS, 1984. Ceramic and mosaic, various sizes.
  Interior and exterior, St. Mary's Houses for Elderly and Handicapped,
  30 Pleasant St.
  Lilli Ann Killen Rosenberg (see Newton: *Five Concrete Mosaic Sculptures*).

MALDEN

THE HIKER, erected 1938. Bronze, larger than life.
  Pleasant and Elm Sts.
  Theo Alice Ruggles Kitson (1871–1932).

   Daughter of the postmaster of Brookline, Theo Alice Ruggles
showed an early aptitude for sculpture and in her teens became a
protégé of the sculptor Henry Hudson Kitson (*see* Lexington: *The Minuteman*). She studied in Paris, receiving at the age of eighteen an
honorable mention at the Paris Exposition of 1889 and another in
1890 at the Paris Salon, first American woman to receive such a distinction. She and Kitson were married in 1893 and collaborated on
several memorials (*see* Commonwealth Ave.: *Collins Memorial*), but
are said to have separated about 1909. About 1915 Theo Alice
moved to Sherborn and then to Framingham, where she maintained a
studio until her death. Creator of a veritable army of military monuments, she had a hand in at least fifty memorial sculptures around the
country.
   Some confusion exists as to whether Mrs. Kitson or her husband,
H. H. Kitson, sculpted the original of this statue; the best evidence indicates that it was she. Part of the difficulty lies in the fact that Gorham Foundry continued to cast reproductions after Theo Alice Kitson's
death; the work was so popular that towns wanting to memorialize the
Spanish-American War began to specify a "Kitson-type memorial." As
late as 1965, a *Hiker* monument was erected—that one at Arlington
National Cemetery. Erected by the City of Malden.

THE FLAG DEFENDERS, 1910.
  At Bell Rock Park, Main St. and Wilson Ave.
  Bela Pratt (1867–1917).

   For many years a teacher at Boston Museum School, Pratt is best
known locally for his seated bronze figures of *Science* and *Art* in front
of Boston Public Library. He was born in Norwich, Conn., studied at
Yale School of Fine Arts, and at age twenty went to New York to work

under the great sculptors of the day, including Augustus Saint-Gaudens. He later studied in Paris. Among his more important commissions are allegorical figures for the Library of Congress in Washington, D.C.

Malden engaged the renowned landscape designer Frederick Law Olmsted to advise on the location of this memorial and to design the park. Funded by the City of Malden with contributions from Malden Chapter of the Sons of the Revolution, Malden Historical Society, and Deliverance Monroe Chapter of the Daughters of the Revolution.

GALLERY: Malden Public Library, 36 Salem St.: Thanks to bequests in 1903 and '04 from Mr. and Mrs. Elisha Slade Converse (of Converse Shoes), Malden Public Library has steadily amassed a small but fine collection of paintings. Copley, Homer, Inness, Turner, Constable, and Millet are among the artists represented; the collection extends from seventeenth-century Dutch and Flemish schools into this century.

MARBLEHEAD

THE SPIRIT OF '76. Oil on canvas, h. 18' × 12'.
Selectmen's Office, Abbot Hall, Washington St.
Archibald M. Willard (1836–1918).

Possibly the most-reproduced American painting of the nineteenth century, this canvas is the original version of *The Spirit of '76*. It was purchased and presented to the town by Col. John Henry Devereux, a native of Marblehead, whose son Henry K. Devereux posed for the drummer boy.

After serving in the Civil War, A. M. Willard returned to his native Ohio and took a job with a wheelwright, painting wagons. He began decorating the wagon boxes more and more elaborately, even painting scenes on them, and in his spare time tried to study painting. Willard achieved financial success with homespun, humorous paintings that could be reproduced by chromolithography and sold in quantity.

This work, at first titled *Yankee Doodle*, was conceived as a money-maker to be reproduced and marketed in connection with the Centennial of 1876; early versions portrayed three lighthearted figures at a rural patriotic celebration. When Willard's father, who was posing as the central figure, became ill (he died before the painting was finished), the painter's concept sobered. This final version proved an overwhelmingly popular expression of American sentiment of the day. The model for the fifer was Willard's friend and war comrade Hugh Mosher, said to be the best fifer in Northern Ohio; Willard chose young Devereux from among cadets at a military prep school in Cleveland. The painter had not dreamed that his work would be exhibited at the Philadelphia Centennial, but the public insisted. The painting then toured the country for an empathetic populace before being bought for Marblehead.

MARSHFIELD

WEBSTER, THE FARMER OF MARSHFIELD, 1986. Forged and welded steel, painted, h. 7'6" × 12' × 20".
In front of Ventress Library, Library Mall, Ocean St. (Rte. 139).
George Greenamyer (1939–   ).

Almost all of Greenamyer's sculptures have wheels, as if they were wacky machines; he has, indeed, "raced" them in the annual Great Sculpture race in Cambridge, usually competing to turn in the slowest time. These humorous welded vehicles refer in multiple ways to old-time Americana, Yankee ingenuity, industrial methodology in fabrication and forging, strength, and implied kineticism. Greenamyer was educated at the University of Kansas and at the Philadelphia Museum College of Art; he has been a fellow of the Center for Advanced Visual Studies at M.I.T. His twenty-plus public works are sited from Maine to Alaska. He lives in Marshfield and teaches sculpture at Massachusetts College of Art.
Statesman Daniel Webster, great orator of the mid-nineteenth

century, owned a 1,500-acre estate in Marshfield, about a mile from this site. Despite his fame, Webster most liked to think of himself as a farmer, according to town historians. Born in New Hampshire of rugged farming stock, Webster early showed such a passion for books that his family educated him, at great sacrifice, at Phillips Exeter Academy and Dartmouth College. He became a lawyer and an orator of clear, massive, gorgeous, overwhelming eloquence. Twice a congressman, he was elected to the Senate in 1827. His presidential aspirations were never fulfilled; he was twice Secretary of State, and the most concrete achievement of his career was negotiating the treaty with England that fixed this country's northeastern boundary in 1842. Funded by Marshfield Arts Lottery Council and gift of the artist.

MEDFORD

ORIENTAL LANTERN. Stone, h. 8½'.
In front of City Hall, Salem St. and I-93.

This Japanese lantern was a gift to the city in the mid-1970s from its sister city, Nobeka, Japan. The inscription reads, "Given by Asahi-Japan to the citizens of Medford." Asahi-Japan is a corporation with a branch, Asahi-America, in Medford.

WORLD WAR I MEMORIAL. Granite, h. 8'.
At entrance to Oak Grove Cemetery, Playstead Rd.
Emilius R. Ciampa (*see* Charles River Esplanade: *Maurice J. Tobin*).

WORLD WAR II MEMORIAL. Bronze angel, h. 11'.
In Oak Grove Cemetery.
Emilius R. Ciampa (*see* Charles River Esplanade: *Maurice J. Tobin*).

At Tufts University:

AZTEC FIGURE, ca. 15th C. Volcanic stone, h. 29".
Lobby, Campus Center.
Mexican, artist unknown.
Gift of Seth Merrin, 1983.

ELEPHANT FOUNTAIN. Bronze, h. 4'.
Outside Wessell Library.
Carl Wilhelm Emil Milles (1875–1955).

MAN AND PEGASUS. Bronze, h. 24".
Inside Wessell Library.
C. W. E. Milles.

COMMON GROUND, 1984. Wool, 6' × 9'.
Cohen Auditorium.
Rhoda Cohen (*see* Natick: *Fiber Revival*).

LONG WHITE CLOUD, 1986. Fabric, 3′ × 7′.
  Wessell Library.
  Rhoda Cohen (*see Common Ground*, above, and Natick: *Fiber Revival*).

GALLERY: in Cohen Arts Center, Talbot Ave. Exhibits thesis shows of
  graduate students of the Boston Museum School, which is affiliated
  with Tufts for the awarding of academic degrees.

MILFORD

GENERAL DRAPER, 1912. Equestrian bronze, larger than life.
  In Draper Park, Main and Congress Sts.
  Daniel Chester French (*see* Concord: *Minuteman*).

  This park was purchased by the widow of Gen. William F. Draper in
  1910 in order to create a memorial to her husband, veteran of the
  Civil War, congressman, and ambassador to Italy. Draper (1842–
  1910) enlisted in the 25th Massachusetts Regiment, was elected lieutenant, transferred to the 36th Massachusetts Regiment, and was
  commissioned captain, served on Burnside's staff, saw action at Antietam and Fredericksburg, was sent West and participated in the capture of Vicksburg and the siege of Knoxville, was promoted to
  lieutenant colonel, wounded in the Battle of the Wilderness, and left
  the army—all before his twenty-third birthday. Draper was later
  awarded the brevet ranks of colonel and brigadier general in recognition of gallantry.

MILTON

IN FLANDERS FIELDS, 1925. Bronze, larger than life.
  In front of Town Hall, Canton Ave.
  ★ Daniel Chester French (*see* Concord: *Minuteman*).

  Every New England town formed a committee to erect a memorial
  to the dead of World War I, and French's services by this time were in
  great demand. For this commission in Milton he needed a new idea.
  The sculptor's daughter relates that a family friend, the sculptor

Malvina Hoffman, suggested the John McCrea poem which ends, "To you from failing hands we throw/ The torch; be yours to hold it high./ If ye break faith with us who die/ We shall not sleep, though poppies grow/ In Flanders fields." She mounted the model stand and struck a pose with a whiskbroom for a torch, and the sculptor made a quick sketch in clay which became the prototype for this work.

At Milton Academy:

WAVES OF ANOTHER DIMENSION, 1978. Cor-ten steel, h. 8′.
On Centre St., between Wigg Hall and Strauss Bldg.
Dennis Kowal (*see* Wellesley [Babson College]: *Ominous Icon #6* and *Yaddo Study*).

MURAL, 1983. Acrylic on homosote, h. 8′ × 116′.
Attached to front of Science Bldg., south side of Centre St.
This student project depicts "windows" on Boston.

FAMILY ALBUM IN BRONZE. Collection of small bronzes.
Inside Science Building.
Robert Cook (1921–   ).

An alumnus of Milton, Cook studied in Paris. His works are at the Whitney Museum in New York and the Hirschhorn in Washington.

GALLERY: Nesto Gallery, basement of Science Building. Rotating exhibitions.

NATICK

FIBER REVIVAL, 1986. Quilt, 36″ × 54″.
Interior, Leonard Morse Hospital.
Rhoda Cohen (1934–   ).

Painter turned quiltmaker, Cohen begins with the quilt form but segues into collage, departing from formal patterning to create imagery. Cohen studied various artistic disciplines at the schools of the De-Cordova Museum and the Boston Museum of Fine Arts before turning to fabric. She has been artist-in-residence at Point Bonita, Cal., and has taught and lectured in the U.S., Europe, Australia, and New Zealand. Her quilts have been exhibited in those countries as well as in Africa, Holland, and Japan. In this work Cohen used as raw material scraps and castoffs given her by batik artist Sharon Engler, who works in Wayland.

NEEDHAM

COLOR SWEEP, 1983. Painted wood, sixty-five posts, h. 5½',
in two lines, 50′ each.
Cooks Bridge, Needham Housing Authority, Evergreen Rd.,
off St. Mary's St.
Virginia Gunter.

A graduate of Massachusetts College of Art, Gunter has had a dual career as creative artist and museum administrator, having been director of exhibitions at Mass/Art. She is a Fellow of the Center for Advanced Visual Studies at M.I.T. and has held grants from Massachusetts Council on the Arts and Humanities. Gunter has exhibited widely, often working in fiber, often creating short-lived environmental works for festivals such as First Night. "Light," she says, "is a primary factor" in her sculpture; "reflections, shadows, and captured color are . . . integral to the sculpture . . . and allow the work to activate the passage of time."

Here Gunter's lines of painted posts function in two ways: they emphasize the contours of the landscape, drawing an arc up each hill, and they record the passage of sunlight, changing aspect with the angle of light and shadow.

VIRGINIA GUNTER PHOTO

WYETH PAINTINGS, various dates. Oil on canvas.
At Needham Library, 1139 Highland Ave.
N. C. Wyeth (1882–1945).

Wyeth, founder of what has become a famous American painting family (son Andrew, grandson Jamie), was a native of Needham. At the age of twenty he traveled to Wilmington, Del., to study at the

Howard Pyle School of Art, Pyle being a famous illustrator of children's books and fairy tales at that time. He married in Delaware and established himself in Chadds Ford, Pa. In 1921 he and his family returned to Needham, but within two years resettled in Chadds Ford. At about this time he received the commission to paint the outsized ship paintings that grace the lobby of Bank of Boston.

NEWBURYPORT

★ THE VOLUNTEER, 1903. Bronze, larger than life.
Atkinson Common, High St. and Moseley Ave.
Theo Alice Ruggles Kitson (*see* Malden: *The Hiker*).

This sensitive portrait has more to say than most about the sacrifice of youth to the exigencies of war; it was reproduced as a Civil War memorial in six other cities. It is unfortunate that vandals have bent the rifle barrel.

GEORGE WASHINGTON, 1878. Bronze, larger than life.
High and Pond Sts.
★ John Quincy Adams Ward (1830–1910).

The initials of J. Q. A. Ward are to be found on a surprising number of late-nineteenth-century sculptures. Along with the younger but better-known Saint-Gaudens, Ward is credited with infusing American sculpture with the vitality of naturalism. Born on a farm near Urbana, Ohio, Ward was offered the best schooling available there, but often played hookey to visit the local potter's workshop. To please his father, he studied medicine for a bit, improving his understanding of anatomy. An older sister who lived in New York introduced him to the sculptor Henry Kirke Brown, who accepted him as an assistant and generously included him in both his work and his friendship. Brown's instruction was at the time the best in this country; Ward made the most of it and rejected the idea of joining the colony of expatriate artists working in Italy. In Washington he modeled portrait busts of a number of notable politicians; then he set up shop in New York. His first really ambitious work, *Indian Hunter*, was done after a journey among the Indians of the West. It was widely acclaimed; its admirers raised funds to erect it in Central Park, and Ward's career was launched. This work was presented to the town by Daniel I. Tenney.

WILLIAM LLOYD GARRISON. Bronze, larger than life.
Pleasant St., across from City Hall.
David French (1827–1910).

David French is apparently no relation to the more famous and
more prolific Daniel Chester French. A resident of Newburyport, he
studied under Stevenson in Boston; this is his best-known work.

Most famous of all abolitionists, Garrison (1805–1879) was born in
Newburyport. Indentured to a printer, he quickly rose to compositor
and then contributor. Rejecting then-current ideas of gradual emancipation and colonization of former slaves elsewhere, Garrison de-
manded immediate emancipation and the rights of citizens for slaves.
Without subscribers or capital, Garrison and a friend founded in Boston the *Liberator*, which became a powerful voice for abolition. Not all
fellow Bostonians sympathized; in 1835 Garrison was mobbed there
and had to be jailed for his own safety until he could escape the city.
The *Liberator* also opposed war, alcohol, tobacco, freemasonry, capital punishment, and imprisonment for debt. Garrison's pro-feminist
views led him to insist on equal participation by women in the anti-
slavery movement.

NEWTON

MARVIN ROSENBERG PHOTO (DETAIL)

FIVE CONCRETE MOSAIC SCULPTURES, 1980–83. Five units, h. 3'–7'.
Newton Centre at Centre and Langley Sts.
Lilli Ann Killen Rosenberg (1924–   ).

A resident of Newton, Rosenberg has produced a number of community art projects and public ceramic murals (*see* South End/Rox-
bury: *Betances Mural* and MBTA [Park St.]: *Celebration of the
Underground*). Trained in architecture, sculpture, and ceramics, she
was educated at Los Angeles City College, Cooper Union, the Art
Students League in New York City, and at Cranbrook Academy of Art
in Michigan. For eighteen years she was director of the art department at the Henry Street Settlement in New York, and in the 1960s,
under a Rockefeller grant, she was assigned by the New York City

housing authority to humanize public spaces through participatory art projects. With her husband Marvin, she has created public murals in Philadelphia, Wilmington, Del., New York City, and Montgomery County, Md. She is the author of *Children Make Murals and Sculpture: Experiences in Community Art Projects*.

Over a three-year period, more than 200 Newton residents—from the mayor to small children—trooped through Rosenberg's ceramics studios, making the clay pieces that compose this work a kind of community autobiography. Sponsored by the Arts in the Park program of the Newton Parks and Recreation Department; funded by a grant from the Massachusetts Council for the Arts and Humanities.

THE 14 VILLAGES OF NEWTON, 1983. Quilt, 9′ × 12′.
In City Hall, left of entrance.

Fifty quilters worked for a year to produce this work to mark the founding of the Fund for the Arts in Newton. Community history and activities are included, from John Eliot, an early preacher to the Indians, to the Boston Marathon, which wends its way through the heart of the city every April. Sponsored by Honeywell Corp.

CHILDREN'S MURALS, 1978–80. Ceramic mosaic, eight units, various sizes.
Lobbies, Administration Bldg., Newton Board of Education, 100 Walnut St.
Lilli Ann Killen Rosenberg (*see Five Concrete Mosaic Sculptures above*).

★ **(1,2) (3,4) 5**, 1985. Cast steel h. 9′.
In front of Newton Art Center, 61 Washington Park.
Mayer Spivack (1936–   ).

Dual interests in architectural design and psychiatry have led Mayer Spivack to become an expert consultant on the influence of architectural spaces and settings upon human behavior. Spivack attended Boston University and the Boston Museum School before taking a master's in city planning at M.I.T.; he has held grants from the Public Health Service and the National Institute of Mental Health to study the psychological and therapeutic aspects of art and architecture. His multifaceted career comprises kinetic light sculpture, objects such as this, photography, and inventions in the fields of optics, medical equipment, prosthetics, tools, papermaking, navigation, toys, and sporting equipment.

This work is sited temporarily at Newton Arts Center pending completion of remodeling at South Station, Boston, where the piece will be placed in the lobby. Its components are railroad car couplings, two-and-a-half pairs, welded together in a muscular totemic vertical. This is a particularly successful example of what is sometimes termed "junk" sculpture, or assemblage—a work formed from found industrial objects (Spivak likes the term "foundiron"). The artist's eye has perceived the resemblance between these functional parts and a human head; he has chosen the repetitions of a totem; he has also seen that three complete heads would be too much and has truncated the top one by using a single coupler. This work is both parody and an entity in itself, a statement at once strong and humorous. Commissioned by Federal Railway Administration.

GALLERY: Newton Art Center, 61 Washington Park.

THE MINISTRY OF THE WHOLE PEOPLE OF GOD, 1983. Ceramic mural.
   Andover–Newton Theological Seminary, 210 Herrick Rd.
   John Moakley (*see* East Bridgewater: *Mural*) and Sonni Waldo (*see* Scituate: *The Heritage of Freedom by the Sea*).

At Boston College:

PHOTO COURTESY BOSTON COLLEGE ART COLLECTION

CONCORD, 1983. Painted metal, h. 8′ × 7½′ × 4′.
   ★ George Sugarman (1912–   ).

Born in the Bronx, Sugarman was the son of an Oriental rug dealer; he says that his aesthetic mindset was influenced by the patterns and colors of Persian and Turkish carpets. After military service, Sugarman used his G.I. Bill benefits to graduate from City College of New York and then to study in Paris from 1951 to 1955. Returning to New York from Paris, he was struck by the "conglomerate but somehow cohesive structure of the city," the energy generated by its unplanned variety. His work is designed to create unity out of disparity, reflection of a reality that is changing and open-ended. His early work consisted of complex, sprawling constructions in laminated wood; in the late 1960s he began to simplify his forms and to design large-scale works to be fabricated in metal. These recent works, which he calls "field" sculptures, reflect his interest in physics and his attempts to unify its conflicting and unlike component theories. Sugarman taught at Hunter and Bard Colleges, has been a visiting professor at Yale, and has held grants from the National Council on the Arts, the Longview Foundation, and the Ford Foundation.

EAGLE, date unknown, installed 1957. Bronze, larger than life.
    In front of Gasson Hall.
    Japanese, artist unknown.

The B.C. eagle displayed at the entrance to the campus is more than a standard college mascot. It was brought back from Japan by Larz Anderson after his service there as ambassador and was part of the estate he bequeathed to the town of Brookline. Arthur O'Shea, town administrator, saw the bronze bird while touring the estate prior to the town's acceptance of it and asked the executor whether Boston College might have the eagle. The column and base used to be in front of South Station, supporting a bust of Admiral Dewey.

GALLERY: Boston College Gallery, in Devlin Hall.

ED MACKINNON PHOTO COURTESY C&R CORP.

LOST BOY WITH DOG, 1975.
    Bronze, life-size.
    In The Mall at Chestnut Hill.
    Cornelius Zitman.
    Commissioned by C&R
    Management Corp.

LES GIRLS, 1975. Bronze, life-size.
    In The Mall at Chestnut Hill.
    Cornelius Zitman.
    Commissioned by C&R
    Management Corp.

THE SUN, ca. 1970. Mural on brick, h. 30′ × 60′.
    On Wasserman Bldg., 271 Auburn St., Auburndale, visible from Mass.
    Pike east of Weston interchange.
    Artist unknown.

This mural was the subject of a civil suit when it was begun. The block of stores has been owned by the Wasserman family for some sixty years; in the late 1960s Ronnie Brooker (since deceased) had a gift shop called The Ends of the Earth in the south end of the block. She commissioned the mural, but neighbors objected to it, claiming (although the mural was unrelated to the shop's logo) that it was an advertisement. The artist's work was halted for a time by court order. The Wasserman family took the case to the state Supreme Judicial Court, contending it was a work of art, and won.

NORTH ANDOVER

PHILLIPS BROOKS, 1916. Bronze, larger than life.
Academy and Great Pond Rds., on Old Andover Common, opposite Merrimack Valley Textile Museum.
Bela Pratt (*see* Malden: *The Flag Defenders*).

SOLDIERS MONUMENT, 1913. Bronze, larger than life.
In front of police station, Osgood St. near Mass. Ave.
Theo Alice Ruggles Kitson (*see* Malden: *The Hiker*).

SHEEP-SHEARING ON NORTH ANDOVER COMMON, 1985. Acrylic on plaster, h. 6′ × 14′.
Senior Center, Main St.
Linda Aubry (1954–   ).

Aubry sought a degree in music before turning to painting, attending the Philadelphia College of Art, Berklee School of Music, and the Boston Conservatory before taking an M.F.A. at Bennington College. She paints murals as a profession. The mural depicts an annual North Andover tradition on the old common. Commissioned by North Andover Arts Council.

NORTON

At Wheaton College:

HEBE, 1983 recasting of original ca. 1850. Bronze, h. 4½′.
Courtyard between Killam and Metcalf Halls.
Thorwaldsen.

Research has revealed that Thorwaldsen was a Scandinavian artist, but not his (or her) first name. The original of this statue was given by Eliza Wheaton, the college's founder, to mark Wheaton's fiftieth anniversary in 1884. Made of lead and painted white, the figure suffered enough damage that it was recast in bronze a century later. Goddess of youth, daughter of Zeus and Hera, Hebe sometimes (as here) appears as cupbearer to the Gods instead of the better-known Ganymede. In legend, she became the bride of Hercules after the end of his mortal life. Her presence here illustrates Wheaton's motto: "Who sips" (from the cup of knowledge) "will thirst for more."

DIRECTIONAL NO. 4, 1966. Bronze, h. 39″ × 31″.
Hood Court, behind Watkins Fine Arts Bldg.
Paul Von Ringelheim.

Von Ringelheim is an Austrian-born American sculptor. Anonymous gift to the college.

GALLERY: in Watkins Fine Arts Center on Rte. 140 (Taunton Ave.), one block east of junction with Rte. 123. Rotating exhibits include works from the permanent collection, student work, and traveling exhibitions.

PEABODY

SOLDIERS AND SAILORS MONUMENT, 1881. Granite and bronze, h. 50'.
In Peabody Sq.
After Thomas Crawford (*see* Cambridge [Harvard University]: *James Otis*).

Among America's early expatriate sculptors in Rome, Crawford re-crossed the Atlantic several times to seek commissions. In 1853 his dreams were realized with a request to sculpt the pediment figures for the U.S. Senate. He accomplished this monumental work at the same time as *Armed Freedom* and a huge statue of James Otis (now at Harvard), although he had begun to suffer from the tumor behind his left eye which ended his life at the age of forty-four. Friends saw to it that *Armed Freedom* was cast during the Civil War; it was hoisted atop the Capitol, to the accompaniment of cannon salutes, in 1863.

The figure crowning the obelisk here is modeled, with some modifications, on Crawford's *Armed Freedom* atop the national capitol. The changes, which contemporary accounts say the committee "thought an improvement," substituted a broken shackle for the coat of arms in Freedom's left hand, and changed the angle of the sword in the right. The monument is dedicated to the fallen from Danvers (now Peabody) during the Civil War.

QUEEN VICTORIA, 1867. Enamel on porcelain, $14'' \times 10''$.
in Peabody Library.
F. A. Tilt.

Largest miniature portrait in history at the time it was painted, this work was commissioned especially for presentation from Queen Victoria to George Peabody (1795–1869), American-born financier, for his philanthropies for the workers of London. Born in the part of Danvers that is now Peabody, he was apprenticed to a merchant and, after volunteering in the War of 1812, formed a dry-goods partnership. By 1830 he found himself the head of one of the largest mercantile concerns in the world. He increased his fortune by buying up American state securities following the panic of 1837; then, establishing himself in London, he became one of the first Americans in international banking. His philanthropies encompassed scientific research, education, and low-income housing which still flourishes in London. The queen offered him a baronetcy, which he declined because it would require loss of his American citizenship; this portrait, in her robes of state, is a substitute.

PLYMOUTH

MASSASOIT, 1921. Bronze, heroic size.
Coles Hill, Water St., directly across from Plymouth Rock.
★ Cyrus E. Dallin (*see* Arlington: *Indian Hunter*).

The survival of the band of settlers from the *Mayflower* was made possible principally by the friendship of Massasoit (ca. 1580–1661), chief of the Wampanoags. His tribe of several thousand had been all but wiped out by an epidemic, thought to be yellow fever, just prior to the arrival of the Pilgrims. Samoset, an Indian who had contact with Europeans and spoke a little English, arranged a meeting in the spring of 1621 between Massasoit and Governor Bradford; the two signed a peace treaty which lasted until 1675.

WILLIAM BRADFORD, 1976. Bronze, life-size.
Water St., just south of Plymouth Rock.
★ Cyrus E. Dallin (*see* Arlington: *Indian Hunter*).

This portrait of the leader of the Plymouth colony, intended to mark the tercentenary of the historic town, was modeled in 1920. The committee ran out of money, however, and the model was not cast. In 1976, as part of the United States Bicentennial celebration, the Plymouth Bicentennial Commission raised funds to cast and erect the statue.

Second governor of Plymouth Colony, Bradford (1590–1657) was elected in 1621 after the death of John Carver and served, with an occasional hiatus, for about thirty years. He was born in Yorkshire of well-to-do parents, joined the Separatists, was imprisoned briefly before emigrating to Holland in 1608, and was among the band of colonists arriving here aboard the *Mayflower*. Biographers credit the success and prosperity of Plymouth Colony in large part to his firm and judicious rule. His *History of Plymouth Plantation* (until 1646) is the major source of information about the colony's settlement and growth. Funded by public subscription.

THE PILGRIM MOTHER, 1920. Fountain and stone figure, larger than life.
Water and North Sts.
C. P. Jennewein (1890–1978).

Born in Germany, Carl Paul Jennewein was brought to the U.S. in 1907, studied at the Art Students League in New York and at the American Academy in Rome. The federal buildings in Washington, D.C., bear many of his marble carvings. His work is owned by the Metropolitan Museum of Art in New York and by the art museums of Baltimore and Philadelphia.

★ THE PILGRIM MAIDEN, 1924.
Bronze, h. 8½'.
West end of Brewster Park,
Water and Leyden Sts., half a
block south of Gov. Bradford's
statue.
Henry Hudson Kitson (*see*
Lexington: *The Minuteman*).
Commissioned by National
Society of New England
Women.

TRAIL OF TEARS, ca. 1984.
    Wood, h. approx. 20'.
    At Tourist Information bureau,
    Exit 5 off Route 3.
    Peter Toth (1947–   ).

Peter Toth was eleven when his family emigrated from revolt-torn Hungary to Ohio. Deeply empathetic with the Amerindian, Toth abandoned his college studies in 1970 and began carving monumental works in stone and wood to honor America's indigenous peoples and to protest their treatment. Traveling across the nation, the sculptor creates his works from materials found wherever he may be. Toth's goal is to place a sculpture from this series in each of the fifty states, all gifts of the artist.

NATIONAL MONUMENT TO THE FOREFATHERS, 1889. Granite and
    marble, h. 81'.
    Allerton St.
    Hammatt Billings (1818–1874), William Rimmer (*see* Commonwealth
    Avenue: *Hamilton*), and others.

Charles Howland Hammatt Billings was born in Milton and educated in Boston public schools and at the workshop of Abel Bowen, Boston's first wood engraver. By the 1840s he was a jack-of-all-arts, turning his hand to architecture, painting, sculpture, landscape design, decorative arts, funerary monuments, fireworks design, and magazine and book illustration—his drawings are associated with such nineteenth-century classics as the works of Louisa May Alcott and Harriet Beecher Stowe.

Billings was responsible for both the design and the fund-raising for this work. Dr. Rimmer made the nine-foot model of Faith, based on the Venus de Milo, but the stonecutter who quadrupled its size for the monument replaced Rimmer's delicate drapery with quantities of material. In an effort to make it a truly national monument, sculptors from elsewhere were engaged to carve the various figures and plaques: Alexander Doyle of New York did Education; Karl Conrad, Morality; J. H. Mahoney, Freedom and Law. Although Billings designed the Monument in 1853, it was not completed until 1889.

A typically Victorian work, this mammoth allegorical group represents the virtues of the Pilgrims. Atop the central pedestal, her arm pointed heavenward, is Faith; she is surrounded by Morality (flanked by a prophet and an evangelist), Law (flanked by Justice and Mercy), Education (flanked by Wisdom and Youth), and Liberty (flanked by

Peace and Tyranny overthrown). Four alto-relief carvings on the base depict the departure of the colonists from Delft Haven, Holland, the signing of the Mayflower Compact, the landing of the Pilgrims, and the treaty with the Indian chief Massasoit. At the time of its erection *Faith* was said to be the largest granite statue in the world; however, statements that it is 216 times life-size are a miscalculation. Its height (36′) and most of its measurements are six to seven times life, the nose being sixteen inches long, for instance. Sponsored by the Pilgrim Society; funded by public subscription.

MUSEUM: Pilgrim Hall Museum, 75 Court St. Although it is a historical museum, Pilgrim Hall contains some important works of art: the only known portrait of a Mayflower Pilgrim (Edward Winslow), three other seventeenth-century portraits of Massachusettsians, the original painting for the Pilgrim mural by Robert Weir in the Capitol in Washington, D. C., and paintings of the landing of the Pilgrims by Henry Sargent and Michel Corné.

QUINCY

CONSTITUTION COMMON SCULPTURE, 1980. Granite, h. 8′.
At City Hall annex, Hancock and Temple Sts.
Edward P. Monti (1927–).

Descended from a line of stoneworkers from northern Italy, Ed Monti owns the granite monument company which his father founded in Quincy after immigrating from Italy. After apprenticing with his father and serving in World War II, Monti graduated from the Barre School of Design in Vermont, then studied with animal sculptor Bonnie Boranda. Experimenting with ways to accelerate the process of stone carving, Monti settled on the quarryman's jet torch, a tool that burns a kerosene-oxygen mixture at 3600 degrees; it forces the stone to spall, or flake off the block, in controllable ways. With this technique Monti has produced fountains, waterfalls, animals, and abstract sculpture for malls, parks, and business complexes on the Eastern Seaboard, in the Virgin Islands, and in Europe.

To commemorate the bicentennial of the drafting of the Massachusetts Constitution, this massive work of Quincy granite was erected in 1980. Oldest democratic constitution in use today and the model for the federal Constitution, the document was written in the Quincy law

offices of John Adams by the Adams cousins (John and Samuel) and James Bowdoin. The three major granite forms represent the three patriot/authors; the interplay of shapes and spaces echoes the interchange of ideas. The monument bears quotations from the document. Commissioned by the City of Quincy.

THE DOUGHBOY, 1924. Bronze, larger than life.
At Adams Academy (Quincy Historical Society), Hancock and Granite Sts.
Bruce Wilder Saville (1893–1939).

Quincy-born, Saville studied in Boston under Cyrus Dallin and in the Quincy studio of Theo Alice Ruggles Kitson. After service during World War I, he set up a studio in Quincy, then at the age of twenty-eight was appointed head of the art department of Ohio State University. Within four years he returned to Boston, planning to devote full time to sculpture, but in 1932 he moved to Santa Fe, N.M., for his health, and died there of influenza at the age of forty-six.

This soldier is a casting of a work Saville created as the central figure of a war memorial for Columbus, Ohio; the City chose it to honor the men of Quincy who served in the first World War.

JOHN HANCOCK, ca. 1900. Gilded bronze bust, h. 5′.
Artist unknown. Casting attributed to Gorham Co., Providence, R.I.
At Adams Academy.

This megascale portrait marks the site of the birthplace of John Hancock (1737–1793), president of the Continental Congress 1775–77, first signer of the Declaration of Independence, and legendary for declaring that he signed "large enough for King George to read it without his spectacles." Hancock was adopted by his childless merchant uncle, Thomas Hancock of Boston, and fell heir to a fortune and a prospering business. With Samuel Adams, he was a "most-wanted man" during the agitation that led to the Revolution; the King's troops marching to Lexington and Concord on April 19, 1775, sought to capture him and Adams as well as to destroy rebel arms. Never really a leader (although he was a militia major-general and repeatedly governor), he was a flamboyant and expansive man and a popular public figure.

This bust was designed to stand over the entrance of a John Hancock Co. building on Federal St. early in this century. In 1922 the company moved, placed the bust in storage, and never found it had a location for it again. When the company built Boston's first skyscraper in 1949, a full-length portrait of the patriot was commissioned for its lobby. (*see* Back Bay: *John Hancock*) At that point the company offered this bust to the city of Hancock's birth, which funded a base of Quincy granite for it. Presented to the City of Quincy in 1951 by the John Hancock Life Insurance Co.

ROBERT BURNS, 1925. Granite, life-size.
Junction of Burgin Pkwy. and Granite St.
Gerald T. Horrigan (1903–   ).

Son of sculptor-stonecutter John Horrigan, Gerald Horrigan studied at the Boston Museum School. Like his father, he frequently assumed a craftsman's role as master stonecutter, translating to stone works designed in clay by other sculptors; John cut major work for Loredo Taft, and father and son both executed large-scale works for the sculptor Grace Vanderbilt Whitney.

In this case the statue, designed by Gerald, was cut by his father. Presented to the City of Quincy by the Burns Memorial Association. Rededicated 1971.

RIVETERS and GRANITE. Bas-relief panels, stone.
CRANES. Bas-relief pediment carving, stone.
    Entrance to Thomas Crane Library, Washington and Coddington Sts.
    Joseph Coletti (*see* East Boston/Logan Airport: *General Logan*).

WINGED MIGRATION #2, 1980–81. Steel, h. 13'.
    Outside offices of National Fire Protection Association, Batterymarch Park, off Granite St.
    Dennis Kowal (*see* Wellesley [Babson College]: *Ominous Icon #6* and *Yaddo Study*).
    Commissioned by National Fire Protection Association.

RANDOLPH

CIVIL WAR MEMORIAL, no date. Bronze, larger than life.
    In front of Stetson Hall, North Main and Union Sts.
    F. Kohlhagen.

REVERE

CHRISTOPHER COLUMBUS, 1892. Bronze, larger than life.
    At St. Anthony's Church, 250 Revere St.
    Alois G. Buyens.

Ceremoniously presented to the Cathedral of the Holy Cross in the South End of Boston, this huge statue overpowered its site; in the 1920s it was discreetly relocated here at St. Anthony's Church to balance an equally large St. Anthony. Commissioned by the Knights of Columbus.

TREE OF LIFE, 1978. Stainless steel, diffraction grating, h. 9'.
At Hebrew Rehabilitation Center for the Aged.
William Wainwright (*see* East Boston/Logan Airport: *Windwheels*).

SPANISH WAR MEMORIAL, 1931. Bronze, approximately life-size.
Broadway and Hyde St., south of City Hall.
M. H. Mosman (*see* Saugus: *Civil War Memorial*).

   Apparently created specifically for Revere, this briskly marching soldier departs from the generic Kitson statue replicated in many other
towns. Commissioned by City of Revere.

CIVIL WAR MEMORIAL, 1931. Bronze, larger than life.
Broadway and Hyde St., south of City Hall.

   The Boston foundry of McGann and Sons cast this work in the style
of Martin Milmore (*see* Framingham: *Civil War Memorial*). Vandals
have bent the soldier's bayonet. Erected by City of Revere.

ROCKPORT

SCENES OF ROCKPORT. Mural in gilded steel, h. 4' × 30'.
At Granite Savings Bank.
C. Fayette Taylor (*see* Government Center: *Upward Bound*).

SALEM

★ HAWTHORNE, 1925. Bronze, larger than life.
Hawthorne Blvd., near Essex St.
Bela L. Pratt (*see* Malden: *The Flag Defenders*).

   Nathaniel Hawthorne (1804–1864), sometimes called the most distinguished craftsman of the New England school of letters, was a native of Salem and periodically returned here to live. Hawthorne's
father died when he was small, leaving him, his mother, and his sisters in a household of genteel poverty and grim Puritanical gloom.
Aloof and a loner, he graduated from Bowdoin College and returned
to Salem to spend twelve solitary years mastering the craft of self-
taught authorship. After some meager literary success he married a

Salem woman, Sophia Peabody; their marriage is one of New England's enduring love stories. Her sister Elizabeth, involved in all the causes of the day, introduced Nathaniel to the great figures of Transcendentalism. For a few years Hawthorne worked unhappily in the customs house in Salem, until *The Scarlet Letter* brought him popular success at the age of forty-six. It was followed by *The House of Seven Gables*, set in a house Hawthorne knew in Salem (now a museum open to the public). Descendant of generations of sea captains, the novelist is depicted hat in hand, gazing toward the sea. Funded by the Nathaniel Hawthorne Memorial Association.

FOUNTAIN, 1977. Stone.
East India Sq.
John Collins.

The pool is designed to display graphically the changes in Salem's topography as the old seaport has experienced dredging and filling. Dry stepping-stone cobbles replicate the original land masses; submerged cobbles trace today's vastly enlarged dry ground. Collins, the designer, is a member of Delta Group of Philadelphia.

ROGER CONANT, 1911. Bronze, larger than life.
Brown St. at Washington Sq.
Henry Hudson Kitson (*see* Lexington: *The Minuteman*).

Roger Conant would be distressed to learn that many visitors mistake his figure for a witch, or at least a warlock, because of his seventeenth-century garb, swirling cloak and tall hat. The fact that he stands in front of the Witch Museum does nothing to dispel the notion. In reality, Conant was the first settler of Salem. The statue has been vandalized by what appear to be bullet holes. Funded by the Conant Family Association.

MOURNING VICTORY, 1947. Marble, h. 30′.
Lafayette and Washington Sts.
Joseph A. Coletti (*see* East Boston/Logan Airport: *General Logan*).

This art deco shaft commemorates the dead of the two World Wars.

CHOATE MONUMENT
West End of Essex St.
J. Massey Rhind (1860–1936).

Rhind was born in Edinburgh, Scotland, son and student of John Rhind of the Royal Scottish Academy. He came to this country in 1889 and won a gold medal at the St. Louis Exposition in 1904. His best-known work is an equestrian Washington in Newark; other works are located in Pennsylvania, Ohio, and elsewhere in New Jersey.

A Parisian-style allegorical monument, this work honors Judge Joseph Hodges Choate (1832–1917), lawyer and diplomat, instrumental in breaking up the Tweed Ring, ambassador to Great Britain, and delegate to the first International Peace Conference in The Hague in 1907. The figure is Liberty in a mobcap, seated, holding up a laurel wreath. A medallion portrait of Judge Choate is affixed to the pedestal. Donated by Henry Clay Frick.

FATHER THEOBALD MATHEW, 1887. Stone, life-size.
Hawthorne Blvd. and Derby St.
Artist unknown.

Father Theobald was an early temperance advocate.

SAUGUS

CIVIL WAR MEMORIAL, 1875. Stone and bronze, larger than life.
Main and Central Sts.
M. H. Mosman.

Although the allegorial War, in stone atop the monument, is different, the sailor and soldier appear to be duplicates of two of the figures on the Civil War monument in Wakefield. Mosman was a Chicopee sculptor. Gift of Henry E. Homer.

SCITUATE

THE HERITAGE OF FREEDOM BY THE SEA, 1986. Glazed ceramic on steel-reinforced concrete, h. 8'.
At Town Hall, Rte. 3A and First Parish Rd.
Sonni Waldo (1938–   ).

Born in Philadelphia, Sonni Waldo studied sculpture there under Frank Gasparro, and later under John Moakley (*see* East Bridgewater: *Mural*). She has most recently earned a degree at the Boston Museum School. She and Moakley have also created a ceramic wall for Andover-Newton Theological Seminary.

Incorporating images from Scituate's history, this work was commissioned to commemorate the town's 350th anniversary. Funded by Scituate Arts Council, the 350th anniversary commission, Scituate Historical Society, and private donations.

SHERBORN

MEMORY, 1923. Bronze war memorial, larger than life.
Rte. 27 and Rte. 16 west (Main and Washington Sts.).
Cyrus E. Dallin (*see* Arlington: *Indian Hunter*).

SOMERVILLE

CIVIL WAR MEMORIAL, 1908. Bronze, heroic size.
Highland St., west of library.
Augustus Lukeman (b. 1872).

Henry Augustus Lukeman was born in West Virginia, studied with Daniel Chester French and then in Paris at the Ecole des Beaux Arts. His name is associated with Augustus Saint-Gaudens, appearing sometimes as assistant and sometimes as competitor. The Angel of Victory here owes its pose to a similar angel Saint-Gaudens created in 1903 for the *Sherman* monument in New York.

SPANISH WAR MEMORIAL, 1929. Bronze, two figures, life-size.
In front of library, Walnut and Highland Sts.
Raymond A. Porter (1883–1949).

Born in Mt. Herman, N.Y., Porter taught in the 1920s at Massachusetts Normal Art School, now Massachusetts College of Art. He also sculpted the Henry Cabot Lodge portrait at the State House.

FLAG, 1985. Phenolic plastic, painted. Mobile screens, three units, each
12′ × 15′.
Overhead, lobby, Public Safety Bldg., Washington and Merriam Sts.
Be Allen (1940–   ).

Somerville artist Be Allen, born in New York City, attended the Boston Museum School and the San Francisco Art Institute.
This building, an MBTA car barn newly converted to a police/fire station, offered a vast open space in its entry lobby. Here Allen's mobile screens, hanging from the skylights, refer in a delicate and fragmented way to the colors and configurations of the American flag. Funded by a Community Development grant.

UNTITLED, 1984. Cast cement statues, life-size.
Davis Sq., Highland St. and College Ave.
James Tyler.

Tyler has studied at Hampshire College, Nasson College (Maine), and at St. Mary's College and Herron Art College (both Indiana). The figures, representing actual local residents, are cast from fondu cement. Tyler has recently moved to New York.

STONEHAM

AERIAL SCULPTURE, 1982.
    Interior, Flynn Rink.
    Linda DeHart (*see* Lexington: *Aerial Sculptures*).
    Funded by MDC 1% for Art.

SPANISH WAR MEMORIAL. Bronze, larger than life.
    Central and Common Sts.
    Joseph Pollia.
    Erected by the Town of Stoneham.

SUDBURY

MENORAH, 1974. Stainless steel, bronze, h. 6′.
    At Congregation Beth El, Hudson Rd.
    Barry Marchette (1939–   ).

    Now on the faculty of the Art Institute of Boston, Lowell native Barry
Marchette studied art at California College of Arts and Crafts and at
Massachusetts College of Art. He held CETA grants in 1979–80 for
environmental study and creation of a cultural community. Commissioned by Congregation Beth El.

BUDDY DOG, 1977. Granite, h. 8′.
    At Buddy Dog Humane Society, 151 Boston Post Rd.
    John Weidman.

    Weidman is an East Pepperell sculptor.

TEWKSBURY

★   WATER, 1985. Bronze, larger than life.
    Town Hall grounds.
    Mico Kaufman (*see* Lowell: *Homage to Women*).

    This work is a memorial to Anne Sullivan, teacher of Helen Keller. It
captures the moment that the teacher finally penetrated the closed
world of the deaf-and-blind Helen, helping her understand the relationship between the word "water" and its physical presence. It is placed
here because Sullivan, at a dark period in her life, was at the Tewksbury State Hospital. Erected by citizens of Tewksbury.

TOPSFIELD

THE WOUNDED COLOR SERGEANT, ca. 1921. Bronze, larger than life.
    On the common, across from library.
    Theo Alice Ruggles Kitson (*see* Malden: *The Hiker*).

    The statue commemorates Topsfield citizens who served in World
War I. Gift of Justin Allen, M.D.

WAKEFIELD

THE HIKER. Bronze, larger than life.
  Main and Common Sts.
  Theo Alice Ruggles Kitson (*see* Malden: *The Hiker*).

   Wakefield's casting of *The Hiker* lacks the usual platform base; his
feet are affixed directly to rock. Backed by a fountain, he enjoys one
of the prettier settings in greater Boston.

CIVIL WAR MEMORIAL, 1902. Stone, h. approx. 30′.
  Main and Salem Sts.
  Sculptor unknown; design by Van Am Ringe Granite Corp.

   Although Wakefield's records fail to show the sculptor's name, it
was most likely M. H. Mosman of Chicopee. Two of the figures, the
sailor with his cutlass and the infantryman leaning on his rifle, are
identical to figures by Mosman in Saugus. Gift of Harriet Newell Flint.

WALPOLE

LIEUTENANT LEWIS MONUMENT, 1911. Bronze, life-size.
  East and Plimpton Sts.
  S. Barnicoat.

   Lieutenant Bachariah Lewis was one of this region's most involved
citizens during his lifetime, 1663–1710. Surveyor, tax collector, tithing-
man, he served as an officer in the Wars of King William and Queen
Anne (conflicts between the French and English colonies in North
America, reflecting the hostilities of those two countries between 1689
and 1713). His aspect here is typical; astride his horse he explored
and laid out roads in the area between Roxbury and Wrentham. Commissioned by his descendants, Isaac N. and Mary F. Lewis.

WALTHAM

★ NATHANIEL PRENTISS BANKS, 1908. Bronze, larger than life.
  Waltham city square, Moody and Main Sts.
  Henry Hudson Kitson (*see* Lexington: *The Minuteman*).

  Born in Waltham, Banks was speaker of the U.S. House of Repre-
  sentatives from 1856 to 1858, Governor of Massachusetts, 1858–61,
  and Major General of U.S. Volunteers during the Civil War. This
  statue, once one of several behind the State House in Boston, was
  displaced by a parking lot and moved to the city of Banks' birth in
  1950. Funded by appropriation of the Commonwealth.

THE HIKER MONUMENT, 1928. Bronze, larger than life.
  Waltham city square, Moody and Main Sts.
  Theo Alice Ruggles Kitson (*see* Malden: *The Hiker*).

  This monument is dedicated to Waltham's veterans of the Spanish-
  American War, 1898. Erected by the City of Waltham and James M.
  Dermody Camp No. 5 Spanish War Veterans.

At Bentley College:

★ PORTAL, 1979. Stone, h. 9′.
  Carlos Dorrien (1948–   ).

  Argentine-born, Carlos Dorrien is now an assistant professor of art
  at Wellesley College. His simple but monumental stone carvings and
  portals are widely placed in the Boston area (*see* Cambridge [Harvard
  Sq.]: *Quiet Stone* and East Boston: *Portal*). Dorrien was sculptor-in-
  residence at Bentley in 1978–79. He has trained at Universidad de la
  Plata in Argentina, and in this country at Lowell Technological Institute, Montserrat College of Art, and Massachusetts College of Art.

★ WALL SCULPTURE, 1963. Copper with patina, h. 50′ × 32′ × 1½′.
  Atrium, Wyman St. Bldg., 275 Wyman St.
  Michio Ihara (*see* Lowell: *Pawtucket Prism*).

"In sculpture I am concerned above all with two things," Michio Ihara has written; "time as a creative element which allows change and motion; and nature, combining forces of light, wind, heat and manpower for constructive ends." Ihara's wall sculpture here is designed to take advantage of the changing light streaming through the atrium skylight. One-foot copper squares are set at angles engineered so that shadow patterns, integral to the visual impact, vary as the sun moves. The copper is colored with heat and flux, a chemical that aids brazing. Vertical grooves in the sandblasted concrete wall are part of Ihara's design.

At Brandeis University:

A partial listing follows:

NEON FOR THE ROSE ART MUSEUM, 1985. Neon.
　　Exterior, Rose Art Museum.
　　Stephen Antonakos (1926–　　).

　　A native of Greece, Antonakos came to this country at an early age and graduated from Brooklyn Community College. He was an early experimenter with neon as an art form; his work is owned by the Museum of Modern Art, the Whitney Museum, and others. He has taught at Yale, the University of North Carolina, and Brooklyn College. Museum purchase.

HORIZON, 1966. Bronze.
　　Rose Art Museum portico.
　　★　Anthony Caro (1924–　　).

　　Caro was for two years in the early 1950s an assistant to England's great sculptor, Henry Moore. London-born, Caro as a teenager apprenticed to another English sculptor, Charles Wheeler, and later studied under him at the Royal Academy. Caro's abstract bolted and welded works first appeared in the late 1950s. Gift of Mr. and Mrs. Max Wasserstein.

END FREE SERIES XV, 1971. Welded steel.
　　At right of Rose Art Museum facade.
　　★　Alexander Liberman (1912–　　).

　　Born in Kiev, Russia, Liberman came to the U.S. in 1941 and joined the staff of *Vogue* magazine. He swiftly rose to art director and then to editorial director of Condé Nast Publications. His steel abstractions are owned by the Museum of Modern Art, the Metropolitan Museum, the Whitney Museum, DeCordova Museum, Storm King Art Center, and many others.

PEGASUS (BIRTH OF THE MUSES), 1971. Bronze relief.
　　Facade of Pollack Fine Arts Teaching Center.
　　★　Jacques Lipchitz (*see* Cambridge [M.I.T.]: *The Bather*).
　　Funded by Lester Avner Foundation and the Jack I. and Lilian L. Poses Foundation.

ISTRA. Mixed media architectural structure.
    In wooded area to right of Rose Art Museum.
    Ed Rothberg.
    New Works Program, Massachusetts Council on Arts and Humanities.

WAND OF INQUIRY, 1983. Stainless steel, h. 15'.
    In front of Rosenstiel Basic Medical Sciences Research Center.
    Lila Katzen (1932–   ).
    Rosenstiel Foundation.

STUDENT, 1986. Bronze and stone, life-size.
    Outside Farber Library.
    Penelope Jencks (*see* Chelsea: *Chelsea Conversation*).

LOUIS B. BRANDEIS, 1957. Bronze.
    Fellows Garden.
    Robert Berks (1922–   ).

    Born in Boston and educated at Harvard, Berks is best known for
his huge bust of John F. Kennedy at Kennedy Center and for his portrait of Einstein, both in Washington, D.C. Berks now lives on Long
Island.
    Justice Brandeis (1856–1941), first Jewish member of the U.S. Su-
preme Court, was born in Kentucky of Jewish immigrant parents who
had prospered here. At the age of eighteen he entered Harvard Law
School, without any undergraduate education, and graduated with
honors in two years. Forming a law partnership in Boston, he found
himself probing economic and social issues behind the legal issues of
the day. Woodrow Wilson appointed him to the Supreme Court in
1916. His image as a dissenter stems from his ability to "state the law
as it was to be interpreted in the future," biographers write. He fa-
vored economic regulation to meet changing social and economic
needs, but opposed curbs on thought, speech, or the press. Of 528
opinions he wrote, however, only forty-four were in dissent. The university named in his honor was founded in 1948. Commissioned, to
commemorate the 100th anniversary of Brandeis' birth, by Lawrence
E. Wien, trustee of the university.

MUSEUM: Rose Art Gallery hosts bi-monthly rotating exhibitions.

AERIAL SCULPTURE, 1981. Fabric, plexiglass, h. 3 stories.
    Atrium, 204 Second Ave.
    Linda DeHart (*see* Lexington: *Aerial Sculptures*).
    Commissioned by Boston Properties Inc.

204 SECOND AVE., 1981. Graphic wall collage, silkscreen on plexiglass,
    fabric, h. 2' × 8'.
    Lobby, 204 Second Ave.
    Linda DeHart (*see* Lexington: *Aerial Sculptures*).
    Commissioned by Boston Properties Inc.

WATERTOWN

SIR RICHARD SALTONSTALL, 1926.
  Charles River Rd. near Watertown Sq.
  Henry Hudson Kitson (*see* Lexington: *The Minuteman*).
  Theo Alice Ruggles Kitson (*see* Malden: *The Hiker*).

  The Kitsons collaborated on several memorial sculptures (*see* Commonwealth Avenue: *Collins Memorial*) in addition to their independent pieces. Although they were said to have separated about 1909, contemporary accounts list them as collaborators on this work.
  Sir Richard Saltonstall led the colony from England that founded Watertown in 1630. This monument commemorates the event that established the principle of "no taxation without representation." A tax of eight pounds had been levied toward the building of a stockade at New Towne (Cambridge); the freemen of Watertown objected. Here, in the bas-relief on the right, the Rev. George Phillips and Elder Richard Browne address them, contending that "English freemen cannot rightfully be taxed save by their own consent." The result was that each town was asked to send two deputies to a General Court, the origin of the Massachusetts legislative body. At left, a colonist and friendly Indians exchange fish and bread. Funded by public subscription.

WATERTOWN PAST AND PRESENT, 1983. Mural.
  Merchants Row, off Main St.
  Elizabeth Carter (*see* Cambridge [Central Sq.]: *Floating Down Mass. Avenue*).

MURAL II, 1984. Ceramic, h. 30'.
  Exterior wall, Metco Tile Corp., 291 Arsenal St.
  Lilli Ann Killen Rosenberg (*see* Newton: *Five Concrete Mosaic Sculptures*).

WATERTOWN PUBLIC LIBRARY owns a number of works by Harriet Goodhue Hosmer (1830–1908), Watertown native and member of the American artists' colony in Rome in the 1850s.

WELLESLEY

At Babson College:

OMINOUS ICON #6, 1976. Cor-ten steel, h. 6'.
YADDO STUDY, ca. 1970. Cor-ten steel, h. 4'.
  Between Horn Library and Kriebel Hall.
  Dennis Kowal (1938–   ).

  Boston sculptor Dennis Kowal maintains his studio in Cohasset on the South Shore. A native of Illinois, he studied at the Art Institute of Chicago, University of Illinois, and at Southern Illinois University under Buckminster Fuller. He received an M.F.A. in 1962. Kowal came East to accept a fellowship at the MacDowell Colony in Peterborough,

N.H., and remained in New England. He has taught at University of Southern Illinois and been artist-in-residence at the MacDowell and Yaddo Colonies, Dartmouth and Amherst Colleges, Milton Academy, DeCordova Museum, University of Georgia, and others. Kowal's training in engineering and design led him to experiment with carved acrylic and steel. Of his twenty-two major public commissions, nine are in the Boston area.

SQUARE THROATED ELBOW. Cor-ten steel, h. 30″.
In front of Horn Library.
David Kibbey (*see* Charles River Esplanade: *Trimbloid X*).

GALLERY: The Gallery at Horn, to the right of Horn Library entrance. Monthly exhibitions of work by contemporary artists, theme shows about the college, or exhibitions arranged by Smithsonian Institute's SITES program. Horn Library also contains works from the college's collection on permanent display.

At Wellesley College:

★ WALKING MAN, 1876. Bronze, h. 7′ (*see* picture on page 122). Academic Quadrangle.
   ★ Auguste Rodin (1840–1917).

Born in Paris, Rodin early in his studies displayed the creative nonconformity that made him the bane of academicians and, eventually, the towering figure of nineteenth-century sculpture. The uninhibited, almost savage, modeling of his late works paved the road for modernism in this century.

Rodin's first major figure had been so masterly that critics accused him of casting his forms directly from the body of the live model. In response, he tried to create his second, *St. John the Baptist Preaching*, in a pose that would be impossible to cast. The *Walking Man*, originally modeled at half scale, was a study for St. John. Rodin wanted to render the progressive development of movement, as if the figure were pushing off the left leg and then transferring weight to the right; thus both feet are solidly planted. *St. John* was completed in 1880; it was not until twenty-five years later that Rodin saw the sketch as a work in its own right. In 1912 it was given to the French embassy in Rome, where its fragmentary nature made it the butt of jokes: Rodin himself said, "A man without a head is the perfect symbol of our diplomacy." This example is from a series of twelve cast in 1969, from Rodin's original 1907 model, by the Georges Rudier Foundry in Paris.

LONG SPREAD, 1973. Steel.
★ Michael Steiner (see Cambridge [M.I.T.]: Niagara).

SCHECHINAH TEMPTATIONS, 1976. Steel.
★ Jules Olitski (1922–   ).

Olitski is credited with the first thorough-going attempt to make a painting out of nothing but pure color. Brought to the U.S. from Russia at the age of two, Olitski served in the U.S. Army, attended various art institutes in New York and Paris, earned a B.A. and a master's at New York University, taught at Bennington, C. W. Post College, and State University of New York at New Paltz. A first prize at the Corcoran Biennial in 1967 solidified his reputation. He turned for a time to sculpture; this is one of several examples.

★ UNTITLED (Filagreed Steel Line for Wellesley College), 1979–80. North of Lake Waban, near college library.
Robert Irwin (1928–   ).

Californian Robert Irwin started out as a painter of poetic, reductive works. Interested in psychological sensory research, he began to create installations in which space was delineated merely with tape, string, or scrim. He is credited with invention of the terms "site-dominant" and so forth (see Introduction) to describe the relationship of works of art with their environment. Here Irwin walked the campus and mused for two days before designing the work, which surely qualifies as "site-determined," responding to the site and visually woven into it. Both this work and Wild Spot, below, were installed as part of a group of environmental siteworks.

★ WILD SPOT, 1979–80. Wrought iron, h. 10′.
North of Whitin Observatory.
Nancy Holt (1938–   ).

All Holt's work is involved in site, time, and orientation in space, often astronomical orientation. Born in Worcester and educated at Jackson College (now Tufts), Holt deals in film, video, and large-scale sculpture and installations. She has held Guggenheim and NEA grants. She was married to Robert Smithson, environmental earthworks artist who was killed in an airplane crash in 1973.

Wild Spot creates a demarcation of the landscape, fencing a tiny wildplant garden, inviting the viewer into its space to view framed vertical slices of the environs. Much of Holt's site-specific work has been done in the West; this more confined piece seems well suited to the less open, more constricted woods of the Eastern seaboard.

GALLERY: Jewett Arts Center.

At Wellesley Office Park (Rte. 128 and William St.):

★ WIND SCULPTURE, 1973. Stainless steel, h. 25′ × 20′ × 8′.
At Building #5.
Michio Ihara (*see* Lowell: *Pawtucket Prism*).

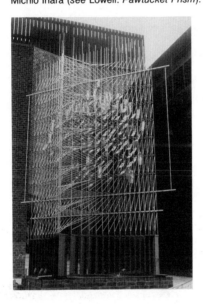

3-D HANGING, M3D6/A, 1979. Textile, h. two stories.
Lobby, 45 William St.
Peter Collingwood.

CASCADE OF CUBES, 1972. Aluminum, h. 20′.
Atrium, 40 William St.
William Wainwright (*see* East Boston/Logan Airport: *Windwheels*).

WESTON

TAVERNSIDE PARK MOSAIC, 1986. Ceramic, h. 3′ × 3′.
In Tavernside Park, Boston Post Rd., south of town green.
Phyllis Biegun (1947–   ).

A native of Boston who lives and teaches in Weston, Biegun earned a bachelor of fine arts degree from Cornell and a master's degree in art education from Rochester Institute of Technology. She instructed in a Buffalo-area high school, and has since taught on many levels from boys' clubs to adult education.

Biegun's mosaic is another example of art designed to reflect the uses of a specific site. For this children's play area, the ceramacist cut the components from clay with cookie cutters: stars, flowers, toy cars, gingerbread children and even (very central) a teddy bear. Matching pairs can be discovered among the forms. Biegun is impatient with art